Peter the Great
Changes Russia

PROBLEMS IN
EUROPEAN CIVILIZATION

Under the editorial direction of
John Ratté
Amherst College

Peter the Great Changes Russia

Second Edition

Edited and with an introduction by

Marc Raeff
Columbia University

D. C. HEATH AND COMPANY
Lexington, Massachusetts Toronto

CONTENTS

IV THE SOVEREIGN EMPEROR AND THE OPPOSITION

V HISTORICAL ASSESSMENTS

FIGURE 1. Profile of Peter I, by J. van Douwen. (From *Starye Gody* [St. Petersburg, February 1914]. Courtesy of Slavonic Division, New York Public Library; Astor, Lenox and Tilden Foundations.)

INTRODUCTION

We call the world we live in "modern"—stressing the fact that it seems to us far different from what the world was to our ancestors of the Renaissance, the Middle Ages, and classical antiquity. And implied in this difference is the belief that what is "modern" has come about through rapid and far-reaching changes in the political, economic, and cultural aspects of Western life. We speak, therefore, of the Industrial Revolution, the great political revolutions of the United States and France, the revolutions in thought and taste associated with the "modern" notions of science, realism, individualism. In short, we have become quite familiar with the idea of revolution and change, and we associate it with innovation, acclaiming it as evidence that things are moving forward, are improving and giving wider scope to man's energies. Even if we disapprove of some specific results of a revolution, we still feel that it is but a perversion of something basically desirable and good, an effort at correcting and improving a bad situation that has gone wrong. We stress the element of innovation, the new direction which the revolution has brought about.

In so doing we tend to forget at times that however radical and thorough a revolution, it must have its foundations in the conditions that preceded it and that its results, therefore, cannot be completely unrelated to what went on before. As time passes, the novelties introduced by the revolution are taken for granted, and we are made aware of the survival of some of the antecedent conditions. We begin to speak of fundamental continuities in the country's history and downgrade the revolution as an accidental and superficial development in the basic structure and direction of a society's evolution.

And yet, something did change, a new turn was taken, no return to the past was possible any longer. There is no denying that something of a break did occur in the continuity of a nation's history.

What at first glance distinguishes the history of Russia from that of most Western European countries is that it has experienced a greater number of profound, "revolutionary" breaks in its history, each one leaving a deep imprint on the nation's consciousness. Like all European nations, Russia experienced its first "revolution" with its conversion to Christianity. Then came the Mongol or Tartar conquest which had a similar impact, though it did not change the Russian people's self-image as much. But it did interrupt contacts with other Christian nations and thereby stop Russia's participation in the life of Europe for two centuries. Whether the reign of Ivan the Terrible (1533–1584) marked a revolution may be a matter of debate. But there can be no question of the profound impact of the reign of Peter the Great, the subject of the present collection of readings. Lastly, without any question, the Revolution of 1917 profoundly transformed Russia and its people. In every instance, but more particularly in the last two (though not to the same extent for all social classes), the Russians felt that they had not only undergone institutional changes but that, as people, they had been transformed spiritually, culturally, psychologically.

The reign of Peter the Great (1682–1725) is known in Russian literature as the period of "transformation" and Peter as the Tsar Transformer [*tsar' preobrazovate'*]. It was only in the nineteenth century, under the influence of the events in France after 1789, that some radical intellectuals began to see Peter the Great as a revolutionary figure who had forcibly pushed Russia onto the path of secularism, rationalism, radical innovation, and modernity. To Russians of the eighteenth century, Peter had been the transformer of his nation, bringing to life a new—modern—type of Russian man, and like God literally creating Russia anew: "Our Lord, Peter the Great, who has drawn us from nothingness into being," a younger contemporary put it. But Peter the Great's work, whether truly "revolutionary" or merely "transforming" did not occur in a vacuum.

The area that was to become the nucleus of what is today Russia had been unified politically and freed from Tartar overlordship in the second half of the fifteenth century. In the course of the sixteenth century the institutional, social, and economic patterns were elaborated and became fixed. The first selection of readings in the present volume gives a summary description and analysis of the major patterns. At this point it need only be stressed that economically, Russia remained quite primitive—underdeveloped we would say today—compared to Western Europe, though it was not quite as backward as is sometimes believed. Socially and institutionally, Russia had none of the complexities bequeathed by the feudal order to Western European nations. Political power was monopolized by the autocratic Tsar, while society consisted essentially of two classes—nobility and peasantry—each equally powerless before the Tsar; but the nobility was gaining more and more despotic power over the peasantry. The city population was relatively small and politically powerless, and in contrast to Western Europe economically poor and socially weak as well. Nor did the Church and clergy play nearly as significant a role in the political and economic life of the country as they did in the West. The cultural life of Muscovy, as the country was then known both to the natives and to foreigners, was dominated by religious concerns, and institutionally it was centered in the Church. The second half of the sixteenth century witnessed an energetic effort at making the basic institutional, social, and cultural aspects of Muscovite life more efficient and better adapted to the political problems faced by the country. The security of the borders was much improved, and in some cases Russia could even embark on a policy of expansion. Ivan the Terrible and his successors, tsars Theodore [*Feodor*] and Boris Godunov endeavored to open Russia to more active intercourse with the West. Boris Godunov even went so far as to send several young Russians to study in England (they never returned, presumably because of the turmoil that broke out in Russia at the death of Boris).

These developments were brusquely interrupted, however, by dynastic and social upheavals which lasted for over a decade and brought foreign invasions in their wake. This period (from about 1603 to 1613), known as the Times of Troubles, was marked by civil and foreign wars, popular revolts, and almost resulted in the destruction of the Muscovite state and the loss of Russia's national and religious independence at the hands of Poland and the Roman Catholic Church. Eventually, the crisis was overcome, a new dynasty

—the house of Romanov—was elevated to the throne, and the national, social, and spiritual integrity of Russia was preserved.

But the experience left a shattering impression on the people, the ruling class as well as the peasantry. In the first place, a very strenuous effort was required of all classes to repair the physical damage and to rebuild the institutional, economic, cultural fabrics of Russian life. This process of reconstruction, extending over more than half of the seventeenth century, brought about a consolidation and hardening of the patterns initiated and developed in the sixteenth century. When a society reconstructs itself following some major cataclysm, it has a tendency to use the past for its standard and model. The Russians were no exception. Because they had come so near to losing their national independence and spiritual identity, the Russians were especially eager to preserve and strengthen the traditional elements of their way of life and exclude the foreign ones that seemed to be a threat. Muscovy became as self-centered as it had been under the yoke of the Tartars; it turned more isolationist and more chauvinistic than it had been at the end of the sixteenth century when its tsars had encouraged active and fruitful contacts with the West.

Of course, Muscovy could not remain self-contained and isolated from the rest of Europe completely. Willy-nilly it had to maintain relations with foreign nations, especially its neighbors. At the time, these neighbors were much more powerful than Russia. Poland, on the eve of her rapid decline, was still one of the largest and most powerful nations in Europe, and Sweden had emerged from the Thirty Years' War as the dominant power in the Baltic. In the south, the Ottoman Turks had not yet spent their offensive energies and together with their vassal, the Khan of the Crimea, threatened the security of Muscovy's richest lands to the south of the capital. Lastly, as a by-product of the conflicts between Turkey, Poland, and Muscovy, the free Cossack Host (occupying the area of modern Central Ukraine) acted both as an irritant and an invitation to penetration. The incorporation of the Cossack Host and its lands into Muscovy in the middle of the seventeenth century created new responsibilities and opportunities. Necessities of national security, as well as diplomatic considerations, required that Russia be on the alert and possess adequate military means. To this end the tsars needed an efficient army and economic resources. To obtain the first, Russia's fighting forces had to be set up along professional, Western lines and endowed with modern equipment. Thus, the Russians had to acquaint themselves with techniques developed in Western Europe. As regards the economic side, Russia needed to exploit more fully and effectively its natural resources and develop its foreign and domestic trade.

Although foreign contacts and the acquisition of Western techniques and knowledge had become a necessity for national survival, the adoption of such a course ran counter to the prevailing mood of isolation, the fear of everything foreign as a potential threat to the traditional values and spiritual identity of the nation. Those who desired to modernize Russia, to open her up to foreign breezes and influences, had to tread very gingerly. Even tsars had to bow to national and religious prejudices, as did Peter's father, Tsar Alexis (Aleksei Mikhailovich, 1645–1676) when he gave up his efforts at creating a permanent theatre and relaxing the prohibitions against foreign dress. The few foreigners who were admitted into the country were prevented from merging into Russian life; they were restricted to a special suburb of Moscow (the so-called "German suburb"), and Russians were not allowed to mix freely with them. Isolationism and bigoted traditionalism were not alone responsible for the very slow and largely ineffective attempts at dealing with basic national needs in an imaginative, "modern" way. The available institutional tools and the country's economic poverty played their role too.

The "primitive" economic resources (because of ignorance and lack of techniques to make greater use of their hidden potential) were strained to the utmost to repair the damage wrought by the Times of Troubles and continuing incursion of foreign raiders; military needs swallowed up the lion's share of the product of the people's labors. As for the institutions, they were proving increasingly more inadequate in dealing with new, unfamiliar, and pressing problems. The old institutions acted on the basis of tradition and precedent, piecemeal, dealing with every case in isolation without an overall view or direction. As long as the problems had been familiar ones, as long as it was only a matter of preserving the traditional status quo, the institutions functioned satisfactorily. But the

challenges and new problems raised by a modern military establishment, diplomacy, international trade, technical and cultural needs,
proved beyond the capacity of the customary operating procedures.
Some far-seeing individuals like the Regent Sophie and her chief
minister and lover V. V. Golitsyn, and the architect of Tsar Alexis'
foreign policy, Ordyn-Nashchokin, were aware of the situation and
endeavored to correct it by attempting to create new institutional
tools. Thus, a corps of professional soldiers—the *streltsy*—was
established; foreign technicians and instructors were hired; a new
code of laws drafted; embassies sent abroad; new administrative
departments set up and their work organized along more rational
and functional lines; finally, some of the most inefficient practices
were being gradually eliminated. Important as these reforms were,
they did not go far enough, for they could not overcome the dead
weight of traditional prejudice nor break through the fear and suspicion of everything foreign that the Russians had developed from
their past experiences, especially the Times of Troubles. The most
dramatic illustration of a violently negative reaction to desirable and
anodyne external changes was provided by the schism of the Old
Believers who rejected Patriarch Nikon's reforms of the ritual in the
middle of the seventeenth century.

This was the situation into which Peter came to power. Awareness
that a transformation was needed had developed in the minds of
many leading Russians. But they had neither the power, the institutional tools, the energy, nor the vision to initiate policies that would
gradually bring about the desired change. It was a matter of the
dynamics of change—its rate had to become such as to make possible a far-reaching transformation—and this is what Muscovy could
not bring about. The task fell to Peter, who carried it out in quite a
different spirit from theirs. Indeed, the enlightened and reform-
minded Muscovites wished to transform Russia, but not at the price
of a loss of its traditional spiritual and cultural identity. For Peter,
on the other hand, this identity did not have any absolute value or
particular meaning, quite the contrary perhaps.

In speaking about transformation we have implicitly meant "modernization." But what did modernization mean for Russia at the
end of the seventeenth century? First and foremost it meant "joining"
Western Europe, becoming part of its political and commercial and

even cultural world. To join Western Europe, to become part of its political system and play in it the role that befitted a country of the size and resources of Russia, meant also to accept the technology and the outlook of the West, for only such an acceptance would guarantee Russia its freedom of action as a nation. The Western Europe of the late seventeenth century, however, was a product not only of the medieval flowering of a Christian civilization and of a social system built around the family (in the broader sense), the corporation, the church, and the common acceptance of norms and symbols that combined the pagan tribal with the Christian imperial legacies. If it were only that, then the world of the West would have been no more strange to the Russians of the late seventeenth century than it had been to their ancestors of Kievan times or to their teachers, the Byzantines of the ninth century. In fact, however, the West implied much more, and in particular those elements that had been developed by the historical events we call—in shorthand fashion—the Renaissance, the Reformation, individualism, and the rise of modern science.

Indeed, the institutions, attitudes, and actions of Western Europe were permeated by "new" elements that were a far cry from the medieval pattern of tradition, slow evolution, the ideal of a static and harmonious order of things designed for the preparation of a life hereafter. To begin with, traditions were in the process of being rapidly subverted and displaced by the commands of reason. Rationality—in the broader sense of the term, that is, clear consciousness of a goal and the search for the most effective means for reaching it —was the principle that dictated the choice and development of the institutional means put at the disposal of the absolutist state, the enterprising trader, the creative thinker and artist. It was the spirit of reason that explained the preference for the general scheme and the readiness to make far-going transformations and to rebuild institutions from anew. We shall see how much of this spirit Peter the Great made his own, and the resistance that it was bound to encounter in a society still living on the basis of uncritically accepted tradition.

The triumph of reason entailed primacy of the individual over the group, for reason could only live in the single person, while the group relied on the workings of uncritically, emotionally held traditions. In the West the old group loyalties were weakening, were even being abandoned outright, for the sake of the triumph of the enterprising and driving energies, the critical reason of the individual. A transformation on the model of Western Europe, therefore, had to accept this new dynamic element and promote the spirit of individualism at the expense of the traditional loyalties and group ties. For Muscovy which still was so much rooted in the traditional family pattern of clannish solidarities, for Muscovy where the single individual counted for blessedly little outside his family and clan, the acceptance of the primacy of individualism signified a revolutionary departure from a centuries-old evolution. In breaking the old group ties Peter unsettled old values and beliefs, disorganized whole strata of society, aroused spirited antagonism on the part of the traditionalists. At the same time, those individuals whom he helped to liberate themselves from the old fetters of the group found themselves isolated, faced with new and difficult problems and very much in need of guidance and help from a strong hand; in the case of Russia it was the hand of the Autocratic Emperor. Thus, Peter's breaking of traditional groupings and the freeing of the individual, at first, served to strengthen the hold of the absolute monarch and his centralized bureaucratic state apparatus.

In the West, rationality and individualism had fostered an active orientation towards life and the solution of its problems. They had stimulated economic enterprise, as well as a belief in progress—in the sense of increasing the realm of human possibilities and the rewards for individual energy. The "modern" period of European history is marked by the expansionist character of European civilization, both internally through economic development and the creativity of the intellect, and externally in the form of the Europeanization of the inhabited world. Acceptance of the patterns of modernization on the Western European model, therefore, implied an acceleration of economic activity, the development of all resources of the country, and the stimulation of the creative powers of the Russian mind. Peter understood this double implication of the process of Westernization and modernization very well. As some of the later readings will illustrate, he devoted much of his energy to this task, a task whose satisfactory (on the whole) fulfillment was to be the major legacy of Peter the Great's reign.

In the West the essential traits of modernity we have just mentioned were put at the disposal of "power"—political, economic, spiritual. Power was the most easily perceptible and most dramatic manifestation of the new spirit of Europe. It was this very modern and Western trait that Peter possessed to a high degree. He had a strong and fervent drive for power, not so much for himself as for his country and his nation. He wanted to bring Russia's power to its peak; and as in his time this could be done by rising to the level reached by the Western European states, Russia would have to go to school in the West and open itself to foreign influences. This was not to be done without difficulty and without creating serious new problems for the Russian body politic, as some of the subsequent readings will show.

Deriving from the rationalistic, individualist approach to power, Peter also had a positive concept of government, while his predecessors had mainly a negative one: Muscovite government policy and practice were negative in the sense that they aimed at preventing the invasion, conquest, destruction of Russia (which did not preclude their taking advantage of opportunities for expansion); they aimed at preserving the traditional values, institutions, and culture of Russia. Peter, on the other hand, wanted to make Russia more powerful, more prosperous, better administered, more enlightened, more progressive, and he wanted it to play a positive and active role among other nations. He wished Russia to become acquainted with and make use of everything that foreign civilizations had to offer of value and benefit. To his way of thinking the state had to play an active role, take a positive stand, and have a general purpose— that of making Russia strong and its people happy. He, therefore, endeavored to impart a positive orientation to the government and to make the administration goal-conscious. His objective did not preclude trial and error, fumbling and improvisation on his part—but he always kept in mind the overall new direction he wished to impart to Russian life. He never was content to let things evolve, situations shape themselves, and transformations to come about gradually, growing out of existing circumstances.

In method, too, Peter differed from his predecessors. The difference did not lie so much in any specific solutions or policies; it was rather a matter of the temper or atmosphere created by Peter. The

Emperor's vitality, energy, driving force have few parallels among the great leaders of history. Not only was he strong physically, he was also a human dynamo: always active, always curious and eager to learn, always driving on; his enthusiasm was unbounded, his will inflexible, and his stamina and working capacity limitless. By contrast, the traditional Muscovite was indolent, slow, timorous, passive (there may have been good reasons for it, but they did not concern Peter). By comparison, the Western European was a more energetic, active, creative, and lively individual. Peter had noticed this very early when he contrasted the interesting, free, stimulating social life in the German (i.e. foreign) suburb of Moscow with the crudeness and boring formality of his own family and court. Intent on bringing out in others the qualities he possessed himself to such a high degree, Peter wanted to change the Russians into active, creative, energetic individuals, like the Western Europeans. He knew, or sensed, that the Russians were as gifted and intelligent as the Westerners, that they only needed the stimulation and opportunity to display their gifts. Western dress—with the greater freedom of bodily movement it afforded—became the symbol of the kind of transformation Peter wanted to bring about. Impatient and driving, himself successful in freeing himself from the shackles of Muscovite patterns, he was determined to lead all of Russia—at least its élite —onto the same path rapidly. Peter cared little for new institutions and policies for their own sake. To him what really mattered was to pull Russia out of its rut, its passivity, to open up channels for the free flow of its people's energies and resources. He wanted to impart motion to Russia—in Pushkin's words, he made the country rear like a steed—and to transform the nation's ways so that it could join the ever-expanding and ever-forward-moving stream of civilization. No wonder that in this attempt he disregarded the psychological resistance of his people, that he rode roughshod over traditional beliefs and values, oblivious to the anguish and suffering he brought to many. In the process, naturally, his personal traits and his ways of doing things became part and parcel of his larger design; they affected the character of his work. For this reason the personal element of Peter has become also an element in the historical destiny of his reign.

To be successful in his own terms, Peter the Great had to take steps leading to a rapid transformation of Russian man, at least of the members of the upper class. All textbooks relate how he went about changing the external appearance of the Russians, and several of the selections in this volume will describe how he initiated their spiritual, inner transformation. Peter wanted the transformation to take place immediately, under his very eyes. The question arises not only whether he succeeded superficially in getting the new values and culture adopted, but also whether he secured their genuine acceptance by the new generations of the Russian élite. Did Peter's contemporaries and their immediate descendants feel that they were in truth different from their Muscovite ancestors? In the realm of political and institutional history, Peter's reign, as some historians have pointed out, may perhaps have had only superficial or ephemeral, albeit striking, results. But did it not have lasting effects on the ways of thinking and feeling, on the way of life of many Russians? Viewing his reign from this vantage point, perhaps Peter's work found its culmination and completion only in the Revolution of 1917 (when the entire Russian people was launched onto the path of full "modernization"), although that revolution was brought about in a spirit far different from Peter's.

Of course, not all Russians were affected equally by the transformation in their way of life. And herein lie both a difficulty in assessing the reign of Peter and the tragedy of modern Russian history. The basic changes affected only the upper classes and those who came to be closely related to their way of life. They did not affect the mass of the people, the peasantry, who continued to live in Muscovite times. It was the formation of this gulf, the appearance of "two nations," that has colored all evaluations of Peter's reign by Russian thinkers and historians. For this reason, too, any and all interpretations of the reign are intimately bound up with ideological presuppositions and political preferences. In Russian thought and historiography Peter's reign has become, and still is, a live political and intellectual issue. The history of the historiography of the reign is actually an account of the intellectual development of the Russian élite over two hundred years. This is also the reason why Peter and his work still await their definitive histories.

If Peter's work affected different social classes differently, the same can also be said of various aspects of his reforming activity.

The elements of modernity and innovation Peter introduced did not affect all branches of public life, nor did they have equal success in all the areas in which they were introduced. Foreign policy and the creation of its instruments—a modern army and navy—were the areas in which Peter appears to have been successful immediately and well-nigh completely. In the domain of economic development, however, or in his social and fiscal measures, the first Emperor was not wholly successful. Even if his measures did affect these areas of Russian life profoundly, they did not always have the results expected by the Tsar. In judging Peter's reign it is, therefore, important to give an order of priority to various areas of his activities. One of the reasons for the disparity in the judgments pronounced by historians on the reign derives from the fact that every historian assigns a different order of priority to the various accomplishments of Peter's policies and plans.

In considering a period of profound and rapid transformation, especially a transformation that gave a new orientation and outlook to many strata of societies and many institutional developments, it is a great temptation to pay attention only to what has survived, to that which seems to lead directly to the present. To give way to this temptation—as advocated by E. H. Carr in *What Is History?*—is to shut oneself off from an important part of reality: that which has not survived, but which at one time may have been equally—if not more—important to contemporaries. Even to understand what has survived, and why, it is necessary to keep in mind the alternatives that were available to previous generations. It is equally important, as noted earlier, to remember that the opinions and reactions of Peter's contemporaries—however wrong they might be "objectively"—were themselves a factor in determining the outcome of Peter's reign, in shaping Russian reality subsequently. The wholehearted and even enthusiastic acceptance of Russia's cultural Westernization by the élite meant that Russian art, literature, music, and thought would be directly influenced and shaped by Western models and values. The rejection of Peter's work by the peasantry, the sullen resistance to it by a large segment of the people, created a gulf between the upper and lower classes. Sooner or later, thoughtful and enlightened individuals, social critics and political leaders would discover the depth of this gulf and attempt to bridge it. In so doing they might be

led to reject all of Peter's work and everything that issued from it
—i.e. the political, social, cultural régime of Imperial Russia—and
advocate either violent and complete revolution or a return to the
allegedly truer national past of Muscovite Russia.

This raises a last general observation. A change that has been
dramatic and rapid, a change that has left a deep impression on the
consciousness of contemporaries, appears to those who have had
to submit to it like a tidal wave or hurricane, an inevitable, elemental force that cannot be resisted. Its results, therefore, must be
accepted without questioning. Such was the effect of Peter's work
on several generations of Russians, and in some respects it lasted
for over two centuries. His impact—due to the energy and ruthless-
ness of his ways—was so profound, his accomplishments so stupen-
dous, that the smaller and more timid men who followed him were
overawed.[1] They did not dare to touch the basic structure he had
left. Consciously or unconsciously they endowed it with an absolute-
ness that imparted great rigidity to the system Peter had helped into
being. This rigidity, this fear of touching the structure, lest Russia's
newly won position crumble and the country revert to its previous
backward helplessness, saddled Imperial Russia with a particularly
onerous heritage. To advocate far-reaching changes in Peter's system seemed tantamount to rejecting it; and this in turn appeared to
call into question the very existence of modern Russia, its power, its
achievements, and its culture. Whether they liked Peter's work or
not, whether they accepted or rejected it, educated Russians in the
late eighteenth century, and throughout the nineteenth, could not
deny Peter's paternity. They operated with the institutional tools
and the modern rational concepts of national progress and welfare
that Peter had first introduced to Russian consciousness.

The problems raised by the reign of Peter the Great, the impact
of his grandiose personality on the destinies of Russia, admit of two
sides. There is, first, an evaluation of the novelty and solidity of the
institutional changes wrought by Peter. It is a task which is amena-
ble to more or less objective and definitive historical analysis. We
can ascertain to what extent the administrative institutions, or economic policies, for instance, had been an elaboration and extension

---

[1] A beautiful and compellingly dramatic illustration of this reaction is A. Pushkin's
famous narrative poem *The Bronze Horseman*

of Muscovite practices; to what extent they were modeled on foreign patterns; how long they survived in the form Peter gave them and how long they remained effective at all. Some of the historians quoted on the following pages will attempt to provide answers, or suggestions, in some specific areas. The other side is more complex and more difficult to come to grips with. Peter's reign must be evaluated in terms of the impact it had on the minds of contemporaries and later generations, of the consciousness Russians had of its significance for them. In this respect the personal characteristics of Peter and of his methods are of particular relevance. The people's awareness of the transformation wrought by Peter and their reactions to this awareness are very much part of an overall assessment of Peter's role in the history of Russia.

This last aspect of the historical problem presented by the reign of Peter the Great gave rise to an analytical and critical attitude among the Russian élite, and this attitude in turn became the source and stimulus to intellectual and artistic creation. Peter the Great, therefore, is both the pretext and the inspiration of modern critical and rational thought in Russia. He also occupies a major place in the history of the artistic and intellectual creations of the Russian mind over the last two centuries. Russian thinkers had to come to terms with Peter and his efforts at Westernization, his wish to see Russia join the family of European nations and participate in Western culture. In so doing the Russian élite—the *intelligentsia*—created the distinctive Russian contribution to the common cultural heritage of the modern world. Whatever their specifically Russian traits, Pushkin, Gogol, Dostoevsky, Tolstoi, Chekhov are unthinkable without Peter's work in Westernizing Russia.

[Note: In this volume, in the selections reproduced from existing translations the original transliteration has been preserved. In other selections which have been especially translated for this volume, the simplified Library of Congress system has been used. The dates are given according to the Julian calendar.]

Conflict of Opinion

... in the eyes of the vast majority, Peter's measures were shaking the very foundation of church and state.

SHMURLO

Peter and his closest aides were not as isolated in their society as some historians assume.

PAVLOV-SIL'VANSKII

In the person of Peter, the supreme state power entered into an implacable struggle with custom, eradicating it without mercy and taking upon itself the entire task of leading its subjects.

BOGOSLOVSKII

What are we to conclude from our study of Peter? Was his activity traditional, or did it represent a sharp and sudden revolution in the life of the Muscovite state for which the country was entirely unprepared? The answer is quite clear. Peter's reforms were not a revolution either in their substance or their results.

PLATONOV

... the conception of reform as the logical consequence of a century-old evolution and the notion that the reform was an artificial contribution were not necessarily irreconcilably opposed to each other. In one sense, Peter's reform had truly been a necessary outcome of a logical development. ... At the same time, however, it doubtlessly had been a personal and artificial accomplishment. ... The reform was at the same time natural and personal, deep and superficial, simple and complex, a single block and a mosaic.

MILIUKOV

Most of what had been done in Peter's day was still in its initial stages. Much was still no more than a blueprint for the future. ... This is why we have spoken of the work begun in the age of reform as a program which Russia is still carrying out and will continue to carry out in the future. ... No people had ever equalled the heroic feat performed by the Russians during the first quarter of the eighteenth century. ... The man who led the people in this feat can justly be called the greatest leader in history, for no one can claim a place of higher significance in the history of civilization.

SOLOVIEV

Peter accomplished a great deal toward the creation and strengthening of the national state of the landowners and merchants . . . and the strengthening of the national status of these classes was carried out at the expense of the serf peasantry, which was being fleeced three-fold.

STALIN

The contradiction in his work, his errors, his hesitations, his obstinacy, his lack of judgment in civil affairs, his uncontrollable cruelty, and, on the other hand, his wholehearted love of his country, his stubborn devotion to his work, the broad, enlightened outlook he brought to bear on it, his daring plans conceived with creative genius and concluded with incomparable energy, and finally the success he achieved by the incredible sacrifices of his people and himself, all these different characteristics make it difficult to paint one painting.

KLIUCHEVSKY

His achievements were not very great, . . . but they constituted a great era of reforms, rushed through at breakneck speed, rather than a revolution in comparison with so all-embracing and far-spreading and profound revolution as that begun in 1917.

SUMNER

I MUSCOVY BEFORE PETER THE GREAT

Sergei F. Platonov

THE HERITAGE OF MUSCOVY

The outstanding specialist on the political history of Muscovy in the sixteenth and seventeenth centuries was Sergei F. Platonov (1860–1933). He was Professor of Russian history at the University of St. Petersburg until the Soviet government established its ideological control over all Russian academic life. One of the first and most important historians to fall victim to Stalin's drive for conformity to the party line, Platonov died in exile in the Ural mountains. Primarily interested in the history of Russia as a state and a great European power, Platonov gave in his university lectures—from which the selection below is taken—the most comprehensive and sympathetic picture of what had been accomplished in the domain of foreign affairs and administration by the predecessors of Peter the Great.

Now let us examine what Peter the Great found on his accession, and what he had to start from. In other words, let us acquaint ourselves with the condition of politics and life in Muscovy at the end of the seventeenth century. A general survey of this condition would take us too far afield. Not all the details of the pre-Petrine era are equally important to us: we are concerned here only with facts that have a bearing on Peter's reforms. Our survey of the seventeenth century will therefore follow the headings under which we shall later examine the various facets of Peter's activity. This activity falls into two main areas: 1) he gave Russia a new political position among European nations; 2) he reformed, to a greater or lesser degree, the organization and administration of the state. We shall briefly review the situation in the seventeenth century under these two headings.

1) Russia's foreign policy before Peter was guided not by chance, but by a long historical tradition. Already in the thirteenth century, we see the emergence of circumstances which shaped both the external aspirations of the Russian people and the Russian state, and their internal organization for many centuries to come. During the early years of the thirteenth century the Germans appeared on the shores of the Baltic Sea; they pressed against the Lithuanian tribes, and at the same time became the enemies of Russia (Pskov and Nov-

From S. F. Platonov, *Lektsii po Russkoi Istorii* [*Lectures on Russian History*], edited by I. Blinov (St. Petersburg, 1904), pp. 367–378. Translated by Mirra Ginsburg.

gorod). The Swedes also began to move against Russia at this period. Under the impact of the German threat, the Lithuanian tribes organized themselves politically and, united by Mindovg, appeared on the stage of history as a principality hostile to Russia. Lithuania subjugated the southwestern part of Russia and threatened its northeast. At the same time, the Golden Horde was formed in the southeast and began to overrun northeastern Russia. Thus, almost simultaneously, the Great Russian people were ringed on three sides with aggressive enemies. Their principal task was now self-defense, a struggle, not for freedom (this had been taken away by the Tartars), but for historical existence itself, for the integrity of the nation and its religion. This struggle continued for centuries. Because of it, the nation was compelled to adopt a purely military [political] organization and wage war perpetually "on three fronts," as one scholar put it.

This struggle dictated the entire foreign policy of the Muscovite state from beginning to end, until the advent of Peter the Great. It may be said that this policy was limited in content: with its nearest neighbors, Muscovy waged a constant traditional struggle; in its relations with the more distant European nations, it sought to increase its means for this struggle. By the time of Peter's coming, the struggle had already brought Russia enormous political successes, but the goal of achieving complete security and establishing natural frontiers had not yet been reached. . . . Moscow did not have equal success in dealing with its diverse enemies.

The Tartars had been the complete masters of northeastern Russia since the thirteenth century. But their attitude toward conquered Russia and the manifest absence (despite the views of several historians) of strong direct oppression permitted Russia to grow in strength and to consolidate itself into a united powerful nation. This nation made its first attempt at rebellion against the Tartars at the battle of Kulikovo (1380), and the success of the attempt raised Russia's national consciousness and helped the further strengthening of Muscovy. This process of consolidation was paralleled by the internal disintegration of the Horde; the latter's progressive decline made it unnecessary for Muscovy to fight a second Kulikovo Battle to overthrow its yoke (1480). The Horde fell apart, the Tartar yoke was gone, but the struggle with the Tartars for the integrity of Russia's borders and the security of its people continued. Instead of one

Horde, there were now several, though weaker than the old. It was essential for Moscow to subdue them in order to achieve security. Ivan the Terrible subjugated the Hordes of Kazan and Astrakhan (1552–1556). His counselors urged him to subdue the Crimean Horde as well. But Ivan understood that Moscow could not defeat Crimea at that time (the talented Stephen Batory thought likewise when he became King of Poland). Muscovy was separated from the Crimea by steppes that were difficult to cross. Besides, the peninsula was then under the domination of a powerful Turkey, which was feared not only by Moscow. As a result, the Crimean Horde survived until the end of the eighteenth century.

In the seventeenth century, after Ivan's death, Muscovy waged a continuous border war with the Crimea (the details of this war are extremely interesting), and every summer it gathered troops along its southern frontiers for defense against Tartar raids. But, in addition to defensive measures, Muscovy acted against the Crimea by increasingly entrenching itself in the southern steppe with fortresses and men. In this way, it was gradually taking the offensive against the Tartars. The development of the Cossack settlements along the lower Don in the seventeenth century provided Muscovy with a new fighting force. Already in the first half of the seventeenth century, the Cossacks captured the Turko-Tartar fortress of Azov, but failed to hold it. The admission of the Ukraine (*Malorossiia*) to Muscovy brought the latter still nearer to the Crimea. At the very end of the seventeenth century (1687–1689), the Muscovite armies for the first time launched campaigns against the Crimea itself. Success, however, still eluded them—the steppe was too formidable an obstacle.

This was the point at which Moscow's policy had stopped before the coming of Peter. As Stephen Batory had estimated in the sixteenth century, and the Cossacks had proved in practice in the seventeenth, Azov was the weakest link in the armor of the Tartars and their masters, the Turks, in the south of the present-day Russia. Peter, who had witnessed the failure of Prince V. V. Golitsyn's campaigns against the Crimea, directed his forces not at the Crimea, but at Azov. Hence, Peter continued the traditional policy of Muscovy. In its struggle against the Tartars, Muscovy had achieved great successes before Peter; now Peter made use of these successes.

During the first two centuries of its existence (until the death of

Vitovt), Lithuania energetically attacked Russia and seized a great many Russian lands; this gave it the character of a state that, both in population and in culture, was predominantly Russian. At the end of the fourteenth century, it united itself dynastically with Poland and came under strong Polish-Catholic influence. The opposition of the Russian Orthodox population to Catholicism engendered internal conflict, which weakened Lithuania without eliminating the Polish influence. The latter triumphed in the sixteenth century, when Lithuania became an indivisible part of Poland (1569).

Before Vitovt's reign, Moscow had yielded to Lithuania. Soon after his death, the respective roles were changed. The strong Muscovite rulers Ivan III and Vasilii III began to wrest the Russian regions back from Lithuania, laying claim to all the Russian lands in the latter's possession. Thus Muscovy had taken the offensive against Lithuania with considerable success. But the final unification of Lithuania and Poland in the sixteenth century brought Poland into opposition to Muscovy as well. The Muscovy of Ivan the Terrible was compelled to yield before their combined forces; Ivan's struggle against Stephen Batory was unsuccessful. Still worse for Muscovy were the Times of Troubles of the early seventeenth century, when the Poles took possession of Moscow itself. In the middle of the seventeenth century, however, after the Poles were expelled and Muscovy had recovered from dissension, it resumed the old struggle to regain the Russian lands, now under Polish domination (1654). Tsar Aleksei Mikhailovich admitted the Ukraine to his rule, fought an extraordinarily difficult war for it, and concluded it with a brilliant victory. Weakened Poland continued to yield to Moscow even after the death of Tsar Aleksei. By the peace treaty of 1686, it ceded to Moscow for perpetuity the lands it had at first only temporarily yielded to Tsar Aleksei Mikhailovich. Peter inherited the relations created by this peace treaty. During his reign, Russia was clearly predominant over Poland, but the historical task of liberating all the Russian lands from Polish domination was not completed either before him, or under him. It was bequeathed to the eighteenth century.

The Germans and Swedes had taken the eastern coast of the Baltic Sea from Lithuania and Russia. Although Novgorod possessed the coast of the Gulf of Finland, it was compelled, for lack of convenient harbors, to depend in its Western trade on the Germans. Having subjugated Novgorod [1478] and inherited all its political relations, Moscow became increasingly aware of this dependence on the Germans. It had expelled the Hanseatic merchants and destroyed their trade in Russia, yet it remained dependent on outsiders; the trade passed into the hands of Livonian merchants. Pursuing its own trade advantages, Livonia was hostile to Russian trade, as it was generally hostile to Russia—a powerful and dangerous neighbor. It sought to erect a strong barrier between Russia and Western Europe, realizing that the education of Russia would double its political power. But Russia itself understood the significance of Western education and knew that the best path to the West was the Baltic Sea. (Because of geographic conditions, the White Sea was of limited usefulness in this respect.) In the sixteenth century, Ivan the Terrible, taking advantage of Livonia's internal weakness, declared war on it with the manifest goal of gaining possession of the seacoast.

Unable to withstand the impact of war, Livonia fell apart, one half of it giving allegiance to Poland, and the other half to Sweden. Ivan the Terrible was unable to hold his own against these powers, and lost not only his conquests, but also some of his own cities (1582–1583). These cities were regained by Boris Godunov, but during the Times of Troubles they were once more occupied by Sweden; by the treaty concluded with the Swedes in 1617, Muscovy was completely cut off from the Baltic Sea. This was a source of enormous pride to King Gustavus Adolphus. In the seventeenth century, Russia was at first too weak, and later too preoccupied with its wars with Poland to take a decisive step toward the Baltic Sea. Yet the idea of the need for this step did not die; it was handed down to Peter, who brought it to realization. In this respect, Peter considered himself the direct successor of Ivan the Terrible.

Our brief survey of the foreign policy of Muscovy shows that, in pursuing its traditional goals, this policy had, by the time of Peter's accession, attained great, though unequal successes. It was more successful in dealing with the Tartars, but less successful with the Swedes, who had followed the Germans as the masters of the Baltic Coast. Muscovy had not achieved an ultimate solution of its problems. And since its objectives were not the fortuitous whim of this or that political leader but vital necessities to our nation, growing out of the age-old conditions of its existence, they demanded solution as urgently under Peter as they had under his predecessors. This was why Peter devoted so much attention to them. We shall later see that his greatest efforts were expended precisely where the action of his predecessors had been least successful—in the struggle for the Baltic Sea.

2) It is generally acknowledged that Peter's activity resulted in substantial changes in the organization and administration of the state in the seventeenth century. On acquaintance with the characteristic features of the state's organization before Peter, we gain the impression that the Muscovite state was one in which the autocratic authority of the sovereign had reached unlimited power. By grouping all branches of administration directly under its control, this authority had created a strongly centralized government, with all of its most important functions located in Moscow, the departments [*Prikazy*] and the Boiar Duma. Despite this centralization, however, the government had not been fashioned into an orderly system of stable institutions, and did not function on the basis of any immutable laws. Guided by purely accidental and external expediency, the tsars governed Muscovy according to the so-called "system of delegation" [*sistema poruchenii*]. They delegated the administration of a given sphere directly to some trusted person. The degree of their confidence determined the degree of power invested in this person, and the latter often combined several offices [*vedomstvo*] under his jurisdiction, in accordance with his abilities. The offices themselves came into being in a haphazard manner: the most diverse affairs were often dealt with by a single office, while, on the other hand, there was much overlapping of functions in offices neither related nor subordinated to one another. This confusion had arisen in the course of history and was the result of the system of delegation of authority. Not being integrated into an orderly system, all offices were subject to easy and frequent change. . . . Nor was there any strict separation of functions between the church and state. The state often acted in the sphere of church administration, as an assistant of the church hierarchy. In turn, the church had jurisdiction over certain categories of lay persons, and the church courts often tried cases of a secular character.

However, this confusion of offices and the absence of integral and stable institutions should not be considered a sign of the disintegration of the state. "A centralized system can function without firm institutions; it can, like Muscovy, rest on a delegative system. There will be no unity and control, and relations will be confused, but it will remain strong by virtue of its closeness to the supreme authority."

Such was the state of the government. In examining the basic features of the social order of the seventeenth century, we shall find that, despite the total absence of warlike tastes, Moscow society had nevertheless adopted a military system of organization. Its upper classes composed the state militia, in which every member of the gentry was obliged to participate. The middle strata of society—the townsmen and merchants [*posadskie liudi*]—were subject to some military duties, but their primary obligation was monetary; they provided the taxes [*tiaglo*] which covered the state's military expenditures. The lower classes—the peasantry—partly shared the tax obligations, and partly assured the economic position of the gentry by their labor, thus making it possible for the latter to serve the state. The position of every estate [*soslovie*] within the state thus was defined by the form of its obligations toward the state, rather than by its rights. . . . The state sought guarantees for the proper performance of obligations by means of a number of restrictive measures in relation to the given estate. These measures are known under the general term of "oaths" [*kreposti*] or "attachments" [*prikrepleniia*]. The noble was bound to service, and through service, to the town in whose district [*uezd*] his estate was located. The urban population [*posadskoe*] was bound to tax duties, and, through these, to the community through which the taxes were paid. The peasants were attached to the land, on which they paid taxes, and to the person of the landowner whom they served by their labor. Because the estates were tied in this fashion to state obligations, their organization was determined by the interests of the state. The local estate associations and the urban and rural tax communities were financial in function and character: the entire purpose of their existence was to allocate the taxes due to the state among their members and collectively to guarantee their payment. The nobility had virtually no autonomous internal organization within their local town communities. Self-administered communities were very rare, and those that existed were very small in size and mere vestiges of sixteenth-century institutions. We may thus say that in seventeenth-century Muscovy there were no independent social organizations, unrelated to state obligations.

These, then, are the distinguishing features one notes at first acquaintance with seventeenth-century Muscovy. A brief review of the
state organization and administration of that time would show the
following scheme: at the head of the state was the Tsar, whose person
was the source of all power—legislative, judicial, and executive. He
was also considered the supreme protector of the church. The Church
Council of 1666–1667 directly acknowledged the primacy of the sovereign's authority over that of the patriarch. If the patriarch's position
seemed at times as high as that of the supreme temporal authority,
as it did during the patriarchates of Philaret and Nikon, this was
merely an accident of history and of the Tsar's favor. In reality, the
tsars of Muscovy wielded absolute autocratic power, although the
substance of this power was not defined by legislation until the period
of Peter the Great.

Until the second half of the seventeenth century, the *Zemskii
Sobor*—an assembly of representatives of the entire land—had held
a place in the government nearest to the throne. Historical conditions
in Russia had brought about a close connection between the supreme
state authority, the Tsar, and the spokesmen of the land. The patriarchal tinge which still survived in the state organization in the
seventeenth century makes it impossible to define precisely the juridical character of our representative assemblies of that period; they
were equally removed from either the limiting bodies or the consultative councils of the West. . . .

The *Zemskii Sobor* had been an occasional extraordinary auxiliary
organ, which assisted the supreme state authority in the task of governing the country. A similar organ, but a permanent one, was the
Boiar Duma. . . .

In the sixteenth century, the Duma had been the political organ of
the boiars aspiring to power; in the seventeenth, it became the principal government institution, merely the Tsar's council. This boiar
council was in charge of all aspects of national life: it drafted legislation, served as the supreme judicial organ and the central administrative institution, and, finally, had charge of all diplomatic relations.
In the seventeenth century (from 1681) the judicial functions of the
Duma were concentrated in the hands of a special commission known
as the Chamber of Justice [*Raspravnaia Palata*], made up of members
of the Duma. Apart from this chamber, the Duma had no other perma-

nent commissions or departments, and all matters were dealt with in the general assemblies. Despite all the changes in the class composition of the Duma in the sixteenth and seventeenth centuries, its rank structure remained the same. The members of the Duma were divided into two categories: the more aristocratic, or the boiars, and the more democratic, or the so-called "men of the Duma" [*dumnye liudi*]. The boiars were of two ranks—boiars and *okol'nichii*; the "men of the Duma" were also of two ranks—Duma gentry and Duma clerks. These were the four highest ranks in the state of Muscovy. With this composition and set of functions the Duma survived until Peter's day and acted as the mainspring of administration even during the early years of his reign.

The central administrative organs—the *Prikazy,* or departments—were subordinate to the Duma. Their number was not constant (from 40 to 50), and the distribution of functions was not systematized. Hence, affairs of the same nature were often within the jurisdiction of different departments, and some departments extended their activities to the entire country. Each department had sprung into being rather haphazardly, in response to historically conditioned requirements for a new agency. The departments were, consequently, in charge of a diversity of matters. Some departments governed specific geographic areas in all matters (Siberian Department, Department for the District of Kostroma, etc.). Others were in charge of specific categories of persons (the Department in Charge of Bondsmen, the Department for *Streltsy,* etc.). Still others had jurisdiction over specific matters (the Brigandage Department dealt with criminal justice; the Department of the Great Treasury dealt with finances; the Department of Rolls [*razriadnyi*] dealt with military affairs; the Embassy Department was in charge of diplomatic relations, etc.). Along with these large departments, there were minor ones, such as the Apothecary Department, in charge of the medical affairs of the court, or the Stone Department, in charge of stone buildings. Finally, there were also palace institutions, of similar structure, which were in effect the household offices of the Tsar's family (workshop chambers, the Funeral Department, etc.).

By the seventeenth century this multitude and confusion of heterogeneous departments had become a vexing problem to the government of Muscovy. The government tried to order and simplify its central administration, and achieved this to some extent by two methods: the merger of similar departments, and the subordination of several small departments to a large one. However, in these mergers the individual departments retained their own internal organization, so that the mergers were merely external. The structure of all departments was approximately the same. They were composed of a board [*prisutstvie*] and a chancery. The board consisted of the departmental chief (often a member of the Duma) and his "associates." These were called judges and were the chief's subordinates; hence, although it was collegial in form, the departmental board was not so in fact. All affairs were decided, not by the majority of its members, but by the chief. In small departments even the form was absent; all their affairs were under the jurisdiction of a single chief, who had no associates. The chancery was staffed with copyists, headed by clerks; their number depended on the scope of the department's work.

Directly subordinate to the departments was the entire regional [*oblast'*] administration. In the seventeenth century there had finally evolved in Muscovy a homogeneous type of local administration—the *voevoda* administration. The *voevodas,* appointed by the Moscow departments to govern the cities and *uezds* (districts), combined both military and civil power. In civil affairs they acted both as administrators and as judges. All aspects of local life were under their jurisdiction. . . . As we trace the activities of the *voevodas* in the seventeenth century, we find that by the end of the century their power over the people had increased, and the circle of their activities was growing. The role of the central government in the provinces was thus becoming increasingly more important, while the role of the local self-government established in the sixteenth century was constantly shrinking. Nevertheless, the relations between the central departments and the local officials remained ill-defined throughout the seventeenth century, and the task of regulating them was left to Peter. . . .

Such were the forms of administration in Muscovy before the launching of Peter's reform. To complete the survey of the state organization and administration, a few words should also be said about the social classes [*soslovie*] of seventeenth-century Muscovy.

The gentry of the pre-Petrine epoch is usually described as a class of persons obligated to render the state personal (chiefly military) service and in return for this were granted state lands in the form of estates of various sizes. The landed gentry's estates were worked by the labor of dependent peasants. Under these social and economic conditions, in the course of the seventeenth century, the gentry achieved a number of improvements in its way of life. On the one hand, with the dying out and decline of the old boiar families, the highest state positions were opening up to the upper strata of the gentry. In the latter half of the seventeenth century, many top-ranking government leaders were members of the rank and file gentry (such as Ordyn-Nashchokin).[1] On the other hand, the economic position of the gentry was greatly consolidated and improved; by legislative act the peasantry was bound to the land and the person of the landowner. (The Code of Laws of 1649 attached the peasants to the land; in the sixties of the seventeenth century a peasant's escape was declared a criminal offense, punishable under the law; and the practice followed throughout the seventeenth century developed into a custom which assumed that the peasant was bound not only to the land, but also to the person of the landowner. This custom was the sale of peasants without land.)

At the same time, the rights of the gentry to the granted estates [pomestie] were steadily extended and came to include the right to dispose of them. Indeed, the estates became hereditary, very similar to the patrimonial holdings [votchina] of the gentry. And, finally, military service ceased to be a duty confined solely to the gentry. A regular army was formed (regiments of cavalry, dragoons, and infantry), consisting of foreigners and lower-class Russians. This army, in which the gentry served as officers, frequently replaced the former gentry militia [opolchenie].

Peter the Great already found the gentry in the position of the upper class of Russian society, and supplying the entire personnel of the upper and lower administration. The old upper class—the

[1] Afanasii Lavrent'evich Ordyn-Nashchokin, died 1690. Son of a small service nobleman from the region of Pskov, he rose to become the architect of Muscovite diplomacy in the reign of Tsar Alexis (Aleksei Mikhailovich). His major achievements were the conclusion of the armistice of Andrusovo (1667), which consolidated Russia's victory over Poland, and the initiation of a policy of reconciliation with Poland.—Ed.

boiars—had not survived into Peter's day either in its former status or its role in the government.

The urban population did not become a separate, closed social class until it was defined as such by the Code of 1649 [*Ulozhenie*]. Consisting of persons engaged in trade and industry, this class was the object of the government's concern in the latter half of the seventeenth century. The government sought to stimulate the development of Russian trade and industries. The ideas of mercantilism, prevalent at the time in the West, appeared in our country as well. There is no doubt that Ordyn-Nashchokin was familiar with them, and this was reflected in the New Trade Statute [*Novotorgovyi Ustav*] of 1667, which contained legislation governing trade and the trading class, and spoke in praise of commerce as a factor of general welfare. However, the development of Russian foreign trade was hampered by the lack of Russian ports and convenient land roads, as well as by the competition of foreign merchants, against whom Russian merchants were unable to hold their own. As for industry and domestic trade in Russian cities, they were also hampered in their development, since the principal consumers—the wealthy gentry—were either concentrated in Moscow or scattered far and wide on their estates, where everything they needed was produced by the skills and labor of their peasants and bondsmen. Hence, urban life could not develop, and the urban population remained small. It is only in the northern part of the country, on the Volga and along the road to the port of Archangel, that as an exception we find a few wealthy cities.

By the end of the seventeenth century, as we have said above, the peasants became completely dependent on their landlords. They differed little from bondsmen [*kholop*] in their subjection to the gentry, but the government continued to regard them as a social class and to tax them. At the same time, the state sought to bring the bondsmen into the tax system as well, and imposed state levies on some of their categories. On the other hand, the owners of the bondsmen began to settle them on the land, allotting them households of their own. In reality then, at the end of the seventeenth century both the peasants of landowners and the bondsmen were dependent husbandmen, subject to taxation by the state. The only difference between them was in the juridical form of their dependence on their owners. Thus, the peasantry and the bondsmen had been brought very close to each other already before Peter. However, the peasants living on court lands (belonging to the Tsar) and on taxed lands (state lands) were far from serfdom. They constituted a class of full citizens, although each was bound to his community.

II PORTRAITS OF PETER THE GREAT

Duc de Saint-Simon
HIS PERSONALITY AND HABITS

The high-ranking French court noble, Louis de Rouvroy, Duc de Saint-Simon (1675–1755) had occasion to observe Peter the Great at close range during the latter's state visit to France in 1717. The following illustrates how an intelligent and perceptive Western observer saw the Russian ruler at the height of his success and fame following his victories over the Swedes.

The Tsar excited admiration by his extreme curiosity, always bearing upon his views of government, trade, instruction, police, and this curiosity embraced everything, disdained nothing in the smallest degree useful; it was marked and enlightened, esteeming only what merited to be esteemed, and exhibited in a clear light the intelligence, justness, ready appreciation of his mind. Everything showed in the Tsar the vast extent of his knowledge, and a sort of logical harmony of ideas. He allied in the most surprising manner the highest, the proudest, the most delicate, the most sustained, and at the same time the least embarrassing majesty, when he had established it in all its safety with a marked politeness. Yet he was always and with everybody the master everywhere, but with gradations, according to the persons he was with.[1] He had a kind of familiarity which sprang from liberty, but he was not without a strong dash of that ancient barbarism of his country, which rendered all his actions rapid, nay, precipitous, his will uncertain, and not to be constrained or contradicted in anything, Often his table was but little decent, much less so were the attendants who served, often too with an openness of kingly audacity everywhere. What he proposed to see or do was entirely independent of means; they were to be bent to his pleasure and command. His desire for liberty, his dislike to be made a show of, his free and easy habits, often made him prefer hired coaches, common cabs even; nay, the first which he could lay his

From the Duke of Saint-Simon, *Memoirs of Louis XIV and the Regency*, vol. III (Washington & London: M. Walter Dunne, 1901), pp. 101–104. Translated by Bayle St. John.

[1] This just appreciation of rank is always vaunted by Saint-Simon as one of the highest qualities a man can possess. No one was so contemptible to him as the person who took off his hat to the same extent to a marquis as to a duke.

hands on, though belonging to people below him, of whom he knew nothing. He jumped in, and had himself driven all over the city, and outside it. On one occasion he seized hold of the coach of Madame de Mattignon, who had come to gape at him, drove off with it to Boulogne and other country places near Paris. The owner was much astonished to find she must journey back on foot. On such occasions the Maréchal de Tessé[2] and his suite had often hard work to find the Tsar, who had thus escaped them.

The Tsar was a very tall man, exceedingly well made; rather thin, his face somewhat round, a high forehead, good eyebrows, a rather short nose, but not too short, and large at the end, rather thick lips, complexion reddish brown, good black eyes, large, bright, piercing, and well open; his look majestic and gracious when he liked, but when otherwise, severe and stern, with a twitching of the face, not often occurring, but which appeared to contort his eyes and all his physiognomy, and was frightful to see; it lasted a moment, gave him a wild and terrible air, and passed away. All his bearing showed his intellect, his reflectiveness, and his greatness, and was not devoid of a certain grace. He wore a linen collar, a round brown wig, as though without powder, and which did not reach to his shoulders; a brown coat tight to the body, even, and with gold buttons; vest, breeches, stockings, no gloves or ruffles, the star of his order over his coat, and the cordon under it, the coat itself being frequently quite unbuttoned, his hat upon the table, but never upon his head, even out of doors. With this simplicity, ill-accompanied or ill-mounted as he might be, the air of greatness natural to him could not be mistaken.

What he ate and drank at his two regular meals is inconceivable, without reckoning the beer, lemonade, and other drinks he swallowed between these repasts, his suite following his example; a bottle or two of beer, as many more of wine, and, occasionally, liquors afterward; at the end of the meal strong drinks, such as brandy, as much sometimes as a quart. This was about the usual quantity at each meal. His suite at his table drank more and ate in proportion, at

---

[2] Mans-Jean-Baptiste-René de Froulay, comte de Tessé (1651–1725), Marshal of France, assistant to Louvois, the Minister of War of Louis XIV, distinguished himself in several military campaigns and also in enforcing the revocation of the Edict of Nantes. In the last years of Louis XIV and during the Regency he was entrusted with diplomatic missions.

eleven o'clock in the morning and at eight at night. There was a chaplain who ate at the table of the Tsar, who consumed half as much again as the rest, and with whom the monarch, who was fond of him, much amused himself. Prince Kourakin went every day to the Hôtel de Lesdiguières, but lodged elsewhere.

The Tsar well understood French, and I think could have spoken it, if he had wished, but for greatness' sake he always had an interpreter. Latin and many other languages he spoke very well. There was a detachment of guards in his house, but he would scarcely ever allow himself to be followed by them. He would not set foot outside the Hôtel de Lesdiguières, whatever curiosity he might feel, or give any signs of life, until he had received a visit from the King.

On Saturday, the day after his arrival, the Regent went in the morning to see the Tsar. This monarch left his cabinet, advanced a few paces, embraced Monsieur d'Orléans with an air of great superiority, pointed to the door of the cabinet, and instantly turning on his heel, without the slightest compliment, entered there. The Regent followed, and Prince Kourakin after him to serve as interpreter. They found two armchairs facing each other, the Tsar seated himself in the upper, the Regent in the other. The conversation lasted nearly an hour without public affairs being mentioned, after which the Tsar left his cabinet; the Regent followed him, made him a profound reverence, but slightly returned, and left him in the same place as he had found him on entering.

Vasilii O. Kliuchevsky
THE ARTISAN TSAR

Vasilii O. Kliuchevsky (1841–1911) is Russia's most eminent modern historian. His reputation rests on his ability to present a perceptive synthesis (based on a prodigious amount of documentation) in the form of vivid pictures drawn with great stylistic brilliance. Interested in basic social trends, at

From Vasilii Kliuchevsky, *Peter the Great* (New York: St. Martin's Press, 1958), pp. 33–56. Reprinted by permission of Macmillan & Company Ltd. and St. Martin's Press Inc. Translated by Liliana Archibald.

times Kliuchevsky sacrificed detail for the sake of panorama, but he had no peer in painting lively portraits of Russia's major rulers. The portrait he drew of Peter the Great is justly considered one of his masterpieces.

Intellectually, Peter the Great was one of those simple-minded people who can be read at a glance and are easily understood.

Physically, Peter was a giant of just under seven feet, and at any gathering he towered a full head above everybody else. During the Easter service he had so much bending to do that he invariably suffered from backache. Not only was Peter a natural athlete, but habitual use of axe and hammer had developed his strength and manual dexterity to such an extent that he was able to twist a silver platter into a scroll; indeed, so dexterous was he that if a piece of cloth was thrown into the air he could cut it in half with his knife before it landed. All the male descendants of the Patriarch Philaret,[1] father of the first Romanov,[2] had been feeble in body or mind. The first marriage of the Tsar Alexis had done nothing to remove this hereditary weakness from the line, but in his son by Natalia Naryshkin it vanished entirely. Peter took after his mother, and was also said to have resembled Theodore, one of Natalia's brothers. Nervous activity and mental agility were characteristics of the Naryshkin family. In later years it produced a number of wits, and under Catherine II a Naryshkin became a very successful court entertainer.

According to a foreign envoy[3] who was presented to Peter and Ivan in 1683, Peter at eleven was a lively, handsome boy. Whereas Tsar Ivan looked at the floor, with the Crown of Monomachus[4] well down over his eyes, and sat like a lifeless statue on his silver throne beneath the ikons, Peter, who sat next to him on a twin throne wearing a duplicate crown made on the occasion of the joint Tsarship, looked eagerly and confidently about him, and found it difficult to keep still. But traces of a serious nervous disorder due either to

---

[1] Philaret had been elevated to the metropolitanate of Rostov by the First Pretender and was Patriarch of Moscow from 1619 to 1633.
[2] Michael, 1613–1645.
[3] Engelbert Kampfer, a German traveler, who was acting secretary for the Swedish Envoy, Fabricius.
[4] The Crown, with the Sceptre and Orb, were originally presents from the Byzantine Emperor, Constantine Monomachus, to the Grand Duke Vladimir of Kiev. They were not used after 1682 because Peter's successors were not merely tsars, but emperors. The Crown and pectoral cross of Monomachus were the visible symbols of the relations of the Muscovite Tsars to the Emperors of Constantinople.

the memories of the bloody scenes of 1682, or to his all too frequent debaucheries, or to a combination of both, ruined his health, so that in later years Peter made a different impression. Very soon, by the time he was twenty, he began to suffer from a nervous twitch of the head; and when he was lost in thought, or during moments of emotional stress, his round handsome face became distorted with convulsions. This, together with a birthmark on his right cheek, and a habit of gesticulating with his arms as he walked, made everybody notice him. In 1697, some Dutchmen who were waiting in a barber's shop in Saardam, and who had been obligingly informed of these characteristics by some of their compatriots who had been in Moscow, easily recognized the carpenter who had just come in to be shaved as the Tsar of Muscovy. At times Peter's face and eyes took on such a savage aspect that nervous people were likely to become demoralized in his presence.

Two of the best-known portraits of Peter are by Kneller and the Dutch painter Charles Moor. The first portrait, commissioned by William III in 1698, shows a Peter with long-flowing locks, wide-open, round eyes, and a happy expression. Although his brushwork is rather insipid, Kneller has captured something of the elusive, cheerful, almost laughing expression which is reminiscent of a portrait of Peter's grandmother Streshnev. The other portrait was painted by Charles Moor in 1717, when Peter went to Paris to try to bring the Northern War to a speedy conclusion, and to try to arrange a marriage between his eight-year-old daughter, Elizabeth, and the seven-year-old King of France, Louis XV. Parisian observers described Peter as an imperious-looking sovereign who, in spite of his fierce and savage looks, could be most amiable to those who were likely to be of use to him. Peter had such a sense of his own importance that he paid no attention whatsoever to the elementary rules of behavior, and behaved on the Seine as he behaved on the Neva. Leaving his Paris hotel one day, he took possession of a carriage that did not belong to him and calmly drove away. But Charles Moor saw him in a different light. The moustache looks as if it has been stuck on and is thicker than that of Kneller's portrait; the set of the lips and especially the expression of the eyes, suggest sickness, sadness and weariness, so the general impression is that of a tired man, overpowered by the sense of his own greatness, who desires nothing more than to be allowed to rest; there is no sign either of his youthful self-confidence or of the mature satisfaction that comes from a job well done. It is worth remembering that this portrait was painted when Peter stopped at Spa, on his way back from Paris, in order to be treated for the malady which eight years later was to be the cause of his death.

Peter was never more than a guest in his own home. His adolescence and youth had been spent either traveling or working out of doors. Had Peter at the age of fifty paused to look over his past, he would have seen that he had been constantly moving about from one place to another. During his reign he had traveled the length and breadth of Russia, from Astrakhan to Derbent, from Archangel to Azov, and from the Neva to the Pruth. As a result of this perpetual mobility, Peter became so restless that he was constitutionally incapable of staying in one place for any length of time, and was always looking for a change of scenery and for new impressions. The haste with which he did everything was now normal. He had such a long stride and used to walk so quickly that his companions had to run to keep up with him. He could not sit still for long, and at banquets he would jump out of his chair and run into the next room in order to stretch his legs.

When he was young his restlessness added to his enjoyment of dancing. Peter was an ever-welcome guest at the parties of noblemen, merchants, or artisans; here he danced a great deal and, though the only dancing lessons he had were "practices" during evenings spent at the Lefort establishment, he danced well. If Peter was not sleeping, traveling, feasting, or inspecting, he was busy making something. Whenever he could he used his hands, which were never free from callouses. When he was young and still inexperienced he could never be shown over a factory or workshop without trying his hand at whatever work was in progress. He found it impossible to remain a mere spectator, particularly if he saw something new going on. His hands instinctively sought for tools; he wanted to work at everything himself. He eventually became so skilled and dexterous that he was able to master new and unfamiliar techniques in a very short time. This attention to technique, which had developed from an intelligent curiosity, became a habit, and Peter felt that he had to master every new technique before he had even considered whether or not it was of any use to him, so that over the years his technical knowledge became most impressive. Even during his first foreign tour, the German princesses who had talked with him came to the conclusion that he was a master-craftsman in fourteen different trades. He felt quite at home in any factory.

After his death, it was found that nearly every place in which he had lived for any length of time was full of the model boats, chairs, crockery, and snuff-boxes he had made himself. It is surprising that Peter ever found enough leisure to make so many knick-knacks. He was so proud of his own skill and dexterity as a craftsman that he believed himself to be a good surgeon and dentist as well. Those of his companions who fell ill and needed a doctor were filled with terror lest the Tsar hear of their illness and appear with his instruments to offer his services. It is said that after his death a sackful of teeth was found—a memorial to his dental practice!

But his favorite occupation was shipbuilding, and no affairs of state could detain him if there was an opportunity to work on the wharves. When he lived in St. Petersburg in later years, he would spend at least one or two hours every day at the Admiralty. He was such a competent marine architect that his contemporaries said that he was the best shipwright in Russia, since he not only could design a ship, but knew every detail of its construction. Peter took a particular pride in this ability, and he stinted neither money nor effort in extending and improving Russia's shipbuilding industry. The Moscow-born landlubber had developed into a real sailor to whom the smell of the sea was as necessary as water is to a fish. Peter always said that sea-air and constant hard physical labor helped to keep him in good health in spite of his overindulgent way of living. It was probably because of this that he had an insatiable sailor's appetite. According to his contemporaries he was always hungry, and whenever he went visiting he was ready to sit down to a meal, whether he had already dined or not. He used to get up at five in the morning and lunch between eleven and twelve, after which he retired for a short sleep. Even when he was a guest at a banquet he would observe this rule, and return after his sleep ready to start the meal all over again.

Because political quarrels during his childhood and youth had kept him from the strait-laced functions of the court, Peter surrounded himself with a motley group of unconventional youngsters, the consequence of which was that when he grew up he could not tolerate ceremonial functions. Moreover he led an essentially active life, and his happiest moments were those spent using an axe, a saw, or a lathe, or "wielding a correctional cudgel." During solemn ceremonies of state this otherwise masterful and self-willed monarch would become awkward and confused; when Peter had to dress up in all his ceremonial finery and stand by the throne in the presence of the court to listen to a newly-accredited ambassador's wordy peroration, he would breathe heavily, grow red in the face, and perspire freely. In his private life Peter lived simply and frugally, and the monarch who was considered by the rest of Europe to be the most powerful and the richest in the world used to walk about in worn-out shoes and in stockings that had often been darned by his wife or daughters. When he was at home he would hold a reception as soon as he had got out of bed, dressed in a very old dressing gown made from nankeen and would then put on a plain, thick, serge kaftan which he seldom changed. He rarely wore a hat in summer, and used to go out either in a gig drawn by two miserable horses, or in such a shabby cabriolet that a foreign observer declared that a Muscovite tradesman would have thought twice about using it. On special occasions, when for instance he was invited to a wedding, Peter would borrow a coach from his foppish Procurator-General, Yaguzhinsky.[5] To the end of his life, Peter retained the habits of previous generations, disliked large, lofty rooms, and during his travels abroad avoided living in sumptuous palaces. Bred on the vast plains of Russia, Peter found in Germany that the narrow river valleys surrounded by mountains oppressed him. It seems strange that a man who grew up out of doors and was used to large spaces could not live in a room which had a high ceiling. When he found himself in such a room he would have a low canvas ceiling put in. It is probable that the overcrowded surroundings of his early childhood were responsible for this particular trait. At Preobrazhensky, where he grew up, he lived in a small, old, wooden house, which, according to a foreigner, was not worth more than one hundred thalers. At St. Petersburg he built himself some small summer and winter resi-

---

[5] For a brief account of his character and career see R. N. Bain, *The Pupils of Peter the Great* (Constable, 1897), pp. 40–41, 45, 75.

dences with tiny rooms. The same foreigner remarked that "the Tsar cannot stomach a large dwelling."

When Peter left the Kremlin he left behind him all the primitive grandeur of court life to which previous tsars of Muscovy had been accustomed. The only other European court which was comparable to his was that of the miserly King Frederick William I. Peter often used to compare himself with Frederick William, and say that the one cared as little for luxury and extravagance as the other. At Peter's court there were no chamberlains, no seneschals, and no expensive plate. The pre-Petrine court cost hundreds of thousands of roubles a year to maintain, while Peter's establishment cost only sixty thousand a year. Peter had ten or twelve personal attendants, young courtiers of obscure origin who were known as *"denshchiki."* Moreover Peter disliked fine liveries and expensive brocades. During the last years of his reign, he established for his second wife⁶ a large and brilliant court which could compare with the splendor of any German prince's court. Though Peter himself could have dispensed with the glitter, he wanted his second wife to be surrounded by it, probably in order to try to make the courtiers forget her humble origin.

Peter was equally free and easy in his relationship to people; but his social manners were a mixture of the habits of a powerful aristocrat of a previous generation and those of an artisan. Whenever he went visiting he would sit down in the first vacant seat; if he was hot he would take off his kaftan in front of everybody. When he was invited to act as Marshal of Ceremonies at a wedding he would fulfill his obligations punctiliously and then, having put his Marshal's rod of office away in a corner, would move towards the buffet, take a hot roast of meat in his hands, and start eating. It was this habit of dispensing with knives and forks at table that had so shocked the princesses at Koppenburg. He had no manners whatsoever and did not consider them necessary.

At the winter receptions at St. Petersburg which were attended by the fashionable society of the town, or at gatherings held in the house of some dignitary, the Tsar had no hesitation in sitting down to play chess with simple seamen, with whom he would drink beer

⁶ Catherine, whom Peter married in November, 1707.

and smoke a long Dutch pipe; he would quite ignore the ladies who were dancing in the same room. Peter spent his evenings either visiting friends or entertaining himself, and liked being surrounded by a gay crowd. At these occasions he was merry, sociable, and talkative, and enjoyed listening to the unconstrained chatter that went on around him as he walked up and down drinking Hungarian wine. He did not like anything to break up these gatherings and would not tolerate malicious gossip, caustic remarks, or brawling. An offender was "sconced"; he had to swallow at a draught either three beakers of wine or an "eagle" (a large ladleful) so that "he would learn neither to lie nor to provoke." This sort of punishment was generally sufficient to stop any tactless talk, though occasionally Peter's free and easy manner would encourage somebody to blurt out exactly what he was thinking. It so happened that Peter was very fond of a naval lieutenant called Mishukov, and thought so highly of him as a naval officer that he became the first Russian to be given command of a frigate. Once at a banquet at Kronstadt (this happened before the affair of the Tsarevich Alexis)[7] Mishukov, who was sitting next to the Tsar, and was rather drunk, suddenly became thoughtful and then burst into tears. This surprised the Tsar who asked him what was the matter. Mishukov explained quite frankly, and loudly enough for everybody to hear. "It's like this," he said, "this place, the new capital, the Baltic fleet, all the Russian sailors, and finally myself, Lieutenant Mishukov, Commander of a Frigate, all know how much we owe to your favor, and realize that this is all your work. When I thought about all this I realized that you are not getting any younger, and so I burst into tears." And then Mishukov added, "and who is there to take your place?"

"What do you mean?" Peter asked, "I've got a Tsarevich, an heir."

"Oh, yes," replied Mishukov, "but he is an idiot and will undo all your work."

Peter was rather pleased with the bitter honesty of the sailor's speech, but, since it was most inopportune and indiscreet of Mishukov to have mentioned this at a banquet, a reproof was clearly necessary. Peter laughed and hit him over the head. "You are a fool," he said, "you cannot say these things in public."

---

[7] There is no discussion of Alexis's conflict with his father in Kliuchevsky. For a brief account see Florinsky, *Russia* (New York: Macmillan, 1953), vol. I, pp. 330–333.

Peter was always honest and direct in his dealings with people, and expected them to be honest and frank with him, and he disliked subterfuge of any kind. The following anecdote is told by Nepluev in his memoirs. On his return from studying in Venice, Nepluev was examined by the Tsar himself and appointed Superintendent of the St. Petersburg Docks, a post which brought him into almost daily contact with the Tsar. Nepluev was advised to be efficient, but, above all, always to tell the Tsar the truth. During his name-day celebrations, Nepluev got very drunk and the next morning overslept, so that he arrived at the docks after the Tsar. At first the frightened Superintendent wanted to go home and pretend that he was ill, but on thinking it over decided that he would go and tell the truth.

"I am already here," said Peter.

"It is my fault, your Majesty," replied Nepluev, "I stayed up too late last night, making merry." Nepluev was shaking as Peter put his hand on his shoulder and said, "Thank you for telling me the truth; God will forgive you; there is nobody who has not sinned. And now let us go and visit a woman in childbed." So the Tsar and Nepluev went to visit the carpenter's wife who was expecting a baby. Peter gave the woman five "grivni," kissed her, and told Nepluev to do the same. But Nepluev only gave the woman one "grivni." Peter laughed, and said "Hey! I see that you do not like to give freely."

"I have not got much to give, Sire," replied Nepluev, "I am a poor courtier, with a wife and children to support, and if it were not for the salary you pay me we would not be able to live." As soon as Peter heard this he asked Nepluev how many serfs he owned and where his estate was. The carpenter brought out two glasses of vodka on a wooden tray for his guests; Peter drank his and ate a piece of carrot pie; Nepluev did not drink and refused the carrot pie. Peter said to him, "Come on man, drink up, or you will offend our host." Then breaking off a piece of pie, Peter added, "Now eat up, this is not Italian, but good Russian food." Peter was a kind man but a ruthless Tsar; and he drove himself as hard as others. As has been shown, the surroundings in which he grew up were hardly likely to encourage in him any care for people's feelings or circumstances. His natural intelligence, his age, and the position he occupied helped to hide these shortcomings, but even so they were sometimes still very much in evidence. When Peter's favorite, Alexander Menshikov, was young, he received the full force of the Tsar's fist in his oblong face more than once. A characteristic incident occurred at a banquet at which a boring foreign artillery officer was boasting to Peter about his knowledge. Peter could not get a word in, and eventually lost patience. He spat in the officer's face, and then turned his back on him. Not unnaturally, behavior of this sort made Peter a difficult man to deal with. But he became quite impossible when he had one of the attacks of nerves which usually ended with convulsions. As soon as his attendants saw the symptoms of such an attack, they sent for Catherine, who made the Tsar lie down, put his head in her lap, and then gently stroked his forehead. Peter soon fell asleep, and as long as Catherine held his head in her hands everybody remained silent. After two hours Peter would wake up quite refreshed, and would behave as if nothing had happened. But not even the excuse of such attacks can justify the failure of this usually frank and outspoken monarch to take other people's feelings into consideration. This lack of consideration often spoiled the easy, unconstrained atmosphere that he enjoyed.

It is true that Peter liked to enjoy himself and make jokes, but it is also true that these jokes often went too far and were either very cruel or just vulgar. During summer feast-days Peter liked to entertain the aristocracy in a grove of oaks which he had planted himself in front of his Summer Palace. Here the guests sat on wooden benches at little wooden tables, while Peter entertained them like a good host, discussing politics with the officials and church matters with the clergy. Unfortunately, Peter's cream choked the cat. He himself was used to drinking vodka neat, and expected his guests, including the ladies, to do the same. Sometimes guards appeared carrying buckets of corn brandy[8] which could be smelt all through the garden, and the sentries were ordered not to let any of the guests leave. It is hardly surprising that the guests were appalled, especially as the guard, all specially appointed, received orders that the guests were to be given corn brandy with which to drink the Tsar's health. Happy were they who managed to slip out of the garden! Only the church dignitaries did not try to avoid the beverage, and they sat at their tables, smelling of onions and radishes, getting progressively drunker. In-

[8] A rough drink used mainly by peasants.

deed, visiting foreigners noticed that at these gatherings it was always the clergy who were the drunkest. A Protestant preacher was dumbfounded by this crude and public behavior. A characteristic incident occurred at the wedding of the elderly widower, Prince U. U. Trubetskoi, to the twenty-year-old Princess Golovin in 1721. Glasses of jelly were served on a large tray at the wedding feast, and Peter, knowing that the bride's father was particularly fond of jelly, made him open his mouth and stuffed jelly after jelly into it; when Prince Golovin tried to close his mouth, Peter wrenched it open again with his own hands. Meanwhile at another table, the host's other daughter, the fashionable and wealthy Princess Cherkasky, was standing by her brother's chair. At a sign from the Empress, who was sitting at the same table, Princess Cherkasky began to tickle her well-brought-up brother in the ribs; he reacted like a calf whose throat is being cut, while the high society of St. Petersburg laughed merrily.

Thus Peter's sense of humor turned his entertainments into unpleasant affairs. Toward the end of the Northern War an important calendar of holidays was compiled, including celebrations of victories, to which, after 1721, the Peace of Nystadt was added. Above all, Peter enjoyed the launching of a new ship, when he behaved as if a new baby had been born. Eighteenth-century Europe drank heavily, and the Russian aristocracy was no different. Generally parsimonious, Peter would spend a large sum of money on alcohol to celebrate the launching of a new ship. Parties on board ship were attended by the capital's high society. These parties inevitably ended with General-Admiral Apraxin bursting into tears and moaning that he was an old, lonely man, a waif with neither mother nor father, and with the Minister for War, the brilliant Prince Menshikov, dead drunk under a table, whereupon his frightened wife, Princess Dasha, and other ladies, had to revive him with massage and cold water. But not all parties ended as simply as this. Sometimes Peter would lose his temper, and would withdraw extremely upset to the ladies' half of the ship. Whenever this happened he had guards posted at the gangways with instructions that nobody was to leave until he had returned. Until Catherine had succeeded in calming him, and he had had a nap, the guests remained in their places drinking and getting bored. The Peace of Nystadt was celebrated by a masquerade which lasted for seven days. Peter was beside himself with joy at the end of the war, and, forgetting his age and his ailments, sang songs and danced on the tables. This celebration took place in the Senate. In the middle of the banquet Peter got up, ordered the guests to await his return, and went to sleep on his yacht which was anchored on the Neva. The abundance of wine and the perpetual noise at these interminable festivities did not prevent the guests from getting bored and tired of staying indefinitely in one place in their compulsory fancy dresses. A refusal to wear fancy dress would have entailed a fifty-rouble fine. For a whole week thousands of masked people walked, danced, drank, and bustled each other, so that when finally the enforced gaieties ended, the participants were all equally relieved.

Though these official functions were oppressive and boorish, there were others which were worse and were openly indecent. It is difficult to know what caused such behavior. Was it a search for vulgar relaxation after a hard day's work or was it merely lack of thought? Peter tried to give his debaucheries an official form in order to turn them into permanent institutions. In this way the "Most Drunken Synod of Fools and Jesters" was created. Meetings were held under the presidency of a chief buffoon called the "Prince-Pope," or the "Noisiest, all-jesting Patriarch of all Moscow, Kokua and Yaüza." There was a college of twelve cardinals, all tipplers and gluttons, who were attended by a large suite of bishops, archimandrites, and other dignitaries, whose coarse and obscene nicknames are too disgusting to print. Peter himself was a deacon of this Order, for which he drew up, with the same legislative skill that he expended on his laws, a charter that minutely defined the method of electing and installing the "Prince-Pope" and the ritual required for the consecration of the rest of this hierarchy of drunkards. The first commandment was that members were to get drunk every day, and might never go sober to bed. The Synod's most important tasks were to offer excessive libations to the glory of Bacchus, and to lay down a suitable procedure to ensure that "Bacchus be worshipped with strong and honorable drinking and receive his just dues." The charter also prescribed the vestments to be worn, drew up a Psalter and Liturgy, and even created an "All-jesting Mother Superior" with "Lady Abbots." It even went so far as to imitate the Catechism, and decreed that, just as a baptismal candidate was asked "Do you believe?," so a candidate for this institution was to be asked, "Do you drink?" Those who lapsed into sobriety after initiation were to be debarred from all the inns of the Empire, and a heretic was to be banned from the society in perpetuity. In short, this was a most indecent parody of religious rites and ceremonial. The pious believed that its members' souls were damned eternally, and that those who resisted this apostasy would become martyrs. Over the Christmas holidays, about two hundred men would descend on Moscow or St. Petersburg in sleighs, and spend a night "celebrating." The procession was led by the mock patriarch wearing his regalia and carrying his mitre, followed by a retinue who jigged along in their overcrowded sleighs, singing and whistling. Those residents who were honored by a visit had to entertain the revellers at their own expense, and, as an eye-witness said, "they drank an awful lot." The first week of Lent was celebrated in a similar fashion, with a procession of penitents organized by the Prince-Pope and his Council for the edification of the faithful. The revelers, wearing their coats inside out, either rode on the backs of asses and bullocks, or sat in sleighs drawn by swine, goats, or bears. In 1699, at Shrovetide, after a particularly sumptuous court banquet, the Tsar organized a service in honor of Bacchus. The patriarch, Prince-Pope Nikita Zotov, the Tsar's old tutor, drank everyone's health, and then blessed the kneeling guests by making the sign of the cross over them with two long pipes, in the same way that a bishop would bless his congregation with a two- or three-branched candelabra. Finally, mitre in hand, Zotov began to dance. The only guest who could stand this ridiculous display no longer, and left, was a foreign ambassador. Generally most foreigners took the view that such behavior served a political or even educational purpose, and that it was directed against the church and its hierarchy, as well as against drunkenness. The Tsar wanted at one and the same time to ridicule an institution which he wished to discredit, and to divert his subjects while trying to make them contemptuous of bigotry and disgusted with debauchery. It is difficult to know how much truth there is in this view, particularly since it is more an attempt to justify than a genuine explanation.

Peter not only ridiculed the church hierarchy and ceremonial, but also made a mockery of his own personal power by appointing Prince Theodore Romodanovsky King-Emperor, and calling him "your Imperial Illustrious Majesty," while Peter called himself "your bondsman and eternal slave Peter," or simply "Petrushka Alexeev." Surely his behavior is the result of a peculiar sense of humor rather than of a particular personal bias. Alexis displayed the same type of humor, only with the difference that he himself did not like being made a figure of fun. Peter and his friends were more intent on playing the fool than in causing trouble. They made fun of everything, ignoring tradition, popular feeling, and their own self-respect, in the same way that children imitate the words, actions, and facial expressions of adults, without meaning either to criticize or to insult them. They did not mock at the church as an institution, but merely showed their resentment of a class which contained so many worthless people. It is not surprising that no attention was paid either to the effect such orgies had on the people, or to the consequences, since Peter was always complaining that while his father had only one damned beard[9] to deal with, he had a thousand, though they were more likely to prove unpleasant than actually dangerous. Moreover, the accusation leveled against Adrian, the last patriarch to hold office, that he did nothing but eat and drink without ever denouncing sin, could also be leveled against the rest of the ecclesiastical dignitaries. But, more serious than this, the people were already murmuring that the Tsar was Antichrist. The administrative classes, who were seriously out of touch with public opinion, hoped that the use of the knout and the torture chamber would stamp out the Antichrist legend. This barbarous usage, though hard to justify, was, after all, in harmony with contemporary custom. It has always been a characteristically Russian habit to make fun of the church and to give an antireligious twist to any buffoonery. Equally familiar was the part played by church ritual and the clergy in popular legend. The clergy had only themselves to blame for their debasement, because, while they expected the laity to adhere strictly to the precepts of the church, they notably failed to do so themselves.

Peter shared the popular attitude to religion; he deplored the hypocrisy of the Russian clergy and the dissension within the church. Yet, in spite of this, Peter was himself quite religious, knew the Liturgy by heart, and enjoyed singing in the choir. Nonetheless, in

---

[9] An allusion to the Patriarch Nikon.

1721, during the festivities celebrating the Peace of Nystadt, he organized a licentious travesty of the marriage service by making the Prince-Pope, old Buturlin, marry Zotov's widow in the Troïtsa Monastery. The ceremony was witnessed by rather merry and extremely noisy courtiers. What can there be political about a wooden receptacle for vodka which reminded the drunken brotherhood of the Holy Bible? This was no subtle political movement directed against the church, although it emphasized what was common knowledge, that the authority of the church was dwindling; it was simply the folly of a group of aristocratic revelers. Because of the monastic tendency of the times and the debasement of the White Clergy,[10] the priests substituted the government of the individual conscience for their proper concern with public morality.

Peter had yet another side to his character; he spent time and money generously in obtaining paintings and statues from Italy and Germany which formed the foundations for the Hermitage Collection at St. Petersburg. The many pleasure palaces which he had built round his new capital indicate his taste in architecture. At enormous cost he hired the best European architects, like Leblond[11] ("my wizard" as Peter called him) who was tempted to leave the French Court by an immense fee. Leblond built the "Mon Plaisir" pavilion at Peterhof, which so excited visitors with its magnificent carved cabinets, its view over the sea, and its shaded gardens.

Peter disliked the classical style, and liked his pictures to be bright and cheerful, so that the pavilion at Peterhof was hung with excellent Flemish landscapes and seascapes. Not even manual labor made Peter indifferent to scenery, and he was very partial to seascapes. He spent large fortunes in embellishing his suburban residences with artificial terraces, cascades, cunning fountains, and flowerbeds. But even though Peter's artistic taste was strongly developed, it was as onesided as his way of life. His habit of going to the heart of the matter and concerning himself with technical details had developed in him a keen eye and a strong feeling for perspective, form, and symmetry. He showed marked aptitude for the

---

[10] That is, Secular Clergy.
[11] For Leblond's contributions to the architecture of Petersburg, see Christopher Marsden, *Palmyra of the North* (Faber & Faber, 1942), pp. 60–67.

plastic arts, and delighted in complicated building plans; but here his artistic appreciation stopped. He himself confessed that he did not like music, and found even dance music unpleasant.

Occasionally, serious discussions were held at the Drunken Synod's uproarious meetings. Peter's discussions of policy with his collaborators were held with greater frequency as the war spread and his own reforms multiplied. These discussions are interesting not only for the ideas that were put forward, and the opportunity they give us to get a closer look at these men, and their motives and attitudes, but also because they go a long way to mitigate the bad impression made by the Drunken Synod on posterity. Through the smoke and above the clinking of tankards, political ideas were thrashed out; and this makes those statesmen look rather better. Once, in 1722, Peter was talking to a group of foreigners, and, under the influence of large quantities of Hungarian wine, told them about the difficulties he had met during the early part of his reign. Simultaneously, he said, he had had to create a regular army and navy, educate his idle, ignorant subjects, and teach them to be courageous, loyal, and honest; all this had been incredibly difficult, but, thank God, it was all in the past and now he could take life more calmly. Peter went on to say that, like all rulers, he must nonetheless still strive to know his subjects better. It seems likely that Peter had had these ideas for a long time, and had given them a great deal of thought. Moreover, it is likely that he himself started the legend about his creative activities. If contemporary evidence is to be trusted, this legend was crystalized in a cartoon which showed a sculptor working at the half-finished form of a human figure carved out of a rough block of marble. This signified that after the end of the war with Sweden, Peter and his collaborators realized that there was still a great deal to do, although as a result of all their efforts, a war had been won and many reforms enacted. . . .

Peter worked hard, both mentally and physically, all his life; he was always ready to adopt new ideas, was extremely observant, and became a highly skilled craftsman. But he had no time for complicated reasoning, and found it easier to grasp the details of a plan than to view it as a whole, so that he was better at devising ways and means of implementing it than at seeing its consequences. He was more a man of action than a thinker, which not unnaturally heavily influenced his way of life and his political program. His early childhood was spent in the sort of company which was least likely to turn him into a responsible and politically minded individual. The court—full of nonentities—and the royal family of Alexis's day were rotten with enmity and petty intrigue. Court intrigues and palace revolutions were Peter's first introduction to politics. Driven from court by Sophia's malice, he was completely cut off from the political ideas of the courtiers. This isolation was in itself no loss. The confused rubbish which served seventeenth-century Russian courtiers for a political system consisted partly of custom and ceremony inherited from previous generations, and partly of those political lies and equivocations which prevented the first tsars of the new dynasty from understanding their true position in the country. It was Peter's misfortune that he had no coherent political understanding, but only a vague, confused notion that he had unlimited power and that somehow this was menaced. For a long time nothing was done to make good this deficiency. His early passion for manual labor and craftsmanship left him no time for meditation, and distracted his attention from those subjects which form the basis of a political education.

As a ruler, Peter knew neither moral nor political restraints, and lacked the most elementary political and social principles. His lack of judgment and his personal instability, combined with great talent and wide technical skill, astonished all foreigners who met Peter when he was twenty-five; their verdict was that nature had intended him to be a good carpenter, not a great sovereign. In spite of the facts, that Peter's early moral guidance had been bad, that he had ruined his health, that his manners and way of life were uncouth, and that he had been unbalanced by the terrible experiences of his childhood, he remained sensitive, receptive, and extremely energetic. These qualities went a long way to mitigate the faults which were due to his environment and way of life. As early as 1698 the English Bishop Burnet had remarked that Peter was doing his best to overcome his passion for wine. However little notice Peter took of the political and social customs of the West, he was sensible enough to realize that it was not the knout and the torture chamber which had given the Western peoples their character and power. The bitter experience of the first Azov campaign, and the struggles around Narva and the Pruth, showed Peter the extent to which he was politically unprepared. He realized that, if he were to effect the improvement he wanted, he must examine more seriously his ideas of state and people, of law and duty, of monarchy and the duties of the monarch. He sacrificed everything to his sense of duty, but never succeeded in changing his personal habits. While the events of 1682 cut him off from the political affectations of the Kremlin, he never managed to rid himself of the biggest fault of Muscovite politics—their arbitrariness.

To the end of his life he never understood the logic of history or the nature of the life of his people. Yet he can hardly be blamed for this. Leibnitz, a clever politician and one of Peter's correspondents, could not understand it either. Leibnitz maintained that the more ignorant a country, the easier it would be to educate it, and he persuaded Peter that this applied to Russia. The introduction of all Peter's reforms was accompanied by force; he thought that only force could bind together a nation lacking in cohesion, and he believed that with force he could completely transform the traditional way of life of his people. His devotion to his people led him to overstrain their resources and waste their lives recklessly. He himself was honest and sincere, and did not spare himself; he was also just and kind to others. But, owing to his interests, he was better with inanimate objects than with people, whom he treated as if they were merely tools. He quickly found out who was useful, but could neither learn not to overtax people nor put himself in another's place. In this respect he differed greatly from his father. Peter knew how to manage people, but either could not or would not try to understand them. These characteristics affected his relations with their own family. He may have had a vast knowledge of his own country, but he hardly knew his own family and home, where he never was more than a guest. He never really lived with his first wife, and he grumbled about his second; he never came to terms with his son, Alexis, the Tsarevich. Moreover Peter did nothing to preserve Alexis from the evil influences which were finally responsible for his destruction and endangered the very existence of the Romanov dynasty.

It is obvious, then, that Peter differed greatly from his predecessors, in spite of a certain family similarity. He was a great statesman who knew where the sources of Russia's wealth lay and understood her economic interests. His predecessors of both dynasties were also statesmen, but they were sedentary men who preferred to benefit from the work of others, while Peter was an active, self-taught master craftsman, an artisan-Tsar.

Feofan Prokopovich

THE HEROIC TSAR

Feofan Prokopovich (1681–1736), a clergyman from the Ukraine, educated at the Theological Academy of Kiev and in Rome, became Peter's most loyal and trusted advisor on matters concerning church affairs and the theoretical aspects of statecraft. Dedicated to Russia's cultural Westernization, a firm believer in the primacy of the state over the church (on the model of the Lutheran states in Germany), Feofan Prokopovich helped to draft the Spiritual Regulation and vigorously defended Peter's policies on all occasions. In defense of Peter's disinheriting his son Alexis and changing the traditional order of succession, Prokopovich wrote his most famous work, the tract "Justice is the Monarch's Will," which was to serve as a justification of the autocratic power of Russian rulers throughout the eighteenth and nineteenth centuries. In his capacity of Archbishop of Novgorod and senior member of the Holy Synod, Feofan Prokopovich delivered the oration at Peter's funeral. It is a good illustration of the uncritical admiration and sense of awe which the collaborators and disciples of Peter displayed towards their great and beloved "Tsar Reformer."

A Funeral Oration for the Most Illustrious and Most Sovereign Emperor and Autocrat of All Russia, Peter the Great, Father of the Fatherland, Delivered in the Capital City of Saint Petersburg, at the Church of the First Apostles, Saints Peter and Paul, by the Right Reverend Theophanos, Vice-President of the Most Holy Governing Synod, Archbishop of Pskov and Narva, on the 8th Day of March 1725.

What is this? O Russians, what have we lived to witness? What do we see? What are we doing? We are burying Peter the Great! Is it

From Feofan Prokopovich, "Slovo na pogrebenie vsepresvetleishago Petra Velikogo, imperatora i samoderzhtsa Vserossiiskogo, otsa otechestva . . ." ["Oration at the Funeral of the Most Illustrious Peter the Great, Emperor of All Russia, Father of the Fatherland. . . ."] in *Sochineniia* [*Works*], edited by I. P. Eremin (Moscow-Leningrad, 1961) (*Izd. Akadaemii Nauk SSSR*), pp. 126–129. Editor's translation.

not a dream, an apparition? Alas, our sorrow is real, our misfortune certain! Contrary to everybody's wishes and hopes he has come to his life's end, he who has been the cause of our innumerable good fortunes and joys; who has raised Russia as if from among the dead and elevated her to such heights of power and glory; or better still, he who—like a true father of the fatherland—has given birth to Russia and nursed her. Such were his merits that all true sons of Russia wished him to be immortal; while his age and solid constitution gave everyone the expectation of seeing him alive for many more years; he has ended his life—o, horrible wound!—at a time when he was just beginning to live after many labors, troubles, sorrows, calamities, and perils of death. Do not we see well enough how much we have angered Thee, O Lord, and abused Thine patience! O, we are wretched and unworthy, our sins are immeasurable! He who does not see it is blind; he who sees it and does not confess his cruelty is obdurate. But why intensify our complaints and pity which we ought to assuage. How can we do it? For if we recall his great talents, deeds, and actions we shall feel the wound from the loss of such a great good, and we shall burst into tears. Alone a kind of lethargy or a death-like sleep can make us forget this truly great loss.

What manner of man did we lose? He was your Samson, Russia. No one in the world expected his appearance among you, and at his appearance the whole world marveled. He found but little strength in you, and on the model of his name he made your power strong like a rock and diamond. Finding an army that was disorderly at home, weak in the field, the butt of the enemy's derision, he created one that was useful to the fatherland, terrible to the enemy, renowned and glorious everywhere. In defending his fatherland he at the same time returned to it lands that had been wrested from it and augmented it by the acquisition of new provinces. Destroying those who had arisen against us, he at the same time broke and destroyed those who had evil designs on us; and closing the mouth of envy, he commanded the whole world to glorify him.

Russia, he was your first Japhet! He has accomplished a deed heretofore unheard of in Russia: the building and sailing of ships, of a new fleet that yields to none among the old ones. It was a deed beyond the whole world's expectation and admiration, and it opened up to thee, Russia, the way to all corners of the earth and carried thine power and glory to the remotest oceans, to the very limits set by thy own interests and by justice. Thine power which had been based on land he also has established on the sea, firmly and permanently.

He was your Moses, o Russia! For are not his laws like the strong visor of justice and the unbreakable fetters of crime! And do not his clear regulations illuminate your path, most high governing Senate, and that of all principal and particular administrations established by him! Are they not beacons of light in your search for what will be useful and what will avoid harm, for the security of the law-abiding and the detection of criminals. In truth, he has left us wondering wherein he has been best and most deserving of praise; was he loved and caressed more by good and honest men than hated by unrepentant sycophants and criminals?

O Russia, he was your Solomon, who received from the Lord reason and wisdom in great plenty. This is proven by the manifold philosophic disciplines introduced by him and by his showing and imparting to many of his subjects the knowledge of a variety of inventions and crafts unknown to us before his time. To this also bear witness the ranks and titles, the civil laws, the rules of social intercourse, propitious customs, and codes of behavior, and also the improvement of our external appearance. We see and marvel then at our fatherland; it has changed externally and internally, and it has become immeasurably better than it had been previously.

And he was your David and your Constantine, o Russian Church! The synodal administration is his work, and oral and written exhortations, too, have been his concern. The heart saved from the path of ignorance heaves a sigh of relief! What a zeal he has displayed in combatting superstition, adulatory hypocrisy, and the senseless, inimical, ruinous schism nesting in our midst. How great his desire and his endeavor to find the best pastoral talent, the truest divine wisdom, and the best improvement in everything.

Most distinguished man! Can a short oration encompass his immeasurable glory? Yet our present sad and pitiful state—moving us to tears and sighs—does not permit us to extend the discourse. Probably, in course of time, the thorns that butt our heart will dull, and then we shall speak of his deeds and virtues in fuller detail, even though we shall never be able to praise him adequately enough.

But at this time, even remembering him but briefly, as if only touching the edges of his mantle, we see, my poor and unfortunate hearers, we see who has left us and whom we have lost.

Russians, it is not in vain that we feel exhausted by sadness and pity, not in vain, even though this great monarch, our father, has left us. He has gone—but he has not left us poor and wretched: his enormous power and glory—manifested in the deeds I spoke of before—have remained with us. As he has shaped his Russia, so she will remain: he has made her lovable to good men, and she will be loved; he has made her fearful to her enemies, and she will be feared; he has glorified her throughout the world, and her glory will not end. He has left us spiritual, civil, and military reforms. For if his perishable body has left us, his spirit remains.

Moreover, in departing forever he has not left us orphaned. How can we call ourselves orphans when we behold his sovereign successor, his true companion in life and the identically minded ruler after his death, our most gracious and autocratic sovereign, great heroine and monarch, mother of all Russians![1] The world bears witness that the female sex is no hindrance to Your being like Peter the Great. Who does not know Your God-given, natural sovereign wisdom and maternal charity! And these two qualities have arisen and developed firmly, not merely because of Your cohabitation with such a ruler—for he cared little to have merely a companion for his bed —but by dint of Your sharing in his wisdom, labors, and misfortunes; so that over many years—like the gold refined in the crucible—he has formed an heir to his crown, power, and throne.

We can but expect that You will consolidate what he has done and complete what he has left unfinished, that You will preserve everything in good order! Courageous soul, only endeavor to overcome Your insufferable pain, a pain compounded by the loss of Your most beloved daughter;[2] Yours is like a cruel wound that has been exacerbated by a new blow. And in this most bitter loss endeavor to be the way everybody has seen You alongside the active Peter, his companion in all labors and misfortunes.

[1] Catherine I, second wife of Peter the Great, Empress of Russia from 1725 to 1727.
—Ed.
[2] Reference is to the death of Nathalie, daughter of Peter and Catherine, that had occurred on 4 March 1725, at the age of seven. (Peter himself had died 28 January 1725.)—Ed.

And you, sons of Russia of all ranks and title, most noble estate, console your monarch and your mother by your loyalty and obedience; also console yourselves with the certain knowledge that in your monarch you see Peter's spirit—as if not all of Peter had withdrawn from you. For the rest, we bow before God our Lord who has thus visited us. Let merciful God, Father of all consolation, wipe the unquenchable tears of our sovereign Lady and her most beloved kin—daughters, grandchildren, nieces, and the whole imperial family; and let His merciful care sweeten the bitterness of their hearts and give us consolation. O Russia, seeing who and what manner of man has departed from you, behold also whom he has left to you. Amen.

III REFORMS OF PETER THE GREAT

Mikhail M. Bogoslovskii

PETER'S PROGRAM OF POLITICAL REFORM

Mikhail M. Bogoslovskii (1867–1929) was Kliuchevsky's successor in the chair of Russian history at the University of Moscow. The outstanding specialist on Peter the Great, he devoted most of his life and work to the study of Peter's reign. At the time of his death he was working on a definitive biography of Peter, of which five volumes of preliminary essays and materials were published posthumously in the 1930s and 1940s. The following passage is taken from his doctoral dissertation which dealt with the reforms in local administration within the framework of Peter's reorganization of the central government and its military needs. In the pages below (taken from the introductory chapter), Bogoslovskii calls our attention to Peter's new approach and method of government. Peter's concept of government was dynamic; he believed that the state should act as leader and driving force in transforming the country and its people. To his contemporaries, used to the traditional and passive approach of the Muscovite administration, this seemed a novel and revolutionary concept, and its all-encompassing nature provoked strong resistance.

The legislation of Peter the Great differs in many respects from that of the preceding epoch, the epoch of Muscovite Russia. One of these differences consists in its manifold, one might even say, its all-embracing character. In Muscovite Russia, the state set itself limited goals, going no further than foreign defense, the levying of means to maintain it, and the maintenance of courts for enforcing domestic security and order. Hence, its laws touched upon few aspects of the private individual's life, affecting it only to the extent necessary for the accomplishment of the few and uncomplicated objectives of the state. It is true that the state of the Muscovite epoch imposed a heavy burden on society: it bound a large part of this society to military duties or taxes; it restricted the freedom of the classes involved in these obligations, forbidding them to change their status and occupations, attaching them to specific communi-

From Mikhail M. Bogoslovskii, *Oblastnaia Reforma Petra Velikogo—Provintsiia, 1719–1727 [Peter the Great's Reform of the Regional Administration—the Province in 1719–1727]* (Moscow, 1902), pp. 1–13, 19–20, 21–23. Translated by Mirra Ginsburg.

ties, and shackling the communities themselves to responsibility for them; and, finally, it attached a certain portion of the taxpayers not only to communities, but also to individual persons. However, the state intervened in the daily life of the persons bound to render services or taxes only to the extent necessary for assuring proper compliance. Indeed, the state did not shun a pedagogical role, but it undertook such a role only on a modest scale, and chiefly in a negative form. It prohibited and prosecuted violations of the few simple norms on which domestic security and order rested, but it did not assume the role of a mentor dictating positive rules. The aspects of private life which did not relate to state obligations and did not endanger internal order were of no concern to it. Private life and private relations were allowed to proceed and develop without state direction. Generally, in the Muscovite state we find only the most rudimentary beginnings of what is known as policing in the broad sense of the word. If the purpose of police activity, as understood in this sense, is to assure the security and well-being of the population, we might say that the concern of the Moscow state with the latter was confined only to the most elementary measures directed toward the attainment of the former. Virtually all that the state did for the welfare of its subjects was to provide them with external and domestic security. Protecting them from enemy invasion from without and from evildoers within, it considered its task fulfilled, leaving it to the subjects themselves to evolve their mutual relations and achieve whatever level of well-being they could on their own.

However, without being a ubiquitous mentor in the affairs of its subjects, and leaving them to their own resources, the state did not leave them without any support. In Muscovite Russia there was one guiding force which rendered superfluous either extensive tutelage by the state or detailed elaboration of juridical norms; this force was custom. Custom was the regulator of both the action of the government machine, and the conduct of private individuals. The Muscovite diplomats guided themselves by it in dealing with problems of foreign ʻpolicy; the Boiar Duma legislated, the judges governed and passed judgment in their departments [*prikazy*], and the governors, in their provinces, with reference to it, always finding in custom a ready answer to the problems arising before them.

"So it has been done from the days of our ancestors!" This sufficed to eliminate all doubt and uncertainty. And if "it has not been done so," then frequently no threat of torture or execution could break the obstinate resistance on this ground. This guiding principle was advantageous in a practical sense, since it lent firmness and clarity to all conduct. By referring to the how and what of custom, the Muscovite knew where and how he was to proceed, and did so without hesitation. But such a principle was useful only within a narrow and enclosed horizon, and at a time when social relations were simple and uncomplicated. It was becoming obsolete in the second half of the seventeenth century, when Muscovy entered into complex relations with the rest of Europe, when the ever-growing foreign influences began to broaden the horizons of the people, and when a stream of new Western ideas began to supplant ancient native tradition. The decline of custom filtered gradually from the top down. While the upper classes increasingly freed themselves of its power, it was still clearly remembered and potent among the common people. Peter's reform, which gave a strong forward impetus to so many phenomena in Russian life, also greatly accelerated the decline of custom.

Reform launched a resolute and implacable struggle against custom. But, of course, it could not limit itself merely to destructive activity. While destroying the foundations which supported the entire order of state and private life, the reformer had to build and determine this order anew, on a different basis. Moved from their age-old customary foundations, state and private relations now needed some legislative norm as a basis for their further existence. And the legislation of the Petrine epoch was many-sided and well-developed. It was many-sided because reform did not remain confined to one specific sphere, but set itself broad objectives of reconstructing both the state order and private life. While seventeenth-century legislation could be called institutional only to a very small degree, Peter's legislation was predominantly institutional [*uchreditel'noe*]. And it was well-developed because the reformer had to foresee both the detailed effects and the subsequent development of the innovations and phenomena which the reform was calling into existence. Legislation had to define and determine everything that was being introduced by the reform. This was why it did not confine itself, as earlier legislation had, to a merely negative indication of the limits that were not to be overstepped by relationships which it had not created, but was merely regulating. Peter's legislation abounds in positive prescriptions, aimed at establishing relationships which had not existed until then, and at determining their further development to the smallest detail. It contained no fewer prohibitions than the earlier legislation, the role of which ended at that point. But the prohibitions were outweighed by positive prescriptions, which were expanded into detailed statutes containing numerous articles. Peter's legislation was regulatory [*reglamentarnyi*] in character. Instead of the former brief items, providing fragmentary rules for individual specific cases and leaving wide gaps to be filled in by reference to custom, it took the form of detailed, exhaustive regulations, foreseeing and seeking to provide for every detail.

With these detailed instructions and regulations, Peter's government developed the widest police activity. Its precepts became the leading strings by which it guided its subjects after depriving them of the immemorial staff—custom—which had helped them in their slow progress in the past. It now surrounded them with the most solicitous care and intervened in every sphere of their existence, subordinating their entire lives to its prescriptions which it viewed as beneficial. The ruling circles of that time were imbued with ardent faith in the efficacy of the police powers of the state—a faith that was, perhaps, best expressed in the tenth chapter of the Regulation to the Chief Magistracy, issued in 1721.[1] This chapter states that "the police promote rights and justice, engenders good order and morality, provides security for all against robbers, thieves, ravishers, swindlers, and their like; it banishes disorderly and licentious living, and compels everybody to work at honest occupations and promotes good husbandry, as well as careful and good service; it regularly plans and maintains cities and streets, prevents high prices, and assures the abundance of all that is needed for human life; it guards against diseases, sees to the cleanliness of streets and homes,

---

[1] The Regulation to the Chief Magistracy [*Reglament Glavnomu Magistratu*] was an ordinance issued January 16, 1721, establishing the new administrative system for the towns. It enumerated the numerous and diverse duties and activities entrusted to the police and government authorities in the towns.—Ed.

forbids excesses in domestic expenditures and all manifest trans-
gressions; it cares for the beggars, the poor, the sick, the maimed,
and all other indigents, and protects widows, orphans, and foreigners; it brings up the young, according to the Lord's commandments,
in chaste purity and in honest studies; in short, above all these, the
police is the soul of civil society and of all good order, and the
fundamental bulwark of civil security and well-being." The chapter
outlines an entire program of police activity which is remarkable
in its scope. It provides for security and public welfare, for sanitary
police, for public education and care of the poor, and also for the
policing of morals. Such were the broad tasks undertaken by Peter's
government, which no longer contented itself with the organization
of external defense and the maintenance of elementary justice.

This program, moreover, was not a mere theoretical tract, allowed
to remain on paper only. A cursory look at the collected edicts of
Peter's time will reveal on almost every page an inspired desire to
implement in practice one or another provision of the Regulation.
The state consciously sought to lead its subjects toward prosperity
and well-being. Entire series of edicts opened up avenues toward
the achievement of various facets of this well-being, and the golden
age was to arrive when all the edict's prescriptions had been fulfilled.
Furthermore, in view of the inexperience of those it led, the state
did not limit itself to setting up infrequent guideposts, sufficient only
to indicate the general direction; it supervised them at every step,
without leaving them for a moment, and frequently intruded into the
most intimate corners of private life.

We shall cite a few examples of such ubiquitous tutelage, which
might, if one wished, be multiplied to infinity. The government took
upon itself the education of its subjects and founded an academy
that was to promote science and train teachers; it established
schools, where these teachers were to instruct the children who
had been forcibly enrolled; it translated and published the books to
be used in the schools, and invented the type in which these books
were to be printed. But it did not stop at these general measures,
and extended its concern with the dissemination of knowledge
among the people to the smallest details. "His Imperial Majesty has
instructed," we read in an edict published in 1723, "that the books to
be published henceforth must, whenever mention is made of the

names of cities known formerly under different names, carry annotations on the margin, indicating the old name, so that the reader might know both the former and the present name of the city."

Adhering to the mercantile views prevalent at the time, the government also assumed the task of enriching its subjects by way of artificial introduction of industry and development of commerce. It did not draw a line at coercion, as if seeking forcibly, despite their will, to make the people rich. "And if," wrote Peter, "there is coercion in that old and experienced country (Holland), which even without this has long flourished in commerce and lives by it, how much more, then, do we require coercion in it, being new to it in every way?" Extensive measures were undertaken with the aim of developing industry and commerce; state factories and workshops were created; industrial and trading companies were founded and supported by state subsidies and various privileges; industrial and commercial education was disseminated by means of sending Russians abroad and importing foreign master craftsmen; private individuals were encouraged, and officials were duty-bound to discover natural resources and seek out new sources of national enrichment, "to search out new sources of revenue without burdening the people."

But the government did not stop at general measures and, besides general supervision over industrial and commercial activity, intervened in details of production and trade relations, making demands and compelling their execution by stern threats. Thus, it prescribed the weaving of cloth only of specified width, in accordance with the samples sent to all the provinces. On fear of exile to the galleys, it prohibited, as of February 1, 1718, the working of leather for footwear with tar, and prescribed that it be worked with blubber oil; accordingly, special courses were opened in Moscow to teach the craftsmen this new method of processing leather. In 1723, the Senate issued an ordinance regulating the processing of hemp: "that the people in the districts [*uezd*] should tear off and cut off the ends and roots of the hemp, and scutch it clean; and that the hemp should not be taken to market damp and with the root stocks [*rhizomes*] and not sold in this condition, but taken and sold dry and without root stocks. The merchants are henceforth forbidden under penalty of fines, depending on the magnitude of guilt, to buy from the peasants hemp that is damp and contains roots and root stocks. And those merchants who dress hemp in the city in their own homes, are to dress it clean and keep a strict watch on the scutchers, making sure there is no woody scutch and no deception of any kind."[2]

All Russia reaped grain with a sickle, as it continues to do to this day. But in the spring of 1721, the president of the College of the Treasury, Prince D. M. Golitsyn, received the following instruction from Peter, who was then in Riga: "In these parts, in Courland and Livonia, as well as in Prussia, the peasants follow the custom of harvesting grain with small scythes and rakes instead of with sickles, which is so much speedier and more profitable that the average workman will do the work of ten men. From which it may be seen what a great help it will be in the work, and how the grain harvest will be increased by it. To this end, we chose suitable people from among the local peasants to serve as instructors and sent them, in groups of several men each, to our grain-growing cities with such scythes and rakes, accompanied by specially detailed officers. And we have written to the governors and *voevody* to assign and send them to such places where the grain grows best . . . which you shall confirm from the College as well, so that by this very summer they shall train as many as possible. Also, have scythes and rakes made up according to the samples, to multiply their number, and see to it that everyone reaps in this manner in the grain-bearing regions next summer (*for you know yourself that, though a thing be good and necessary, if it is new, our people will not do it unless forced to*)." In September and October, the *voevody* had to submit reports on the number of scythes and rakes manufactured, and the quantity of hay harvested in the new manner.

It is also difficult to imagine how much energy the government had to expend to introduce the building of river boats of a new type, which it considered more suitable, and to wean the shipowners from the "old-fashioned" ships. "The vessel known as the *kolomenka*," wrote Peter on February 14, 1718, "which I have rebuilt, is to be sent to Dedinov (a village on the Oka River, known for its

---

[2] The College of Manufactures appointed special inspectors from among the district service classes to see that the decrees concerning hemp and wide cloth were properly complied with. In the province of Orel, for instance, there was one such appointee for each district [*stan*]. They were officially called "gentry for the oversight of hemp work and the making of wide cloth."—Ed.

shipyards, where the famous *Orel* was built), on paying the master in money. There she is to be docked and all the other boats are to be made accordingly, on fear of lifetime banishment to the galleys for building otherwise." During the five years from 1718 to 1723, not less than 14 edicts were issued, banning the use of vessels of the old type, which had proved hazardous for sailing Lake Ladoga and had often perished there. But the new models, as Peter complained, were not readily accepted, owing to the stupidity and stubbornness of the owners, who thought to benefit from the lower cost of the old boats, without reckoning how many of them are lost. Despite the threats of confiscation of the entire property of those who disobeyed and their banishment to the galleys, and despite orders that the "old-fashioned ships" be destroyed, resistance continued.

In 1721, the Tsar noticed that on the river freight boats, used to carry materials, through the thoughtlessness of their builders the spill-windows were made so low that they were no more than two inches, or even less, from the water line. This caused them to be flooded in bad weather. Orders were issued, by Imperial edict, that such windows should not be made again, that the existing ones be closed up, and that the water be pumped out overboard with a pump.

Passenger travel on the Neva was to be by sailing ship only, and residents were forbidden to use rowboats. Since the use of sails was unfamiliar and therefore presented great difficulties, detailed instructions as to their use were issued, and the boat owners were ordered to gather every Sunday on a given signal to practice sailing under the direction of a commissioner appointed for that purpose. Despite the fact that the compulsory use of sails took a considerable number of lives every year, since many people could not learn to manage them, Peter insisted on it.

Numerous measures were adopted toward improving the cities. The police indeed began regularly to plan and maintain cities and streets. Regulations and instructions to magistrates, instructions to the General Police Chief [*general-politseimeister*] of Petersburg and the Police Chief [*ober-politseimeister*] of Moscow, as well as a great number of individual edicts contain numerous rules, bearing not only on the maintenance of public order and the preservation of civil security, but also on the sanitary state of the city and the building police. The latter were especially stressed. Peter entered personally into all details of the construction work on private buildings. By Imperial edict, he ordered that ovens be set on foundations, rather than directly on the floor; that chimneys be wide enough to permit a man's passage; that ceilings be finished with clay, rather than left with beams exposed; that roofs be covered with tile, sod, or shingles, rather than boards or laths, and so on. He brought in specialists in shingle-making and laying from the Ukraine and Smolensk to give free instruction to the residents of the capital. And the edict explained that one log could be made into twenty, thirty or even more, shingles. In 1723, the General Police Chief, Devier, proclaimed to the people of the city that His Imperial Majesty had commanded that those who build the entrance-way to their house with a ceiling, should finish those ceilings in the same manner as the ceiling in the house, as prescribed by edict, the old manner being henceforth forbidden. Building regulations affected the villages as well. An Imperially approved plan, specifying dimensions, was sent out throughout the provinces. All peasant houses were to be built according to this plan, in order to protect them against fires.

But the law did not confine itself to concern with the quiet, the order and cleanliness of streets, and the safe and solid construction of buildings. It did not stop outside the walls, but insistently sought to enter the house, trying also "regularly to plan the private life of its inhabitants, enmeshing them in a net of instructions as detailed as those that governed the building of walls, roofs, and ceilings. The appearance of the inhabitant of the house was subjected to the same compulsory regulations as the façade of the house itself. The hair growth on the face, the material, cut and color of clothing, and footwear—all this was minutely regimented by edicts. There was a category of men who were forbidden to wear beards and clothing of the old style; another category was forbidden to wear anything but the old style of dress—and not only old, but the most ancient, long, "with a long collar and stripes sewn across the chest . . . slits with loops on the hem, and a high hat, also with slits and tails."

Peter's struggle against beards and clothing is too well known to be repeated here. It was no less stubborn than his struggle against the "old-fashioned" ships. It was continued under his successor, who issued an edict on May 31, 1726, instructing that all officers who were fully retired and living in the countryside, as well as those on temporary leave or occupying civil posts—in short, all members of the gentry not currently in the army—should undeviatingly preserve the appearance prescribed for those in military service: i.e. they were to wear German clothing and swords, and shave their beards. The edict entered into a detailed enumeration of all the obstacles to its execution that might be encountered in the countryside. "If there should be none in their village," the edict stated, "who know how to shave, then they must clip their beards with scissors close to the skin twice every week, and every man must always maintain himself in cleanliness." Those who were too poor to purchase German cloth for their dress were permitted to make it of Russian drab cloth, but under strict orders that the coat sleeves have cuffs of a different color.

After dressing its subjects in clothing of fixed pattern, the state turned its attention to their entertainment and diversions. The present government arranges public entertainments in a manner it considers beneficial. In the early eighteenth century the state lacked the means to do this, but it frequently intruded into private entertainments and regimented them in detail according to its own ideas. On November 26, 1718, the day of the famous decree establishing the capitation tax, a ruling was also issued concerning the organization of "assemblies" in private homes.[3] This decree began with an explanation of the term itself, and then went on in seven paragraphs to enunciate the rules "by which such assemblies should be planned until they become customary." The rules determined the time when assemblies should be called, the order of invitations, the duties of the host, the actions of the guests, who were permitted to sit, walk, and play games during the assembly, and the conduct of the servants. The games were regulated by the decree of 1717, which forbade playing for money.

Having reconstructed the amusements of higher society along the European model, the law turned to the diversions of the plain people, the most popular of which were bouts of fisticuffs. Catherine noted that, during these bouts, "it sometimes happens that many take out knives and chase the other fighters, and some put lead, stones, and iron balls into their mitts and beat their opponents

---

[3] "Assemblies" [*assamblei*] were social gatherings or dancing parties introduced by Peter the Great among St. Petersburg high society.—Ed.

mercilessly with deadly blows, so that the bouts are not without cases of killing, which killings are not even considered murder or sin among the common people, and it also happens that they throw sand into the eyes." Not venturing to abolish this popular entertainment entirely, Catherine attempted in 1726 to regulate it, forbidding the organization of fights without special permission from the office of the Police Chief, establishing supervision over them, and defining a set of rules which, among other things, prohibited the hitting of a man who was down.

Teaching its subjects to amuse themselves according to given regulations, the government also taught them to cure themselves in cases of illness according to similar regulations. In 1717, from abroad, Peter instructed the Senate to see to it that springs be searched out in Russia, similar to those he had seen abroad, whose waters were useful in the cure of illness. The search proved successful. The Olonetsk chalybeate springs were declared curative. Peter himself repeatedly made use of them, asserting that they helped him better than the foreign springs. Therefore, "caring for his subjects as a father," he ordered the establishment of detailed medical rules concerning their use. These were published for everyone's information, in order that, as stated in the decree accompanying the regulations, "one might not, through ignorance, bring worse harm instead of benefit, to his health, and thus subject this God-sent gift to disparagement on the part of unreasoning simple men." Water cures were made obligatory for the aristocracy and the courtiers, and the Olonetsk resort became fashionable. However, since not everyone found there the expected cure, and disparagement of the springs had indeed begun to be voiced by some, an Imperial decree followed, explaining the lack of desired effect in certain cases by failure to observe the Imperially prescribed rules, and censuring those who "like true boors, without thinking of their irregular and stupid actions," dared to disparage the gift of God. Even when the cure ended in total failure and death, the regulations did not cease. The government did not leave the dead without its tutelage, as it had not left him in his lifetime. It forbade the burial of the dead inside the city limits, making exceptions only for "highly placed personages"; it forbade the use of oak coffins, specified the kind of gravestone to be erected, and banned the building of wooden booths on graves for the reading of the Psalter. It also ruled that, where the "stones laid over human bodies in Moscow and in other cities, near parish churches, and in monasteries, are not level with the ground, such stones are to be dug up and lowered so as to level them . . . and henceforth, no stone is to be laid over a grave otherwise than level with the ground."

The government even extended its concern for its subject's fate in the world beyond the grave, and took steps for the compulsory salvation of his soul, not hesitating to touch upon the most intimate aspects of his spiritual life. Under threat of fines, it commanded him to attend church and go to confession and Holy Communion. "It has come to the knowledge of our Great Sovereign," we read in a decree of 1718, "that many persons of diverse origin [*raznochintsy*], tradesmen, and villagers are accustomed to live idly, and never attend divine service in church, not only on Sundays, but even on the Lord's great holidays; nor do they go to confession. He therefore commands that all the above-named persons should attend church on the Lord's holidays and on Sundays, for matins and vespers, and most of all for Holy Mass (unless prevented by sickness or some other disability) and that all must go to confession yearly." The priests were instructed to keep special records for all who came or failed to come to confession, to impose monetary fines, and to report to the lay authorities, governors, and *landraty* [local police officials] all cases of obstinate resistance. These authorities were to punish the recalcitrants and compel them to go to confessions.

The conduct of the worshippers in church was also regulated by Imperial edicts, which instructed "men of all ranks . . . to stand silently and listen with all reverence to the singing of Holy Mass," under threat of fines, "a ruble from every man, without allowing him to leave church until he pays." The law did not shrink even before commanding the priests themselves, including those invested with the special aura of the Holy Spirit—the bishops—"to exercise in divine meditation during the liturgy." Regulating the attitude of its subjects toward the church and their conduct in church, the temporal power intervened in the service itself. Its last step in this spiritual realm was the command to the church authorities that they compose special chants for the celebrations of particularly significant victories won in the Northern War. . . .

During the preceding period, the government had been content with a narrower sphere of action, concerning itself with but a few aspects of life and permitting the rest to be fashioned and guided by custom. In the person of Peter, the supreme state power entered into an implacable struggle with custom, eradicating it without mercy and taking upon itself the entire task of leading its subjects. But what did the supreme power guide itself by in this task of directing its subjects? The principle, the light, in the name of which it fought "stupidity and ignorance" and armed itself against custom was the principle discovered by the philosophy of the sixteenth century, proclaimed in the seventeenth, and virtually worshipped as the highest good in the eighteenth. It was reason. In Peter's reform, we see an absolute supreme ruler leading the people and reconstructing its life in accordance with the dictates of reason. Reason would not reconcile itself with custom, but sought to refashion life by its own light. This was why this reform assumed the character of an all-encompassing assault on the old way of life. It had to look into every dark corner where custom reigned in order to drive it out. It had to touch upon all phenomena of contemporary life in order to build for each of them a new foundation. . . .

*　*　*

During the first quarter of the eighteenth century, there was in Russia a good deal of blind, mechanical imitation of the West, unconscious, as a child's unconscious imitation of an adult, or a savage's attempt to imitate a civilized man. But there is no doubt that the borrowing from the West also had a certain conscious significance, being regarded as a means for attaining a specific ideal. The ideal itself, which the reform was endeavoring to realize, the model, along which Russia was to be transformed, was inevitably close to the image of the European, regulated state of the same period. It was composed of elements derived from acquaintance with the Western European state system and political ideas, which furnished a rich and ready source of material for creative political thought and action, such as native Russian life, which by the eighteenth century had proven itself impotent and bankrupt, could not provide. All Russian reformers, all who were not stubborn diehards, clinging to ideals drawn from the ancient order, with its dim and nebulous notions, all who were not ideologists capable of creating political constructions solely from the resources of their own mind, and drafting constitutions with their eyes and ears closed, inevitably had to be caught up in the general European stream, swept on by the force of its current, but also consciously appreciating the superiority of its direction. They not only accepted the direction of the stream which carried them along, but also nourished themselves on its aroma. They not only began to adopt Western European ways of life, but also guided themselves by new political ideas.

And, indeed, this was not difficult. Peter was not an independent political thinker and had no time to study contemporary political theories. But, possessing a lively, curious, and penetrating mind, he could not fail to observe the workings of the Western European political systems, despite his concentration on shipyards and workshops during his trips abroad. And it was inevitable that he should be influenced, at least to some extent, by the political ideas widely current at the time, permeating the very air of Europe like bacilli, and sparing from their contagion only those who were completely deaf and blind. True, the abstract elements in these ideas were beyond his grasp, as were all abstract systems, and he did not engage in leisurely studies of the origin of the state, but, as a predominantly practical man of action, he clearly assimilated their practical side.

In clumsy and awkward expressions, but with complete clarity, he expressed his views concerning the general good as the goal of the state in his speech of October 22, 1721, at the Troitskii Cathedral, in reply to the congratulations of the senators on the conclusion of the Peace of Nystadt. He said at the time that the sovereign's task is to "labor for the general benefit and profit." It was the same view he had proclaimed in 1702 in the manifesto on the summoning of foreign experts, where it was offered in more polished form, perhaps lent it by a foreign pen. The manifesto spoke of the Tsar's intention "to govern the state in such a manner that all our subjects shall be brought to a better and more prosperous life through our solicitude for the *general good.*"

This view of the "general good" as the ultimate objective of the monarchy also reached the people in Feofan's tract on "The Justice of the Monarch's Will." This noble goal was pursued everywhere in Europe by the absolute rulers—absolute in practice, and necessarily absolute in theory. And now Russian autocracy was given a clear and exact definition for the first time in Peter's words: "His Majesty is an absolute monarch, who need not answer for his acts to anyone in the world. But he has power and authority, as a Christian Sovereign, to govern his states and lands according to his will and his benevolent understanding. . . ."

The legislative reform, guided by the dictates of reason, began to speak to the Emperor's subjects in a language quite different from that of the old laws, a language which also bore the stamp of the rationalist epoch. This difference in language stemmed from the different conception of the means necessary to assure compliance with the law on the part of those to whom it was addressed. The legislation of old knew of only one method—stern threat. In directing society by legislation, the supreme authority assumed the role of a laconic and strict pedagogue, who expressed his commands or injunctions in few words, but with a knout or lash in his hand. Read the Code of 1649 or the numerous edicts which followed it, and you will encounter at every step the threat that "if there be people who do such and such . . . those people shall be punished without mercy," or "those people shall be punished and given the lash, so that others, beholding this, shall desist from doing likewise."

The legislative acts promulgated by Peter are attended by as many, if not more, threats. But they are also accompanied by explanations, stating the reasons for and objectives of the measures adopted, and aiming to instruct those who are to comply with them. Pre-Petrine legislation had acted only upon the sense of fear. Peter's legislation sought first and foremost to appeal to the reason of the subjects, and resorted to threats only in the event of its failure to convince. It not only threatened the subject, but endeavored to persuade him. In almost every one of Peter's decrees, we inevitably find the conjunction *as* which leads to the reasons for the law. "In St. Petersburg, persons of all ranks are enjoined from allowing their cows, goats, pigs, and other cattle out into the street without shepherds . . . *as* such cattle, wandering in the streets and other places, deface roads and spoil trees." And it is only then that the law goes on to threaten strict fines and irrevocable confiscation in the event of noncompliance. The riding of unbridled horses is forbidden, "*as* this leads to much harm to people, for an unbridled horse cannot be quickly curbed." All laws and regulations must be faithfully complied with, "*as* nothing is so necessary to the administration of the state as firm observance of civil laws; for it is vain to write laws if they be not observed, or if they be played with like cards, matching suit to suit, which is not done anywhere in the world, as it was done, and is still partially being done, in our land. . . ."

Along with the abolition of the custom of using self-derogatory diminutives in petitions and bowing to the ground on meeting the Tsar, the use of this small word (*as*) is an important index of the new relationship which, divesting itself of its former mystical aura, was seeking to establish with the society it governed. It was now striving for conscious and intelligent compliance with the law for the sake of its rational goals, instead of slavish obedience based on fear of the lash. Whenever Peter wrote a law, he reasoned, and sometimes this reasoning was expanded into entire tracts on politics, law, or even natural science—in accordance with the teaching of Thomasius[4] that "the wise are governed more by good counsel than by stern command." The reasoning of the reformer is occasionally naive; it seeks to persuade of things that are self-evident. But what is clear and evident to us today was often beyond the understanding of Peter's contemporaries, who had to be taught the rudiments, like children.

---

[4] Christian Thomasius (1655–1728), a German jurist, who endeavored to give a practical form to natural-law concepts in jurisprudence.—Ed.

Paul N. Miliukov

SOCIAL AND POLITICAL REFORMS

Until the end of the nineteenth century all those who wrote about Peter had been mainly concerned with his successes in military and foreign affairs and with his personal role in bringing about Russia's greatness and glory. At the end of the nineteenth century, however, the interest shifted to social and economic problems. Assuming the existence of historic laws of inevitable social progress, historians examined Peter's reign from the point of view of the population's material condition and of its place in Russia's social and economic evolution. Paul N. Miliukov (1859–1944) exemplified this new orientation in his dissertation for the degree of magister, a massive and exhaustive study of the relationship between Peter's economic and administrative policies, from which we quote part of the conclusion. While recognizing the necessity of Peter's reforms in that they helped to turn Russia towards Europe and progress, Miliukov believed that in terms of the well-being of the Russian people the price had been much too high. So high, as a matter of fact, as to jeopardize the future economic and social progress of Russia and as to negate in part Peter's political and military successes. Unwilling to give much credit to Peter for any constructive transformation of the country's structure, Miliukov felt that the social and economic changes which occurred in the first Emperor's reign were not the result of any conscious policy of Peter's but only the unavoidable by-products of his military and diplomatic efforts.

Had Peter lived a few years longer, he would undoubtedly have gone still further along the road of Russifying his reform of the state—a road he had taken from the very first when he introduced his reform in 1718–1719. But Peter died, and the task of adapting the reform to Russian conditions had to be completed by the Supreme Privy Council. Did this alter the fate of the reform? Hardly. In essence, it was still in the hands of the men who had carried it out during Peter's last years. As we follow the changes in the field we have selected for observation, we become accustomed to seeing reform without the reformer, and this is true of the years when Peter was still alive. Substantially the same impression was gathered by the

From Paul N. Miliukov, *Gosudarstvennoe Khoziaistvo Rossii v Pervoi Chetverti XVIII Stoletiia i Reforma Petra Velikogo* [*The National Economy of Russia in the First Quarter of the 18th Century and the Reform of Peter the Great*] (2nd ed., St. Petersburg, 1905), pp. 542–543, 545–546 (1st ed., St. Petersburg, 1896), pp. 730–732, 734–736. Used with permission of the literary executor of Paul N. Miliukov. Translated by Mirra Ginsburg.

better-informed contemporary participants and observers. It was only people remote from the field of action who later naively identified Peter with his reform and paved the way for the view that Peter was the sole creator of the new Russia.

Unfortunately, there is not a single piece of sincere contemporary testimony by any of Peter's closest Russian aides regarding Peter's last years. However, the numerous reports and memoranda of foreign envoys consistently convey the same impression, which coincides with the results of our own study and, it seems to us, with the facts: an impression that the sphere of the Tsar's personal influence was relatively narrow. This was stated briefly, clearly, and with his usual intelligence, by Vockerodt,[1] one of these observers. This is how he described the gradation of Peter's personal interests, which determined the extent of his personal intervention. "Particularly, and with all his zeal, he sought to improve his military forces. At the same time, the wars, which occupied his entire life, and the pacts he concluded with foreign powers in connection with these wars, compelled him also to give attention to foreign affairs. In this, however, he relied in most part on his ministers and favorites, who usually managed to influence him in favor of the side which paid them best. His favorite and most pleasant occupations were shipbuilding and other activities related to navigation. This provided him diversion every day, and even the most urgent affairs of state had to yield to it. . . . Internal improvements in government, justice, economy, revenues, and trade concerned him little or not at all during the first thirty years of his reign. He was content, provided his admiralty and army were adequately supplied with money, firewood, recruits, sailors, provisions, and ammunition; and this was easy enough, since his troops found ways and means for many years to maintain themselves at the expense of others, without burdening the state."

We know that all of this was not as easily achieved as it had seemed to Vockerodt, and that the Tsar was therefore, willy-nilly, compelled to concern himself with increasing his revenues. But we also know that his reform aspirations in the sphere of internal state

---

[1] Johann Gotthilf Vockerodt, Secretary of the Prussian legation in St. Petersburg, in 1734 wrote a memorandum to the Prussian Crown Prince Frederick (the future Frederick II) on his observations and experiences in Russia where he had resided for 25 years.—Ed.

organization did not go beyond this involuntary concern. After 1714 the legislator's horizon broadened noticeably. His domestic policy ceased to be exclusively fiscal. But even here his lack of preparation and of a general outlook and system continued to lead to innumerable contradictions, which manifested themselves not only between borrowed forms and native reality, but even among the borrowed forms themselves, and among their various facets. As we trace this endless chain of errors and misunderstandings, documented in archival records, we cannot help recalling the words which slipped from the lips of a person whose competence in this case is beyond question. They are the words of the Empress Catherine, who made the first thorough study of the papers of Peter the Great for her own practical purposes: "He did not know himself what laws were necessary to the state." Of course, this comment is too general and sweeping. Yet it is much nearer the truth than the schoolbook rhetoric of some recent scholars, who assert that "Peter took with him to the grave the key to his great schemes, and those who continued his work were unable to find this key. They assimilated only the outward forms of his transformations, but were unable to grasp the content of these forms. They were unable to revive the spirit of the first Emperor."

All that we know about Peter's reform of the state contradicts this rhetoric. Prepared by the elemental flow of history and collectively discussed, this reform not only was hidden deep in the Emperor's "spirit," but, on the contrary, reached his mind only at second hand, in chance fragments. . . .

Peter's social and state reforms have been least studied. Indeed, one can scarcely speak of Peter's "social" reforms. With the exception of the measures in favor of the urban class, promulgated during his last years under the influence of mercantilist ideas, Peter introduced no social reforms as such. The great changes observable during his reign in the position of other social classes were merely the indirect by-products of his legislation, which he himself had least foreseen. When he introduced the capitation tax, he never thought that he was tightening the knot of serfdom. And when he imposed life-long service duty on the service class and introduced single inheritance [*edinonasledie*], he least imagined that he was furthering the creation of the corporative spirit of the Russian nobility and the privileged property rights of the gentry. Russia's social evolution was bound, to an even greater extent than her cultural development, to historic precedents, and was thus even less dependent than the latter on the will of the lawmaker.

There remains the aspect of the reform which has been the subject of our study. Its place, it seems to us, lies somewhere in the middle, between those aspects of the process which developed under the direct influence of the reformer, and those which developed independently of, or even counter to his will. It is more difficult to alter the state system than to dress some of the people in new styles of clothing, to form new regiments, or build new ships; but it is easier than changing customs or the class structure. The political reform was not prompted by the lawmaker's personal plans or predilections as were his navy or the German style of dress. Nor was it the product of the spontaneous historical process alone. Peter's will was, of course, necessary for its accomplishment; however, this facet of his reform went beyond his essential horizon and was carried out by him almost by necessity. The facts of history had also prepared the ground for the state's reorganization, yet this reorganization did not follow spontaneously. The reform was not brought about either by personal initiative or by historic precedent, although both elements combined to produce it. It was dictated by the exigencies of the moment, which were themselves the product of both personal initiative and historic precedents.

In this sense, the reorganization of the state appears to have been a secondary, a derivative phenomenon. And, indeed, this is what Peter held it to be, regarding it not as a goal in itself, but only as a means. This means was a necessity to the extent that the objectives set by Peter were necessary to the state; it was timely to the extent that objectives were. It would be too late and generally idle today to question the necessity of the objectives, as they were questioned by Peter's contemporaries. As for their timeliness, there can unfortunately be two answers, depending on whether we examine them in relation to the domestic or to the foreign position of Russia. In connection with Russia's external position, the timeliness of these objectives is proven by their successful achievement; this timeliness will probably be confirmed by the juxtaposition of facts of European politics, from which Russia could not be absent. However, in connection with the domestic situation, the question as to the timeliness of the reform must be answered in the negative. New problems and tasks of foreign policy were thrown upon the shoulders of the Russian people at a moment when they did not as yet command sufficient means to deal with them. The political progress of the state once more outran its economic development. The tripling of the taxes (from 25 to 75 million in our money) and the simultaneous decline of the population by at least 20 percent are facts that prove our assertion more eloquently than any details. Russia had been raised to the rank of a European power at the cost of the country's ruin.

Peter I. Lyashchenko
THE NATIONAL ECONOMY

The selection below is from the pen of the distinguished Soviet economic historian, P. I. Lyashcenko (1876–1955). Following the official interpretation of Marx's periodization of Western history, Lyashchenko would like to see in the reign of Peter the Great the formative period of Russia's capitalist development. But in spite of the establishment of new industries and the modernization of some sectors of Russian economic life, Lyashchenko cannot call Peter's reign the beginning of true capitalism in Russia, since the labor force continued to consist mainly of unfree serfs and the capital was obtained from noble landowners and state subsidies. In spite of his questionable theoretical framework, Lyashchenko gives an informative summary of Russia's economic development in the eighteenth century and of the contribution made to it by Peter's legislative activity.

The Reforms of Peter

"When Peter the Great," says Comrade Stalin, "was confronted with the more advanced countries of the West, and feverishly went about building factories and mills to supply his army and improve the defense of the country, it was a peculiar attempt to jump out of

Reprinted with permission of The Macmillan Company from *History of the National Economy of Russia to the Revolution of 1917,* by Peter I. Lyashchenko (New York, 1949), pp. 267–270, 283–288, 291–295, 296–297. Translated by L. M. Herman. Copyright 1949 by American Council of Learned Societies.

the framework of backwardness." In this respect "Peter accomplished a great deal toward the creation and strengthening of the national state of the landowners and merchants. It should also be stated," Comrade Stalin says further, "that the exaltation of the landlord class, the cooperation with the incipient merchant class, and the strengthening of the national status of these classes was carried out at the expense of the serf peasantry, which was being fleeced threefold."

The Moscow state of the end of the seventeenth century (at the beginning of Peter's reign, 1682) already embraced nearly all Russian territories, including Smolensk, Chernigov, and the east-bank Ukraine, and was rapidly pushing its frontiers toward the east, into Siberia. It was, in the expression of Marx, "a system of local annexations, appropriate for continental areas; for a general offensive the use of the sea was necessary." The wars of Peter I during the late seventeenth and early eighteenth centuries pursued precisely this new aim—to obtain outlets to the seas (the drives toward the Azov and Black Sea, and the conquest of the Caspian shores), and to the western seas in particular, which would make possible "the opening of a direct passage to Europe" (Marx). The transfer of the nation's capital to the shores of the Baltic Sea (in 1713) was the culmination of this drive toward the western seas.

By his sharp break with the old political and social order, Peter created the political, military, and material foundations for the "Europeanization of Muscovy," and its transformation into a European empire. But at the basis of this "Europeanization," Peter was unable to provide anything beyond the old system of serfdom, the same social serf institutions. The influence of Europe, inevitably, indeed, awakened among the progressive elements of Peter's associates the idea of the advisability, in the interests of the state, of abolishing the practical slavery of a vast portion of his subjects. From the foreign reports we now have on the last years of Peter's reign, it appears that Peter was repeatedly advised to abolish serfdom and to introduce even a "limited freedom" for his submerged subjects.

The influence of the bourgeois ideas of mercantilism on the urgency of promoting industry and commerce, and the importance of the personal freedom of the peasantry from that point of view were reflected in the well-known views of the first publicist of the Petrine era, Pososhkov. "The landowners," he said, "are not the permanent owners of the peasants. . . . Their direct owner is the all-Russian autocrat, while they own only temporarily."

Peter was, however, incapable of changing the existing social conditions. Therefore, while he was fully capable of seeing the negative features of serfdom, he was powerless before his own serf-holding nobility. He could find no other sources of revenue for his reforms besides the serf economy, and no other sources of personnel for his army or for his industrial construction aside from the same serf population. Having once become upset, for example, by the sight of the retail sale of serfs, where men were sold like chattels, "a thing unheard of in the whole world," Peter issued a decree to the Senate in 1721 in which he limited himself merely to the wish that "this type of sale cease, or should that be impossible," then, at least, they should be sold in whole families.

His decrees sounded, however, a great deal more authoritative on occasions when they made the raising of revenue their objective, and when their full burden fell on the taxpaying population in general, and the serfs in particular. A vital part in this connection was played by the capitation census of the whole taxpaying population taken by Peter (the first revision, or census of 1718) for the purpose of ascertaining and increasing the number of the taxpayers and of introducing, on the basis of this census, a direct "per capita" tax for everybody, "excepting no one, from the aged to the very last babe" (Senate decree of 1718). His fiscal aims—an increased tax— were achieved, but from the standpoint of the national economy and the taxpaying public the effect was negative. First, the quotas of persons reported by the census and subject to the per capita levy were raised through the inclusion of not only all various "idling" and "free" persons, but also of categories of the population which had previously not been subject to the per capita tax—palace peasants, state peasants, one-yard men [*odnodvortsy*], taxpaying tradespeople, commonland [*chernososhnye*] peasants, Siberian agricultural service people, and others. Secondly, among the serf population itself, the census and the per capita tax introduced a change whereby the decree of 1723 "placed" the *kholops* within the per capita impost equal to the serf peasants. In this manner occurred the apparent elimination of the *kholop* class. It was not accomplished, however, by way of abolition, but by joining the *kholops* to the peasants in the general "census affidavit" and in the general per capita levy. The inclusion of the *kholop* in the census affidavit meant his complete bondage, whereas formerly the "service *kabal*" [indenture] and "residence record" [*zhilaya zapis*] afforded him some opportunity for earning his freedom.

Thus, henceforth, their mere official entry into the census record fixed the taxpaying position of two main groups of the taxable population: the "royal" tax-liable persons and the serfs of the landlords. The fiscal aims of these reforms of Peter were such that among the taxable population "no one . . . shall belong to the idle," and that each "shall be attached to some service or in someone's domestic service, and not roam without serving," and that "none shall remain without being included in the tax."

We shall not dwell here on the other phases of Peter's reforms, on his measures for the promotion of industry related both to his reform and military problems, or on his "Europeanization" in the spirit of the mercantilist ideas of his age. These shall be discussed separately at a later point. Here, to raise the general problem, we shall merely indicate that, in any event, the enormous successes of Peter in this respect required new methods and means for developing industry— the attraction of "new people," new initiative, new technique, capital, and a new organization of industry. And here, too, as we shall see subsequently in greater detail, Peter was still incapable of functioning outside the general conditions of serfdom within which he was compelled to propagate industry.

Clearly, on the basis of what we have just said, the reforms and wars of Peter, despite their advantageous significance, were of necessity a heavy burden on the national economy of the mass of the people, who were being "fleeced threefold." Diverted from their work to endless wars, to build towns and a navy, for hard labor on industrial enterprises, and to all types of general "royal service," the population was impoverished, forced to curtail or completely abandon its economy. Even an apologist and theoretician of the reforms of Peter like Pososhkov refers to the "soul-killing per capita head levies" (the capitation tax), and also to the fact that the peasantry, due to the burdensome levies, "quit their homes and ran, some into the lowlands, some toward the borderlands, and others beyond the frontier, and thus settled foreign lands while leaving their own wasteland." It must be noted, however, that the per capita duty had one advantageous aspect: the peasant who paid one poll tax of 70 kopecks per person, regardless of the amount of land he cultivated, could by hard work increase his acreage. This did, in fact, occur: the arable land of the country increased in the course of the first half of the eighteenth century, regardless of other circumstances.

His huge military expenditures compelled Peter to initiate, in addition to the per capita tax, a variety of other duties, leaving nothing untaxed which could be used as a source of revenue: the sale of salt, the wearing of beards, the sale of oak coffins or cucumbers, the keeping of bees, the grinding of knives and axes. The total amount of tax collected over several years of Peter's reign increased five times. In addition to money duties, the populace was extremely overburdened by heavy obligations in kind—by the requisitioning of horses and carts for the military supply, by chopping wood for shipbuilding, by work on the construction of fortresses and towns, by work in factories, and so forth. For the fortification and construction of Petersburg alone, tens of thousands of peasants were driven together from all parts of Russia to perish in that swampy region from exhausting labor. Moreover, the dragnet of military recruiting caught annually tens of thousands of the peasant youth.

The Serf Manufacturing Industry of the Eighteenth Century

General Characterization of the Manufacturing Period. In the economic history of Russia, the beginning of the eighteenth century and the reforms of Peter were of great importance for the development of industry. In this particular period began the "manufacturing" stage in the history of Russian industry, which continued within the framework of serf industry until the middle of the nineteenth century, when feudal manufacture changed into capitalist manufacture, and afterward into the capitalist factory. In the industrial development of Russia the prehistory of this period of serf manufacturing of the eighteenth and nineteenth centuries may be found on the one hand in the development of the serf manorial industry in the Moscow state of the seventeenth century, and on the other hand in small handicraft and *kustar* [artisan] industry.

While the early eighteenth century may be considered the first line of demarcation of the "manufacturing" period in the sense that Russian manufacturing and its budding large-scale industry emerged only in the early eighteenth century, created only by Peter and, furthermore, "artificially" propagated by him without any preliminary economic preparation (as originally believed by one of the historians of Russian industry, Korsak, and later by many writers of Populist tendencies). On the contrary, from our preceding presentation we have seen that, as early as the second half of the seventeenth century, "large" (for that age) industry began to come into existence in the Moscow state alongside the prevailing small urban handicraft production. Its first infant steps were taken on the large manorial economies by a variety of industrial enterprises working for a wide market (the enterprises of Morozov and others), or in the enterprises of foreigners, created chiefly for the military and other needs of the state.

Still, these early steps and peculiar forms of "large" industry were not sufficient in the seventeenth century to lay the foundation of the manufacturing period in Russian industry. This foundation can be traced specifically to the reforms of Peter, inasmuch as the distinct elements that had come into existence earlier and functioned as the prerequisite premises for manufacturing were by the age of Peter I molded into a developed system.

The bases for the creation of capitalist manufacturing in the West were: the expropriation of the agricultural population and the emergence of a class of hired workers; the accumulation of capital and the rise of the industrial capitalist; the existence of a market for mass production and wide exchange on the basis of social division of labor; and the well-known advanced level of manufacturing technique founded upon the division of labor within the workshop.

In the circumstances leading to the rise of serf manufacturing industry in Russia, these preliminary conditions assumed a very different character in consequence of the very existence of the social-economic relationships of serfdom, within which serf manufacturing in Russia originated during the eighteenth century.

The existence of large fortunes and the accumulation of capital in the sixteenth and seventeenth centuries arose, as we have seen, on the basis of the substantial accumulation of money by the land-owning class, as well as by merchants and industrialists. Large commercial capital became the chief source for the emergence of our first manufacturing during the age of Peter. Among these "manufacturers" of Peter may be found many names of the former Moscow "guests"[1] and merchants. To them we should, indeed, add a number of large landowners, a few foreigners, and other persons. A majority of these persons, to be sure, owing to a lack of personal capital, obtained assistance from the treasury in the course of establishing their industrial enterprises. But the amount and number of these contributions were not especially impressive: according to the calculations of Tugan-Baranovsky, no more than fifteen to twenty private enterprises per hundred established during the age of Peter obtained loans for their enterprise amounting to 15,000 to 30,000 rubles.

Clearly, the "large" manufacturing industry emerging in Russia during the eighteenth century was, by its very nature, most intimately connected with the state, with the latter's military and economic problems, and, hence, with such financial assistance as the state might render an infant industry. Likewise, in Western Europe, even in the case of an advanced industrial state like France, the participation of the state with its investments and the erection of fiscal industrial enterprise were known to have occurred and exercised a strong influence on the development of private capitalist industry. There, too, private enterprise found support in the government by means of various industrial privileges, tariff protection, and so forth.

In this same respect we should examine the question of the formation of the large-scale exchange and wide market required by a system of manufacturing. The serf economy with its natural and consumption character, as well as its poorly developed social division of labor, could not function as an extensive consumer market for our nascent manufacturers. Nevertheless, manufacturing under Peter to a large extent did cater to a wide market, preparing wool cloth, linen, nails, dishes, and so forth. This aspect of feudal manufacture developed even further in Russia than in Western Europe, owing to

[1] "Guests" [*gosti*]—big merchants who in Muscovite Russia were alone entitled to engage in foreign trade.—Ed.

the backwardness of handicrafts and the earlier emergence of extensive market connections and a wide market. Obviously in Russia, as in Western Europe, the state and its military-industrial orders served, especially during the earlier phases, as the largest consumer of the products of manufacturing industry. The artisan could not satisfy this type of demand either as to the nature of such products or as to their volume. Therefore the large government contractors, in Western Europe and in Russia alike, faced with an increased demand on the part of the state, arrived at the natural conclusion that for such large deliveries they must depend only on unified manufacturing production rather than on the small handicrafts. Nor should we, despite all this, exaggerate the connections between manufacture and government orders and consumption during the age of Peter.

Finally, another preliminary condition for the development of manufacturing was the evolution of the class of the industrial proletariat. In this respect we observe a most significant distinction in the industrial development of Russia compared with Western Europe. The economic conditions of serfdom and the bondage of a considerable part of the agricultural population offered little opportunity for the substantial and rapid formation of the class of free manufacturing workers required by manufacturing. Another source were the enterprises employing seasonal peasant labor [*otkhozhye*] of the serfs who paid *obrok* [quitrent] and were released by the landlord. At times these seasonal enterprises outside the villages provided the manufactures with the relatively skilled labor of the *kustars,* who, after engaging in industrial processing in their own homes, brought their technical skills to manufacturing. Finally, the most skilled among the free laborers were the foreign master workmen. All this limited the availability of a technically trained worker force equipped for manufacturing production.

However, even under Peter, industry had already found the number of these free workers inadequate for its purpose. At times a newly established factory would obtain, along with assistance from the state, experienced masters and workmen from old state plants. Additional forces of hired workers needed by the entrepreneurs were recruited with great difficulty from various elements: fugitives, retired soldiers, children of the soldiers, the poor, the vagabonds, and others. Although in Western Europe persons of this type likewise filled in part the ranks of manufacturing workers, the bulk of such labor was recruited among the mass of proletarianized free rural population, while the more skilled labor elements came from the former artisans. In Russia, under conditions of a poorly developed system of handicrafts, industry had no access to such sources. For this reason the problem of labor organization became particularly acute for the manufacturers of Peter. The solution of this problem was marked by lack of absolute clarity or consistency. The well-known Petrine decree of 1721 permitted "mercantile people" to buy fully inhabited villages for their factories and works "upon the condition that those villages remain forever inseparable from those factories." But even the use of another method—the "assignment" of peasants to the "merchants' factories"—still left unsolved the problem of hired or serf labor in industry. Although the "assigned" factory workers were not formally serfs, the practice did, in fact, encroach upon the nobility's monopolistic class rights to the compulsory labor of the serf. The struggle for industrial manpower between the nobility and the merchants became, therefore, a matter of supreme importance during the eighteenth century.

Social Composition of the Workers. Our latest sources enable us to assume that even for the eighteenth century one must not exaggerate the prevalence and significance of serf labor in our industries. Despite the earlier opinion of Tugan-Baranovsky concerning the expansion and profitability of serf labor from the standpoint of the factory-owners of the period (for which reason they sought the right to acquire serfs), recent historical publications (still fragmentary to date) assign much less significance to serf labor in many branches of industry than had been previously assumed. Thus, according to the surveys [*enquette*] of 1737–1740, for the manufacturing enterprises of the Moscow, Yaroslavl, and Kazan provinces (a small number of thirty-four enterprises and 6,992 workers, to be sure), the social composition of the labor force in the various branches of production is characterized by the figures (in percentages) in the table below.

As suggested by this table, "peasant children" proper often constituted no more than between one-third and two-fifths of the total number of workers. Such "declassed" proletarianized groups as the

TABLE 1

Social Groups of Workers	Wool Cloth	Linen and Cotton	Silk	Other[b]
Peasant children	23.5%	41.2%	36.1%	46.9%
Tradespeoples' children[a]	23.2	22.3	33.4	20.9
Soldiers' children	27.8	11.1	11.6	6.0
Mill hands' children	11.0	13.3	5.6	9.0
Total[c]	85.5%	87.9%	86.7%	82.8%

[a] Included in the group of tradespeople [*posadskiye*] were the tradespeople proper, "taxpaying peasants of the various settlements," artisans, clerks [*podyachiye*], and others.
[b] Included in the group of "other" manufactures are sailmaking, button-making, the manufacture of red lead, glass, pipe and other products.
[c] No breakdown is available for the others.

children of soldiers and tradespeople together constituted about one-half or more of the labor force. Furthermore, during these years, the "hereditary proletariat" proper, as represented by the "mill hands' children," held a position rather prominent for that era, comprising about one-tenth of the total number of workers in the said branches of production.

On the whole, then, serf labor played a prominent role in the industry of the eighteenth century. In contrast with Western Europe, therefore, the first growth of Russian manufacturing industry came within the milieu of serfdom. This circumstance was fraught with important consequences. Once a solution for the basic manpower problem in the organization of production was found, "industrial development" and the establishment of serf-operated manufactures began to be undertaken not only by merchant capital, but also by the manorial nobility with their abundant supply of serf manpower. As the result of the nobility's struggle to preserve its monopoly over manpower, the decrees of 1762 forbade nonaristocratic enterprises to buy peasants for their manufacturing mills. And although permission to buy peasants for industrial enterprises was restored in 1798, the latter measure was of little significance by that time, inasmuch as the merchant industries began to change to hired labor from the turn of the century. But the industries of the nobility continued for a time to operate with serf labor. In view of their privileges, the branches of manorial industry connected with raw material produced on the estates proper, in the production of wool cloth, for example, or in linen and paper production, began more and more to crowd out the mercantile industries. By the end of the eighteenth century, for example, of the forty wool-cloth industries nineteen belonged to the nobility (Tugan-Baranovsky). The situation was reversed in cotton, silk, and leather production.

Some elements of the commodity-capitalist character of these [large-scale] manufactures and their technically centralized organization may be clearly observed. Generally speaking, the technique and centralization of production were not too far advanced, to be sure. These problems remained uppermost in the organization of industry for some time to come. It became necessary to adopt measures, not always successfully, for improving production technique through the centralization and mechanization of production. Thus in 1712, with a view to "better discretion and speed" in the armament business, Peter I ordered the construction at the Tula factory of an "armament yard, in order that arms shall be produced by all masters at the same armament yard without stoppage, whereas in the home, where some of them might live, no guns shall henceforth be made." Consequently, guns were manufactured until that time by masters in their own workshops, and only several operations (the boring of the muzzle) were performed in the factory shops and at the factory benches. The armament yard was completed in 1718, but evidently centralized production somehow failed to occur, since working at home was permitted even afterward, and in 1733 a substantial part of the buildings within the armament yard were carried away for scrap.

Thus it may be noted that manufacturing under Peter produced no revolution in technique, and developed largely on the base of the old technique of handicraft and *kustar* production. This does not, indeed, diminish the importance of the Petrine era as a period that brought into view the trend and organizational forms of later industrial development in all its characteristics and peculiarities.

State Manufactures. The first and simplest form of big-industry organization to which Peter I turned his attention was the construction of state industrial enterprises. The military needs, the creation of a navy, the reorganization of the army, and the construction of cities demanded swift measures for the increase of industrial production. In this manner emerged the armament and metallurgical plants; the Petrozavodsk, Sestroretsk, Okhta, and Tula. The Urals and Perm witnessed the creation of state mining units, the largest of which were at Uktuss and Kamensk. Other large state enterprises were the sail plant at Moscow, the saltpeter plants in Kazan and in the south, a number of glass factories (including the largest and well-known Petersburg plant still in existence today), cotton cloth, wool cloth, tobacco, silk, and other plants. The size of these state enterprises may be judged by the following figures: 9 mining establishments in Perm had 25,000 peasants assigned to them, the Sestroretsk plant employed 683 workers, the Tula factory had 508 peasant households assigned to it, while 1,162 persons worked at the sail factory in Moscow. Built at government expense, these factories operated with the aid of foreign masters and Russian workers, along with peasants assigned to the factories as their "royal service."

Merchant Manufactures. It became necessary, however, at an early date to abandon this type of government industry, evidently because of its wastefulness. Gradually a large part of such enterprises, especially in the field of light industry, were transferred to the use of private persons on fixed terms. Along with a small number of previously existing enterprises, thus emerged, on the one hand, a special group of private merchant manufacturers employing hired labor, and, on the other, the so-called "possessional manufactures."

A general order was issued in 1723 to the effect that the "state factories" should be transferred to "particular persons," individually or in companies. The main elements among such companies and individual entrepreneurs were merchants, tradespeople, foreigners, and, occasionally, noblemen. Thus the state wool-cloth manufacture at Kazan was transferred to the merchant Miklyayev, another to the merchant Shchegolin, a paper manufacture at Petersburg to Maslov and Solodovnikov, the Moscow linen factories to the merchant company of Andrey Turk, Tsimbalshchikov, and others. Of the industrial companies maintained by the nobility, the largest silk industry was organized by Count Apraksin, Shafirov, and Tolstoy. The largest entrepreneur among the foreigners was Tames, the owner of several industries and the head of a company of large Russian merchants.

In general the "undistinguished" names of the merchantry, almost exclusively Russian at that, predominate in the lists of entrepreneurs during the age of Peter. This was true with respect both to private enterprises erected independently, and those leased from the state. A part of the factories was built entirely by "personal expense," another part with some assistance from the treasury. Thus, in the above-named large company of Shafirov, the founders invested a capital of 81,300 rubles, while the assistance from the treasury amounted to 36,700 rubles. In the Tames company the founders invested 46,000 rubles (including 12,000 rubles by the largest shareholder, Miklyayev), while 5,000 rubles came in assistance from the state. The capital of the Tomilin needle factory company consisted of 3,000 rubles, and that of the linen factory of Goncharov of 142,000 rubles.

Thus, bearing in mind the high value of money during that period, it may be considered that the organization of industrial enterprises involved the investment of large capital, about a million or more rubles in terms of present-day money. "Primitive accumulation" had evidently attained a substantial volume for that time. The development of the manufacturing industry occurred, however, under conditions of the economic system of serfdom. The basic problem remained the shortage of the free and skilled industrial worker. Merchant manufacturing, employing freely hired labor, had therefore not shown any significant development, prior to the early nineteenth century at least.

"Possessional" Manufacture. Serf manufacturing first emerged on the basis of the decree of 1721, which granted permission "in the interest of increasing the number of factories. Both the nobility and commercial persons shall be entitled to buy villages for those factories upon the permission of the Mining and Manufacturing Collegium only on this condition: That these villages shall remain inseparable from these factories." Thus came into existence a special type of manufacturing, afterward known as the "possessional." The name "possessional" was applied to factories of private merchants or former Crown enterprises which had been transferred to the use of private persons, together with their buildings and land, and sometimes including a loan as well as the right to buy peasants on the above-named conditions. The "possessional" owners obtained exemptions from obligatory government service and taxes, special customs privileges, and so forth.

The peculiar features of the organization and position of the "possessional" workers were as follows. The peasants were "bound" not to the owner but rather to the enterprise; they could not be sold apart from it, and constituted one indivisible entity together therewith. All production in the "possessional" factories was under the control of the government. The volume, articles, and quality of output, including the regulation of the width and quality of wool cloth, for example; the terms of sale of the product, the level of wages, and conditions of work were all subject to control and regulated by the government.

Clearly, the "possessional" enterprises were under these circumstances a rather unprogressive and wholly noncapitalist apparatus. The owner was tied down by the terms of the production of goods, their pricing, delivery, and so forth. He was tied down by the availability of a fixed number of workers assigned to the enterprise. The conditions of the "possessional" and assigned workers were quite difficult, and disturbances and uprisings were very frequent among them. Wages were negligible: men received between 4 rubles 50 kopecks and 8 rubles 50 kopecks a month; women 2 to 3 rubles a month. Some factory-owners maintained their workers at full room and board and paid their taxes, as did the landowner for his serfs, while the workers were obliged to labor for him at a fixed rate of pay. The money earned was subject to the deduction of taxes, and only a few kopecks fell into the hands of the workmen. Each "possessional" worker spent about 260 days of the year in factory work, and some were released to do field work for one or two months. The length of the workday usually was 11, 13, and even 15 hours a day, or more. A system of "tasks" was adopted, as a result of which it was necessary for an annual quota to be performed, and by the minors and the aged as well. Child labor was employed rather widely. At the same time the factory-owners had no right to discharge their workers or curtail production. Nor was there any permanent force of professional and qualified workers.

Under the economic conditions of serfdom, many "possessional" factory-owners were evidently interested not so much in industrial production itself as in a chance to acquire serf labor which they frequently used for purposes other than industrial production. The Factory Investigation of 1740 discovered a number of "false factories," that is, factories provided with serfs, but not actually functioning and hence, subject to closure. Nevertheless, the "possessional" enterprises, in some branches of industry particularly such as the Ural mining industry, for example, existed throughout the entire era of serfdom and were liquidated only by a general order in 1861.

Manorial Manufacturing. Finally, the last type of serf industry was the "manorial" manufactures of the landowners, operated exclusively by serf labor of the seignioral peasants. The manufactures of the nobility, which were almost nonexistent during the reign of Peter, began to develop only with the second half of the eighteenth century, during a period of intensified protectionist policy on behalf of the nobility, and continued until 1840–1850, when they finally began to pass out of existence.

*   *   *

The Quantitative Results of the Development of Manufacturing under Peter I. The above were the main types and trends of industry evolved since the time of the Petrine manufactures. They did, as we have seen, appreciably expand industrial production in existence at that time both in number and in new branches of production. The bulk of manufacturing under Peter I consisted of mining and iron works, arsenals, sailmaking, linen, wool cloth, cotton, glass, leather, silk, mirrors, wallpaper, chinaware, and other industries. Many of these branches had existed prior to the reign of Peter I, but were strongly stimulated in their development during the Petrine era. Regrettably, there are no exact data as to the number of manufactures launched during the reign of Peter I. The frequently cited figures of Kirillov list 233 industries at the end of Peter's reign, but these figures are obviously quite low for some branches, while they include, on the other hand, some enterprises of a nonmanufacturing type. According to other data, among 195 of the largest industries were included 10 wool-cloth, 19 linen, 7 silk, 5 leather, 4 cotton, and 3 armament-making enterprises.

Still more important was the fact that large-scale manufacturing, regardless of its rather low level, contributed to a rise in the general level of production forces. This was especially true, for example, of an industry like metallurgy. In volume of production of pig iron, Russia at that time, if we accept the figures of the same Golikov, held a foremost position among the countries of the world, producing under Peter 6.5 million poods [approximately 116,500 tons] of pig iron; this figure, however, appears to be considerably inflated.

Alexander Gerschenkron

THE ECONOMIC POLICIES OF A MODERN AUTOCRAT

The nature and implications of Peter's economic policies are subtly and searchingly analyzed by the eminent economic historian Alexander Gerschenkron, Professor of Economics at Harvard University since 1948. Professor Gerschenkron not only places the Petrine policies in their contemporary European context, but suggestively reflects on their relevance for a better understanding of the fundamental process of economic "modernization" (or Europeanization) in the last two-and-a-half centuries.

Turning . . . to Russian mercantilist experience, I propose to deal exclusively with the reforms of Peter the Great. To confine the presentation in this fashion does not imply that Peter had no predecessors. Some elements of his policies no doubt were visible during the successive reigns of his father, brother, and sister. In the more remote past certain similarities can be discerned in the second half of the sixteenth century. But those inchoate attempts rather pale into insignificance when compared with what followed them. I know that continuity is an "O.K. word" with historians. Continuity, however, is a term that has more meanings than its users are usually aware of, and so has its antonym of discontinuity. If we use the term in the sense of a sudden change in the rate of change—meaning a kink in the curve of investment and output—then there is no doubt that the first quarter of the eighteenth century in Russia was marked by a momentous discontinuity. It opened a new chapter in the economic history of the country.

Reprinted with permission of the author and publisher from *Europe in the Russian Mirror—Four Lectures in Economic History*, by Alexander Gerschenkron (Cambridge: Cambridge University Press, 1970), pp. 69–96. For footnotes containing original calculations and polemics, the reader should refer to the original text.

Militarily, the period was marked by continual wars, even though the intensity of the conflicts varied. Overshadowing the wars against the Turks—one victory and one ignominious defeat in which the fruits of the earlier conquest were lost—and saying nothing of the Persian War—there was the Great Northern War which started with the Russian debacle at Narva (1700), lasted for most of the reign, and eventually put an end to Sweden's *stormaktstiden,* the Swedish Age of Empire. Viewed from the shores of the Atlantic Ocean, Sweden may not have stood in the forefront of Western civilization, but for Russia this was the struggle against the West, against an enemy immensely superior in culture, both spiritual and material. In the process of Russian expansion this was the crucial drive to the open seas, that is to say, the push toward the West into Europe. The Black Sea proved unattainable, for the time being, but the Baltic, which Ivan the Terrible had craved, but could not hold, was the object of the war and the prize of victory. But while the task facing the Russian government—or, more personally, the Russian autocrat—was modern in the contemporaneous sense of involving him in a conflict with a modern power, all the resources at his disposal were abysmally backward. The problem, therefore, was to lift the military and economic potential of the country to a level more consonant with the nature of the task. In principle, this was the standard mercantilistic situation. In dealing with the economic policies of the Petrine state, I have to point out first the standard ingredients of mercantilism and then touch on its specific Russian aspects.

There is first of all the unification policy. Administratively, pre-Petrine Russia had already been centralized to an astonishing degree. Still Peter's administrative reforms greatly tightened the grip of the government over the territory of the state. Weights and measures became more uniform; some old measures were abolished, others were adjusted, as were some measures of length in order to accommodate the foot and the inch which Peter brought to Russia from his trip to England. By contrast, no attempt was made to remove the internal duties. They were not abolished until nearly three decades after Peter's death (1753). This, however, is not surprising. The Renaissance monarchy in France at times even raised the internal tolls and tariffs, the fiscal needs seeming more important than the goal of unification. It is such conflicts and inconsistencies, including that between investment and military expenditures (see below), that bedevil simplistic views of mercantilism which are indeed vulnerable to criticism. But inconsistencies of this sort essentially reveal instability of time horizons of statesmen, and they need not detract from the validity of broad interpretations. But physical unification—the problem of communications—was given great attention. Roads and bridges were built. So were canals. The Baltic Sea was linked with the Caspian by a system that hit the River Volga rather far upstream, but still provided an essential connection with the eastern tributaries of the Volga and, by the same token, with the mines and mills of the Ural Mountains. The project to connect the Baltic with the Azov and Black seas by a Volga–Don canal was begun, but remained unfinished; but the canal around Lake Lagoda was started as the first step to other and more effective inland waterways between the Neva and the Volga basin, although its construction took longer than anticipated and its completion did not occur before 1732.

As in the West, there was the previously mentioned problem of choice between immediate war expenditures and investment outlays to provide the basis for larger military resources after some lapse of time. This was the Colbert-Louvois dilemma. There are some indications in the papers of the Tsar that he was aware of the problem. But it is precisely at this point that something *sui generis* becomes visible in the Russian experience. For the impression that one receives, particularly from actions during the first part of the reign, say until 1715, is that the answer to the problem was not a calculated allocative decision, but the daimonic feeling that development was a function of will power translated into pressure and compulsion. The result was the simultaneity of effort in all directions: constructing and equipping the navy; building harbors; creating a new capital in the swamps of the Neva estuary; prospecting for minerals, opening mines and erecting blast furnaces and building factories, even though when it comes to plants that really deserve the name, the numbers were much less than had been assumed by earlier historians; and at the same time reorganizing and re-arming the army and reshaping the administrative machinery of the government. The new civil service was designed to push, press, and squeeze, to overcome resistance, indolence, and dishonesty, except that the deeply ingrained habits of government graft and corruption ate their ways into the new machinery, however ready the Tsar's whip, or rather the heavy cudgel he favored, was to fall on the shoulders of the guilty dignitaries—the fledglings from Peter's nest, to use Pushkin's phrase —to say nothing of torture to which some of them were submitted, of prisons to which they were sent, and of gallows on which they ended.

The very magnitude of the effort, its vigor, amplitude, and persistence endow the Petrine reign with unique features. Nowhere else in the mercantilistic world do we encounter a comparable case of a great spurt, compressed within such a short period. Nowhere else was the starting point so low; nowhere else were the obstacles that stood in the path of development so formidable. And along with differences in the vehemence of the process were the differences in its character. Nowhere else was the state to any comparable extent the demiurgos of economic development. Nowhere else was it so strongly dominated by the interests of the state. Hence came the composition of the nascent industry with its concentration above all on production and working of metals as well as on plants producing uniforms for the army, sails, ropes, and timber for the ships, and powder for the guns. Hence it came that the large-scale plants were established and run—at least for some time—by the state; that for those plants the state supplied everything: land and entrepreneurship and management, capital and labor (about which something more will be said presently), and, finally, the demand. It is true that at times, in a sudden flight of fancy, Peter would order the establishment of a factory producing Venetian mirrors or of a workshop producing Gobelin tapestries, but those short-lived although costly escapades must be seen as aberrations from a goal that in general was pursued with unswerving constancy. The *manufactures royales* in France did cater to the luxury demand of the court where that demand served an important social and political function: the splendor of the court was to reconcile the nobility to its loss of power to the monarchy. In Prussia, much poorer than France, the problem, during a certain period, was solved by granting the Junkers increasing rights over the peasantry and by appeasing them in this fashion. But in Russia the problem did not exist at all. The Russian state was poor but strong.

The combination of poverty and strength of the state resulted in pressures that were incomparably greater than those produced by mercantilistic policies in other countries. The budgetary revenues were but one of the forms these pressures took, but the fiscal policies reveal them with particular clarity. The bulk of the revenue came from direct taxes and the internal tariffs, the latter partly being in the nature of a sales tax and even a turnover tax. But nothing indicates the desperate urge of the government to squeeze additional money out of the population than the crop of new indirect taxes. An immense amount of ingenuity went into designing them. A new office—that of *pribyl'shchiki,* literally "profiteers," that is, people working for the profit of the state—was created. Those were men whose job it was to suggest new revenues. It was one of them who had the idea—speedily put into effect—that every petition to the authorities was to be written on a special paper with an eagle stamped upon it, the petitioner having to pay for the value of the stamp. The requirement of this "eagle paper," incidentally, remained on the statute book until the revolution of 1917. Everything imaginable was taxed: watering horses and beehives, peasants' private bathhouses and their beards as well as "illegal," that is, "un-German," dress of people in the towns. It is doubtful whether all these flights of fiscal imagination actually produced results that were consonant with the effort involved in inventing and collecting these taxes. According to Miliukov, the "eagle paper" in 1724 brought about two per mille of total revenue and the proceeds of taxes on dress and beards amounted to about one-quarter of one per mille of the total. But no source of revenue, however small, was disdained. The fiscal edifice was finally crowned in the penultimate year of the reign by the introduction of a poll tax or "soul tax" based on regular censuses of the population, this tax, too, remaining in force for nearly 160 years. The precise evolution of the tax burden over the period of the reign is still a matter of controversy. A well-known Soviet economist, Strumilin, even argued that it was lower per head in 1724 than it had been in 1680. But this extreme position is based on very questionable computations and the only thing that can be concluded from the debate is that the rise in the per capita tax burden, while perhaps somewhat less than that computed by Miliukov in his standard study of Peter's budget, was still disastrously large.

Strumilin, for rather obvious reasons, is at pains to show that Peter's reforms did not lead to a "ruination" [*razorenie*] of the Russian peasantry. It should be noted first that the tax burden of 1680 was already intolerably heavy, and Kliuchevsky said with reference to that year that "the paying forces of the population had been stressed beyond the point of exhaustion." On the other hand, it is natural that after the end of the Northern War (1721) some relief of the tax burden, as compared with the previous years, could, and in fact had to, take place. But a comparison between 1680 and 1724, interesting as it may be for some reasons, is of limited importance when the problem is to measure the weight of the fiscal burden imposed upon the peasantry during the first two decades of the eighteenth century. Using wherever possible data contained in Strumilin's study and making most conservative assumptions, I have computed the tax burden at the beginning of the second decade of the century, that is, *after* the decisive victory at Poltava in 1709, as amounting to 64 percent of the grains harvested from the peasant household's allotment of arable land. This is surely a most shocking result, and whatever admiration Strumilin felt for the great achievements of the "Transformer" on the throne, should not have prevented him from making a similar computation. I may be not wrong in assuming that this making light of the disastrous cost to the people was designed to suggest and justify the inference that also Stalin's superindustrialization and collectivization policies were altogether tolerable.

Yet, compulsion went far beyond confiscation of a huge portion of the population's income which even Strumilin—very implausibly in the light of his own data—believes to have been around 20 percent of total national income. Also 20 percent would be quite excessive in a country where the standard of living was probably below anything that would have been considered subsistence minimum in the West. Supply of manpower for army and navy, for construction projects for mines and factories, for forest work and transportation was the area where brute force was most clearly displayed. The Tsar's lack of concern for the cost of his projects in terms of human lives was absolute. It may be an exaggeration that hundreds of thousands of workers perished in the construction of the—subsequently lost—port of Taganrog on the Sea of Azov, but the figure was plausible enough for a qualified acceptance by Kliuchevsky. And similar statements were made of the Baltic ports. It is probably natural that horrors of this sort appear to be of little weight to people of Strumilin's ilk who have lived through the contemporary experience of the Soviet industrialization.

As in the West, there were the stern measures against vagrants and beggars. Even in this respect, the Petrine state went one better on the West by attempting to punish not only the receiver, but also the giver of alms, a step that was bound to remain ineffective in a country where a beggar was considered to be a representative of Christ and possibly Christ himself. But the impressment of beggars represented only one aspect of the labor policy, even though in the factories in Moscow and two other cities (Yaroslavl' and Kazan) in the 1730s more than 21 percent of the labor force apparently had been beggars before being brought to the factory. Year by year, orders went out to local authorities all over the newly established nine provinces of the huge country to send men—state peasants—to places many hundreds of miles from their native villages. Mines and factories received whole villages assigned to them, many of those villages located far away from the place of employment. In the later part of the reign the government began to transfer mines and factories into private hands; individuals had to take them over whether they wanted to do so or not, or as Peter put it, "be it willingly or unwillingly." Thus even the private entrepreneur—so unlike the Schumpeterian image of him—could be, and at times was, created by appointment, by a fiat of the state, just as Molière's Sganarelle was made a *médecin malgré lui* by having been beaten with a big stick. It was in this later period (1721) that the private entrepreneurs were given the right to purchase villages of serfs, the latter to be tied permanently to the factories.

There has been a debate going on among the Soviet historians as to whether the enterprises established under Peter were capitalistic or feudal. The faith in the usefulness of such ambiguous labels is more remarkable for its childlike quality than for its explanatory power. There is no doubt that skilled labor—masters and foremen—

imported from abroad were contractual workers who earned very high wages and were extremely well-treated. Many of them proved ignorant and inept, quite unworthy of their hire. Some of those who came were just the jetsam and flotsam of foreign shores. But Peter did not follow the angry advice he received to send such men away in disgrace. Foreigners were needed, and there should be no tales told abroad about their ill treatment in Russia. Krizhanich may have been Peter's forerunner, but the xenolasia of the learned Croatian priest was altogether foreign to Peter whose concern for economic development was not blurred by ulterior motives.

By contrast, native workers were exposed to an entirely different treatment, both with regard to income and personal freedom. Even to the extent that so-called free labor was used, the adjective must be taken with the greatest possible caution. There is a regrettable tendency of some Soviet historians to speak of free labor as soon as a wage was paid. Apprentices were tied to the factory for seven years plus three more years after the completion of their apprenticeship. More importantly, delinquent debtors were sent to the mines, if they were able-bodied males (old people and minors, who as heirs also could be delinquent debtors, were to be put to less strenuous jobs); if they were females, they were dispatched to the weaving sheds. Criminals of both sexes naturally were used as heavy laborers. Prostitutes were sentenced to labor "without limit of time and if necessary until death." What mattered more was that time and again large numbers of artisans were forcibly collected in Moscow and other towns and sent to the Urals. A salter could ask the government for delivery of 9,000 laborers and, after some bargaining, receive 5,000. Year in, year out, ukazes were issued ordering mobilization of 40,000 workers to be sent, under guard to St. Petersburg from all over the country, including Siberia; while the home villages and home towns of the laborers were held to pay for their sustenance. Thousands of artisans were forcibly brought to St. Petersburg for permanent settlement. At times promises were made designed to attract contractually hired labor to factories and other projects, but when, later on, the census for the poll tax caught the so-called free workers in factories, they were subsequently tied to the factories for good, that is to say, enserfed. Children of soldiers as well as older soldiers were forcibly used as laborers, the service of a soldier in the Petrine army and afterwards being for lifetime and ending only with incapacity by illness or old age. Strumilin must admit that "after 1726 in state factories also recruits conscripted beyond the military needs of the army were added to the labor force." "But," he goes on to say, "they received wages just as other workers and fulfilled the same functions as the others." By this line of reasoning also a peasant serf put into a gentry factory and given money to keep body and soul together would be regarded as a freely hired laborer and the enterprise would become a "capitalist" enterprise. This is a fairly foolish position, stubbornly maintained in order to make a rather irrelevant point. What matters, of course, are not terminological quibbles, but the historical fact that it was the power of the state that was used in the historical process of creating the industrial labor force. Wage or no wage, the labor was essentially a coerced, forced labor, created as an industrial labor force by the fiat of the state. It is not surprising, therefore, that most of the mines and factories looked like fortresses and were guarded by detachments of soldiers in order to prevent escapes.

Nor is it surprising that industrial labor should be essentially unfree labor in a state that was a "service state," or as the Russian phrase runs, a "serfdom state." For it was not only the peasantry that was enserfed to the gentry. The gentry, created by the state, was under the obligation to serve the state, and the serfdom of the peasantry had a clear social function, that is, to pay for the services of the gentry, both military and civil. By serving the gentry the peasant was serving the state. Therefore also the never-ending cogitations of Marxian historians in Russia about the class nature of the Petrine state—was it a gentry state or was it a merchants' state?—miss the essential fact that the state was not the state of this or that class. It was the state's state.

The Marxian approach which has yielded extremely useful insights in appropriate periods and circumstances—say England of the nineteenth century or Austria in the interwar period, to illustrate at random—becomes altogether sterile when applied to the Russian demiurgos state. Marxism at all times had difficulty with explaining dictatorial power. Even when, as in the case of Napoleon III, the state that was not dominated by a certain class could be presented as *originating* from an equilibrium of class power, the problem still remained that once the dictatorial state was established, it was able to pursue an independent policy of its own, because it had become a power in its own right. Engels, who created the "theory" of equilibrium of class forces, was at pains to present such equilibria as "exceptional," situations arising from the special conditions of a moment ["*momentan*"]. Even Engels's own examples, which include two centuries of absolute monarchy, do not fit his definition too well. But when it comes to Russia, it is not only that the use of terms such as "exception" or "moment" is patently unsuitable to characterize the course of Russian history and the role of the state in it. The overriding consideration is that it would make little sense to regard the autocratic state as emerging from equilibrium of class power. It was not class power relations that created the state. The obverse was true: it was the state that was creating the classes: labor, and even the entrepreneurs, although soon more and more men became ready to make use voluntarily of the great benefits that were held out to them by the state. And even though the state did not create the peasantry, it was the policy of the state through its methods of repression, its passport system, introduced by Peter, as well as its fiscal arrangements which kept the peasantry put and tended to reduce, though not to stop, its escape from oppression into the wide open spaces of the East. But without classes as independent forces, the materialistic conception of history becomes sterile because the phenomenon of the independent state involves the primacy of the political rather than of the economic factor, the latter playing an instrumental role in the service of the former. Marxism in general found it difficult to place the mercantilistic state within its conceptual framework, but the degree of the difficulty varied from country to country, reaching its maximum in Russian mercantilism.

Before I proceed to summarize the comparison of Russian mercantilism with that of the West, I must refer to an aspect of the former that was, by contrast to others, not more but less in evidence in Russia. I am referring to the fact that the Russians, among their manifold borrowings from the West, did not include the Western preoccupation with foreign trade and precious metals. To some extent, this is reflected in the lexical changes in the Russian language and a word thereon may be in order. As a result of the intensive borrowing from abroad, things never seen before and often even never heard of before made their appearance in Russia. New things—and concepts—required new words, and the language was therefore flooded with foreign words, very frequently quite imperfectly Russified. It is interesting to note then that of some 3,500 foreign words that entered the language during Peter's reign about one quarter of them were shipping terms; another quarter was occupied by terms connected with government administration; the third quarter was held by military terminology; the balance was taken up by miscellaneous words with a preponderance of luxury terms imported from France, either directly or via Germany and Poland. But what is striking is the absence of both economic terms and business terminology. There were perhaps two dozen borrowed words which could be stretched to suit the concept. In particular, accounting terms were missing altogether. This is as it should be. The economic enterprises created during the Petrine spurt were not oriented toward any careful calculus of costs and revenues. The state, that is, the Russian people, were to foot the bill, and profitability or its absence aroused little interest. The ingenuity of the previously mentioned "profiteers" that went into invention of new minute taxes, each of them requiring special collecting apparatus, was not matched by a comparable endeavor in the sphere of industry, except, of course, for the perennial struggle against deceit and corruption. Incidentally, the "profiteers" themselves often showed excessive interest in their private profits. One of them died on the wheel for taking bribes, and the inventor of "eagle's paper," the king of the profiteers, died in prison before his trial for the same offense.

Very similarly, no terms were allowed to enter the Russian language from the mercantilist literature of the time. And indeed the interest in foreign trade and the balance of payments as well as in precious metals was clearly subordinated to the problem of economic development and foreign policies. An active balance of trade was indeed a matter of considerable importance. The export surplus was to finance the subsidies and bribes given to allies in the war against Sweden. It was needed to pay the foreign technicians. Foreign trade in a number of basic commodities (the so-called forbidden goods, such as potash, caviare, rhubarb, ship timber, furs, and others) was maintained as a government export monopoly, although most of those commodities were released to private trade in 1719. There were some import prohibitions, mostly directed against luxury goods, and there were some very loosely enforced measures of control of movement of precious metals. At one point Peter tried to find out in which way foreign prohibitions against exports of precious metals could be evaded. In addition, there was throughout concern for the terms of trade, and particularly for the low prices offered for Russian goods by foreign traders in Russia. Peter tried to order establishment of merchant companies in Russia, precisely in order to raise export prices, but did not pursue the matter and the project bore no fruit. But at no time did Peter in this field exhibit the boundless energy which was so characteristic of his actions elsewhere. Essentially, it was only in the last years of Peter's life, particularly after his visit to France, that foreign trade began to attract more serious attention, resulting in the first protectionist tariff in which the degree of protection varied directly with the ratio of domestic output to total consumption, the duty rising up to 75 percent *ad valorem*. This was the very opposite of an infant industry tariff and probably reflected the high cost of output in those branches of industry on the development of which greatest emphasis had been placed in the preceding years. It is reasonable to assume that those industries were subject to increasing rather than decreasing cost, and in some way the tariff, crude as it was, may have been broadly adjusted to such patterns of quantitative restrictions of imports as existed prior to its introduction. The main point, however, is the one previously made. Something that seemed to stand in the very focus of Western mercantilist thought appears to have played a very subordinate role in Russia.

A distinctive feature of Russian mercantilism was the almost complete absence in it of general theorizing. At the beginning of this century social policies in Australia were once described as *socialisme sans doctrine*. Similarly, the Petrine policies were *mercantilisme sans doctrine*. But one of a couple of exceptions to this proposition may be mentioned here, because it tends to confirm the conclusion just reached. The reference is to the curious literary document of the period, composed by Ivan Pososhkov—*The Book on Poverty and Wealth* (1724). Soviet and also some pre-Soviet enthusiasts liked to describe Pososhkov as one of the great economists of all times.

This is fairly ludicrous. But the book of this auto-didact of peasant origin (1652–1726) is remarkable in many respects and may be considered the only contemporaneous comprehensive mercantilistic tract on Russian economic policies, as one may well abstract from the memoranda of F. S. Saltykov,* who was influenced by his long residence abroad. It is, therefore, instructive to observe Pososhkov's distribution of emphasis.

Pososhkov does indeed deal with foreign trade. He is interested in improving the country's terms of trade by exerting pressures on foreign merchants. In the process, he incidentally assumes very low price-elasticity of foreign demand for Russian goods, and obversely very high price-elasticity of Russian demand for foreign commodities. He is interested in expanding the volume of Russian exports and applies an infant-industry argument of sorts to them by suggesting that exporting at a loss for some time will be profitable in the long run. On the import side he calls for drastic steps against luxury goods and at one point even objects to purchases of foreign cloth for soldiers' uniforms, despite the existing price differentials, arguing in this and in a couple of other cases the advantage of keeping money at home. But all this is far from playing a central part in his argument. The balance of trade is never mentioned explicitly and there is never the remotest hint that the export surplus as such is the source of the country's increase in wealth. For Pososhkov's main interest is directed to problems of economic development.

Here the range of subjects he treats is very wide: training of workers; improvement in the quality of products and introduction of severe penalties for shoddy goods; technical innovations and protection of inventors; location of industries, with regard to which he, curiously enough, considers cheapness of food as exercising the strongest pull in determining the place of production; development of chemical industry; suggestions for efficient prospecting for minerals; criticism of inefficiency in collecting indirect taxes and proposals for reform of Peter's direct taxation of peasants so as to increase the state's revenues. It was in the latter connection that he issued to the gentry a stern warning not to exploit the peasantry excessively with a clear understanding of the existing competition

* Saltykov died in 1715 in England, where he had been sent to purchase ships. He is the author of several plans for the "modernization" of Russia.—Ed.

for the product of peasant labor—and for that labor itself—between the state and the gentry. What in fact was intimated was a threat of "reversion" [*reduktionen*] of gentry lands to the crown upon the then recent Swedish model. Pososhkov said: "The landlords [*pomeshchiki*] are not permanent owners of the peasants. Their direct owner is the autocrat of all the Russias, and the landlords possession is a temporary one. . . ." And Pososhkov went on to say that peasants must be protected by imperial edicts, because "the wealth of the peasantry is the wealth of the Tsar." Pososhkov made a number of suggestions designed to improve the lot of the peasantry, so as to prevent the peasants' flights "southward and to the border regions, and even beyond the frontiers, populating foreign territories and leaving their own land empty."

There is more, however, to Pososhkov's book than the important priority assigned in it to economic development. The book was finished in 1724, a short time before Peter's death. By that time, Russia's position as a great power had been assured, but at the cost of an effort that—very visibly to the eyes of contemporaries—had led to the impoverishment of the country. Hence came Pososhkov's insistence that continuation of economic development must be accompanied by increases in popular well-being.

A specific Russian pattern of economic development was reaching completion. And in this sense Pososhkov's book, while characteristic of Russian mercantilism, bears the mark of a precise historical moment in its evolution. We have, of course, no proper statistics to measure the speed of industrial growth during Peter's reign, let alone what happened to national income over the period. Even the estimates of the growth of pig iron are quite uncertain. Still, it may be assumed that it had grown at about 8 percent per year between 1700 and 1725. It is most unlikely that any other industrial commodity could boast a similarly high rate of growth. But even if we assume the whole industrial establishment to have grown at the same rate, such an increase in what after all still was a tiny portion of the total economy was compatible with great reductions in national income, the disposable incomes of the population decreasing even more. What certainly increased was the wealth of the state that was designed to support the power of the state. As Kliuchevsky put it: the state grew fatter and fatter and the people grew leaner and leaner. The great historian was referring to the seventeenth century, but his pithy conclusion fits the Petrine period with particular force. In attempting to draw conclusions from the preceding discussion of Russian mercantilism, the following points appear to stand out:

1. if we wish to conceive of mercantilism as a common European phenomenon, it is power policies and subordination of economic policies to the exigencies of power that provide the common denominator; the economic policies centering on economic development in general, and industrial development in particular;

2. for the rest we observe deviations from the basic pattern. The role of vested interests in co-determining the policies of the state varied from country to country. In viewing the Petrine experience no one possibly could claim with Adam Smith that "the sneaking arts of underling tradesmen have been erected into political maxims" or that "the merchants and manufacturers have been by far the principal architects . . . of this whole mercantile system." They were the objects rather than the agents of Petrine policies. Even so, the emphasis on foreign trade, active balance of trade and the resulting influx of precious metals, and, finally, protectionism was enormously strong in some countries and tended to be fairly insignificant in others;

3. in dealing with deviations of this kind, it is possible simply to register them as such and let it go at that. Then the economic history of Europe appears in a rather fragmentized fashion, the deviations greatly detracting from, and even destroying, the unity that was so dear to Heckscher and his teacher. Yet something more can be said on the subject. As one reviews once more in one's mind the history of the Petrine era in Russia and looks for reasons for the overwhelming role of the state, the ubiquitousness of compulsion, the weakness of vested interests, and the single-minded concentration on power, the economic backwardness of the country surely suggests itself as the main, if not the sole, explanatory factor. But if this be true, then the Russian experience does provide a clue to the understanding of mercantilism westward beyond the borders of Russia. The intensity of the deviations from the basic pattern, beginning from the greater role of vested interests and the consideration of wealth as an independent goal of policies

are then to be regarded as a function of the decreasing backwardness of the countries concerned. If this proposition holds, as I believe it does, then it becomes possible to arraign mercantilistic countries according to the degree of their economic backwardness, starting probably with the Low Countries and continuing over England and France to Prussia, and finally, Russia. If the resulting picture should be one of a fair degree of continuity in the sense of gradual increase in the significance of the basic pattern until the naked power point is reached in the east of the continent, then indeed the European economic history in the mercantilist period may be conceived as a unity, although not a uniform, homogeneous unity; but a diversified, graduated unity, which, however, is comprehensible as such because of its relation to the degree of economic backwardness which serves not only as an organizing but also as an explanatory principle.

Assuming that this view of European development in the mercantilist period is at all defensible, it would seem to accomplish two things: it conceives of Russia as a part of Europe and by the same token it uses Russian history to add to our understanding of the economic history of Europe. It constitutes an attempt to move backward in time my general conception of European industrial development in the more modern period, that is to say, in the eighteenth and nineteenth centuries. But before addressing myself to the question as to how Russian industrial development in the later period may help us to understand the industrial development in the West, one final point must be made concerning Russian mercantilism with regard to its effects on the country's subsequent development.

Heckscher's well-balanced and judicious appraisal of mercantilism emphasizes both the contrast and the concord between mercantilism and *laissez-faire*. Leaving aside the field of intellectual history, the field of doctrines and ideology, and riveting our sight to economic processes, it may indeed be said that in the West in some respects, mercantilist policies prepared the soil for modern industrial development while in others they had created obstacles that had to be removed, at times requiring a considerable effort. Incidentally, some of those obstacles may have originally been in the nature of factors promoting rather than retarding economic development. . . Whatever the meaning of Marxian dialectics and, as we know, it is quite elusive, if it means among other things that in the course of historical development the nature of something that for some time had a positive effect, may over a rather short time change to its opposite, this is a most useful reminder which an historian will ignore at his own peril.

I am not in a position to demonstrate here how the problem of obstacles created by mercantilist policies actually presented itself in the individual countries of Europe. But I should like to volunteer a general hypothesis and then say a few words on the conditions in Russia in this respect. The general proposition, or rather a surmise, I can offer is this: the less backward, economically speaking, was a country when it went through its mercantilist experience, the less formidable were the obstacles for subsequent development that resulted from that experience and the more easily they were overcome.

Let me try to illustrate: the Austrian monarchy undoubtedly occupied an intermediate position with regard to its economic backwardness between Russia and the West. In Austria, Joseph II (1780–1790) was the great mercantilist on the throne, the man who liked to say that every single thread of the clothes he wore on his back came from indigenous material and labor. One of the outstanding features of Josephine policies, greatly intensifying those pursued by Maria Theresa, was unification. "The whole Monarchy will become one mass of people ruled in the same fashion," he wrote to his brother. But unification meant, first and foremost, the creation of a strong centralized state. In the process the power of the bureaucratic machinery was greatly increased, most notably at the expense of the gentry diets and its local apparatus in the individual provinces, both German and non-German. There is little doubt that these policies under Joseph II favored the economic development of the country and facilitated the introduction and enforcement of economic reforms. But when in the nineteenth century the enlightened despotism of Joseph was replaced, in the period of reaction between 1815–1848, by the unenlightened despotism of Metternich, and economic progress began to be viewed with great suspicion and the railroads came to be regarded not as the welcome carriers of goods and persons, but as the carriers of the dreaded revolution, then the centralized state, the outgrowth of mercantilistic policies clearly became an obstacle to the economic development of the country. If the same sequence was reproduced in France by the absurd tariff policies of the Napoleonic bureaucracy after the demise of the Continental System, the intensity of the phenomenon and its negative effects were undoubtedly a good deal weaker and less damaging than was the case in Austria.

But a comparison of Austria with Russia is also illuminating, although in different respects. The effort of economic development and general reform produced by Joseph II, strong as it was, cannot be compared in magnitude and intensity to that of Peter the Great. This is as it should be as the vehemence of the spurt, the magnitude of the change, can be expected to vary with the backwardness of the country. But, in particular, the problem in Austria was not to establish a general service state, subjugating the gentry and forcing the peasantry to serve both the gentry and the state. Quite the contrary was true. The burdens of the peasantry were not increased but reduced. By Joseph's edict of 1781 personal subjection of the Austrian peasantry was abolished. As a piece of what aptly was called imperial propaganda the edict spoke of the abolition of *Leibeigenschaft,* that is, slavery, which was exaggerated as the Austrian peasant was enserfed rather than enslaved. But abolition of personal subjection meant, in addition to the right to marry without consent of the seignior and the discontinuation of the hated house services by the members of the peasant's family, also, and most importantly, the right to leave the land and choose their trade freely. This was surely an approach to the problem of forming a modern labor force that was radically different from that followed in Russia. It is true that peasant obligations to the lords as attached to the land rather than to the person remained. But also in this respect, Joseph II tried a rather radical reform of compulsory commutation on a national scale. Under the terms of his edict of 10 February 1789—significantly five months before the start of the French Revolution—labor services to the seigniors were to be abolished and instead the peasant was to pay in money a fixed proportion of his gross income to the seignior and another fixed proportion to the state. This reform was never carried out for a number of weighty political and economic reasons. But the effect of the reform was perhaps not entirely nil. It left the gentry with the feeling that eventual emancipation was inevitable and as a result encouraged some of the seigniors to conclude private redemption agreements with the peasants and to replace bonded labor with freely hired labor. Thus, at least in this respect the mercantilistic policies left no obstacles for the future.

The effect of the Petrine policies was very different. Peter, of course, was in no way the creator of serfdom in Russia. The last legal measures sealing the condition of enserfment were administered by Peter's father in the code of 1649. And yet, it is fair to say that it was Peter's policies that in a very real sense greatly increased the effectiveness of the system of serfdom. The great improvement in the efficiency of the administration, the introduction of the passport system, and, last but not least, the reform of the fiscal system by the establishment of the poll tax with its regular censuses as a form of registration of the peasantry for the first time rendered it extremely difficult for the peasants to escape from the yoke of serfdom. In the longer run, once the crisis of the last years of Peter's reign and of the few following years was overcome, the chances of a successful flight were very greatly reduced, unless indeed it be a flight from a poorer seignior to a high and mighty one who often was in a position to use his influence in order to prevent the return of the refugee to his rightful owner. In addition, as a result of Peter's policies the burdens imposed on the peasantry increased very greatly, and this not only by extending peasant services far beyond the sphere of agriculture to industry, construction, and transportation; but also within the area of agriculture. As never before, the burdens the peasants bore were regarded as work for the state.

When the great experiment was over; when after some stagnation, the country's growth was resumed at very moderate rates; when finally the Industrial Revolution in England ushered in a new era in industrial history, then it was precisely the institution of serfdom, so greatly reinforced by Peter and one of the carrying pillars of his edifice of economic development, that became the major block in the path of Russia's participation in the new industrial progress. For in the interval the nature of serfdom had profoundly changed. The reform work of the Petrine period, combined with the size of the country in area and population, effectively and long-lastingly liberated the rulers of the country from the necessity to undertake extraordinary efforts in order to maintain the military power of the country on a level sufficiently high for the purposes of expansion. For a full century after Peter's death, the Russian arms and Russian power basked in the sun of continual successes. In the south, the steppes of Novorossiya and the Crimea were wrested from the Turks, and the Russians firmly established themselves on the shores of the Black Sea. In the West, in the course of the Seven Years' War, Russian Cossacks had penetrated into Berlin. The partitions of Poland meant enormous territorial expansion westward. Finally, the failure of Napoleon's invasion of Russia which in the end brought the Russian troops into the streets of Paris crowned this series of astonishing triumphs. . . .

My usual way of looking at the Petrine experience (and applying the same idea to some earlier periods of Russian history) was to discern in it a series of sequences which I regarded as a specifically Russian pattern of economic development. To summarize the sequences briefly: 1) economic development was placed in the service of the country's military needs and was a function thereof; 2) as a result the development assumed an uneven, jerky, spurt-like character and was compressed within a relatively short period; involving 3) imposition of high, if not intolerable, burdens on the population who had the misfortune of living in those particular periods; and 4) introduction of special repressive measures, designed to force the population to bear those burdens; 5) continuation of the spurt until the decrease in military pressures and/or the exhaustion of the population led to the termination of the spurt which was followed either by stagnation, or, at any rate, by a considerable decline in the rate of growth.

I do feel that this summarizes correctly the course of the Petrine experience. The crucial problem in the preceding sequences, from the point of view of this presentation, relates to point 4: the introduction of special measures of enforcement, that is to say, the enserfment of the peasantry. It is really this point that made me feel that quantitative differences apart, here lay the peculiar qualitative specificity of the Russian pattern. While the main purpose of the Russian development was to modernize its economy, and, in fact, much of its social and political framework, that is, to bring it closer to Europe in some of its most significant respects, it was by the force of the selfsame development that Russia was being forced in other, no less significant respects, away from Europe, towards the despotisms of the Orient with their service states, which involved enslavement of the population by the state.

I do not feel that there is anything wrong per se with this presentation. It is a significant fact that as serfdom was on the wane in the west of Europe it was greatly increasing in Russia. If human freedom is one criterion of civilization, then Russia was becoming less civilized as—*and because*—it was aspiring to move closer to Europe, or, as Hjärne would say, to enter the community of European civilization. . . . I have tended to view the decisive "Europeanization" of [the] Russian economy as pertaining to a much later period—the last three decades before the outbreak of World War I. And yet, I have begun to wonder whether even the Petrine period and the policies of Russian mercantilism could not be regarded as an integral part of a general European experience, and this in a sense that goes a good deal beyond the fact that the Russian experience can be subsumed under a general European concept of mercantilism and that actually looking into the Russian mirror has helped us to develop such a concept. What I am referring to now is the problem of the deviations in the individual countries and the chance of systematizing these deviations into a general pattern. The hypothesis then is as follows: everywhere mercantilism in promoting economic development was creating obstacles to the perpetuation of development, and the magnitude of these obstacles varied in a comprehensible fashion with the backwardness of the country.

A. A. Kartashev
CHURCH REFORM

Of all the reforms of Peter the Great, the abolition of the Patriarchate and the establishment of the Holy Synod was the most radical in form. It also had the most widespread and immediate repercussions, for it provoked bitter resistance among the people. In Muscovy, the church had enjoyed great influence and its head, the Patriarch of Moscow, was the most influential and powerful individual after the Tsar. Peter decapitated the church and made it into a mere government department. Recalling that in the nineteenth and twentieth centuries the church—as an institution—exercised little influence on the people and none on the educated élite, and remembering that it offered but little resistance to the Revolution of 1917, one is tempted to blame the situation on Peter's subjection of the church to the state and its transformation into a tool and handmaid of the government and police. Professor A. A. Kartashev (died 1960), a leading figure in the revitalization of church life on the eve of the Revolution, who became dean of the Russian Orthodox Theological Seminary in Paris after the Bolshevik seizure of power, dissents from the traditional view. He argues that after Peter's reform the church successfully raised its cultural standards and expanded its missionary activities. It may be worth noting, however, that perhaps Kartashev's analysis fails to take adequate account of the general rise in literacy and in the level of Russian cultural life in the two centuries following Peter's death. For the traditional view and interpretation, see the excerpts from an article by Professor N. Zernov, below.

Along with other events which unquestionably marked turning points in Russian history, such as the introduction of Christianity by St. Vladimir and the Tartar conquest, the revolutionary reform of Peter the Great must be regarded as an event setting a boundary between major epochs and opening a new period in the history of the Russian Church, known as the Synodal period.

Our leading historians (Soloviev, Kliuchevsky, Platonov, and Miliukov) have tried to eradicate the mythological patina upon the epoch of Peter the Great by elaborate demonstrations of the continuity of the historical process, in which there are, according to them, no breaks or fantastic leaps. However, after all their critical scrubbing, the dividing line drawn by our forebears in Russian history and also,

From A. A. Kartashev, *Ocherki po Istorii Russkoi Tserkvi* [*Essays in the History of the Russian Church*], vol. II (Paris: YMCA Press, 1959), pp. 311–312, 313–314, 317–320. Translated by Mirra Ginsburg.

by that token, in church history, became still more indisputable. Our history falls into two periods—the period before Peter, and that after Peter. The Synodal period is not a scholarly convention, but a naturally formed and uniquely new epoch in the development of the Russian Church. And the essential point here is not merely in the new form of the supreme administration of the Russian Church (a form, incidentally, which is canonically defective), but in the novelty of the legal and cultural principle which had been brought into Russian history from the West, and which profoundly altered and distorted the "symphony" between church and state normal for the East.

Thus, both because of the historically established link between the destinies of the church and the state (as in the other free national churches of the East), and because of the novelty of the system of church administration introduced by Peter the Great, after the death of Adrian, the last, Eleventh, Patriarch of Muscovite Russia (died in 1700), we entered a new period—that of Imperial Russia. . . . It would be denying historical truth to close our eyes to the powerful grip of the temporal rulers upon the reins of church administration or to lull ourselves by the clerical illusion that nothing had changed in Orthodox Russia, and that the church had lost neither its former primacy, nor its style and color.

In reality, everything was changed so radically that no church historian, of whatever school or trend, can any longer write church history in terms of this or that head of the church. The plan of the Tsar-Reformer had succeeded. There were no longer any heads of the church. The church was decapitated in the most literal, technical sense of the word. For a brief while, the titles of President and Vice-President of the Synod flashed on the horizon. They were meaningless, entailed no powers, and were quickly succeeded by the equally nominal title of senior members [*pervenstvuiushchie*]; in the late eighteenth and early nineteenth centuries, these were placed entirely under the jurisdiction of the ministerial figures of the Chief Procurators. It might be possible, with some slight justification, to trace the history of this period in terms of individual Chief Procurators, but certainly not in terms of the Synod members, who were appointed and dismissed by the Chief Procurator at his own discretion. However, the most appropriate and logical method of narrating this history is in terms of reigns. On this level, it will be possible also to capture the characteristic features of the process of historical development, determined by the person of the absolute sovereign and those who surrounded him. . . .

Fundamental Character and Appraisal of the Synodal Period

The brilliantly vivid and masterful personality of Peter was both the conductor and the executor of the drastic break in the inexorable, world-wide historical process of changing relations between church and state, a break for which Russia had been ripe since the middle of the seventeenth century. The essence of this break consisted in the repudiation of the antiquated forms of medieval theocracy, not only in its extreme aspect of Roman papal-caesarism, but even in the milder form of Byzantine caesaro-papism. In the West, the process of the breaking up and rejection, embodied in the sharp conflict between the two authorities, manifested with utmost clarity its positive tendency—the tendency to the overthrow of the sacred primacy of church authority and its replacement by the secular primacy of state authority and, in general, lay culture. In the humanistic atmosphere, the human principle was emancipating itself from the divine principle; it not only asserted its independence, but it insisted on its pre-eminence, or even more than that—its absolutism. This was the popular counterbalance to the absolutist tendency of the waning theocracy.

The dualist discussions about *jus divinum* and *jus humanum* were, by the sixteenth century, overshadowed by the monistic idea of the *jus naturale,* the "natural law," as the supreme principle, embodied in the national state, which occupied a definite territory. Everything existing on this territory, including all religions, churches, and sects, was declared subordinate to the state and subject to its administration. And it was this legislative, administrative, and judicial power of the state that was seen as the basis of its primacy over the religious sphere. In principle, religious life, with its body of dogma, its mystique and ethics, goes on at depths that are independent of the external power of the state. In fact this dependence is very real and palpable historically, much like the mysterious bond between body and soul.

In canonical law, the above form of relations between church and state is known as the "territorial" system. In the days of Peter the Great, this system had been dominant and, from the point of view of the modern monistic humanitarian *Weltanschauung,* it was normal in the West, especially in Protestant nations. In the age of "enlightenment" (seventeenth-eighteenth centuries), canonical "territorialism" set itself up chiefly against the obsolete Roman Catholic clerical theocracy. It was inevitable that Peter the Great, along with a part of the intellectual elite of seventeenth-century Moscow, would fall under the spell of the secular "enlightenment" philosophy, and that his impetuous reforming temperament would lead him to introduce this secular territorialism in Russia as well, applying it to the Russian Church, which in its Byzantine manner, was also profoundly theocratic. The result was a radical breaking up of ideological and canonic forms and ways of life, whose seriousness neither Peter nor his collaborators understood to the end. In the light of the new, extra-religious philosophy, there was born a new form of supreme authority in the Russian state, as well as a new form of supreme administration within the Russian Church. These were embodied in Imperial Russia and the Synodal Church. . . .

In comparison with the preceding Patriarchal period, the Russian Church expanded numerically almost ten-fold during the Synodal period. Out of a population of 21 million under Peter the Great, some fifteen million belonged to the Orthodox Church. In the Russia of Nicholas II, with a population, according to the census of 1915, of 182 million, 115 million were Orthodox Christians. During the Patriarchal period, Russia had twenty bishoprics and twenty bishops. At the end of its Imperial period, the Russian Church had sixty-four bishoprics and some forty vicarates under more than one hundred bishops. It had more than fifty thousand churches, one hundred thousand priests, and up to one thousand monasteries, with fifty thousand monks. It maintained four Theological Academies, fifty-five Seminaries, some one hundred ecclesiastical schools, and one hundred diocesan schools, with an annual student body of seventy-five thousand. This numerical growth was not only the automatic result of an increased population, it was also the product of the active and systematic domestic and foreign missionary work of the Russian Church, carried on more extensively than ever before. The conversions resulting from missionary activity and unrelated to the natural increase of the Orthodox Russian population may be estimated at several million. Traditional tolerance toward all religions, nationalities, and tribes inside Russia precluded the rapid development of the foreign mission of the Russian Orthodox Church. By tradition, Islam, Judaism, and Buddhism (lamaism) were even protected by the special privilege of inviolability from Christian missionary work. However, in the regions which had been newly annexed to Russia, the missionary efforts were more active. In the course of the three partitions of Poland and the gradual return to Orthodoxy of the originally Russian population, which had been artificially drawn into the Uniate Church, some five million persons were gradually restored to the Russian Church. The gradual conquest of the Caucasus also led to efforts to reestablish Christianity, which had prevailed there in ancient times. In the Kazan region, the mission of Baptized-Tartars adopted the practice of Professor Ilminsky's system of translating the Orthodox service into the native languages; this automatically became the rule during the voluntary mass conversions of Letts, Estonians, and Finns (Karelians) from Lutheranism to Orthodoxy in the middle of the nineteenth century. The Russian Orthodox mission also carried their work beyond the borders of Russia—to Japan, North America, and even Persia (Urmiia).

But historically, the more significant fact, which brought the Russian Church out of the confines of a modest, nationally limited life onto the highroad of universal action and universal responsibility, was not so much its outward expansion, as the inner growth of its forces and the forms of its existence. The element of culture [*prosveshchenie*], pointed out by the late Academician Golubinsky,[1] is only one of the marks of the broader and more lasting achievement of the Russian Church—its general historic maturation and ascension "unto the measure of the stature of the fulness of Christ" (Eph. 4, 13). During its early period, the Russian Church had already manifested within itself the presence of the mighty forces of Christian consecration and holiness, but it was still in many ways theologically infantile. Having mastered during the Synodal period the technique and methodology of scholarly theology, it rapidly became the highest

---

[1] E. E. Golubinsky (1834–1912), prominent historian of the Russian Church.—Ed.

and strongest pillar, one might even say, the supreme leader of all Eastern Orthodoxy. And this was so because it had become in sufficient measure equipped from a scholarly point of view for competition and cooperation with the Western Christian churches, which had formerly looked down on the Christian East precisely on the ground of its own scholarly and cultural superiority. From this point of view, the excessively drastic and painfully revolutionary reform of Peter the Great proved to have been a beneficent ordeal to the Russian Church, stimulating its creative energies. To paraphrase the well-known saying, "Peter threw out his challenge to Russia, and she answered him a hundred years later with the appearance of Pushkin," we might add, "and, in the church, by the appearance of Philaret."[2] Just as behind the image of Pushkin we see the entire wonderful Olympus of Russian literature, so behind Philaret there rises the iconostasis of all our brilliant ecclesiastical lights, the theologians, preachers, and writers of the Russian Church of the eighteenth-nineteenth centuries.

Our Orthodox brethren—the Greeks, Slavs, and Syrian Arabs—dazzled by the glitter of Western civilization, studied theology with the Western representatives of various denominations, and particularly with Protestants. But the flowering of Russian theological schools opened their eyes also to this new, healthy, Orthodox source of theological scholarship. An ever-growing number of Orientals studied, with the aid of Russian stipends, in Russian ecclesiastical academies. This also furthered a new and vital contact between the Orthodox churches, so unfortunately separated by their political and national destinies.

The educational and theological upsurge in the energies of the Russian Church during this period was also stimulated by another original cultural phenomenon. And the latter became once and for all the distinguishing characteristic of Russian culture, both general and ecclesiastical. We have in mind the prominent participation of Russian lay forces in creative theological activity. None of the Orthodox churches boasts of the same number and caliber of secular theologians. We are not speaking of the professionals—professors

---

[2] Philaret (1782–1867), Archbishop of Moscow from 1821 on, prominent theologian and a leader in the religious and spiritual revival of the first half of the nineteenth century.—Ed.

of theological academies—but of representatives of secular culture who became creative contributors to Orthodox theology and religious philosophy. These include the Slavophiles Khomiakov and the Aksakov brothers, the Westernizer Vladimir Sloviev, the synthetic school of the Trubetskoy brothers who followed him, and a number of our most recent contemporaries.

Along with this we must also cite the religious-Orthodox force in Russian literature, which has become a world literature. This Christian breath of our literature, carried by it over the entire world, is a direct product of the thousand years of educational influence of the Russian Church. In the wake of our literature, the whole world has come to see the Orthodox light in Russian art as well. We need not speak of the specific and, in certain respects, supreme achievements of Russian icon painting; throughout the realm of Russian art—in music, in architecture, in religious observance and in culture generally, the Russian Church has called forth such a wealth of creative values that its primacy within the chorus of Orthodox churches is scarcely subject to question.

In recent times in connection with the emerging trend toward oecumenical unification, the Russian Church has become the object of particular attention in the West. First, the Protestant world, as represented by Anglicanism in the eighteenth and nineteenth centuries, knocked at the door of the Petersburg Synodal Church. The Old Catholic [*starokatolicheskoe*] movement of the nineteenth century gave the Russian Church a place of first importance in this oecumenical question. And, despite its present ruinous condition, the role of the Russian Church in the newest phase of the oecumenical movement is, at any rate, not inferior to that of its other, unshaken Eastern sisters.

To avoid excessive doubts and hesitations in appraising the history of the Russian Church, we may apply the unquestioned criterion for all churches and all times, the criterion of sanctity. The Russian Church from its very cradle has been a zealous advocate of the glorification of its own saints. Conferring on its native land the exalted title of "Holy Russia," the Russian Church strove to justify this claim by diligent canonizations, the number of which had reached 230 by Peter's time; if we add to this the names of saints locally revered, this number will rise to 500. The constraints of

Peter's legislation temporarily halted this generous flow of official canonizations. But the nationwide communal worship of the revered leaders of Orthodox piety took no account of official legislation. The church authorities sanctified only ten new names during the Synodal period, but individual attempts to gather information (such as that of E. Poselianin) and the materials of church journals show that more than one hundred new candidates for canonization were proposed during this period. If we add to these the hundreds of martyrs of communist persecution, the testimony of the wealth of accumulated charisma of holiness in the Russian Church of the Synodal period will be beyond question. To the catalogue of five hundred revered names of the first seven hundred years of its history, the Russian Church can boldly juxtapose its new calendar and martyrology for only 250 years, numerically larger than the old, and graced by the heroic and imperishable crown of martyrdom for the Christian faith.

Another living testimony to the abundance of holiness in Russia, which justified its audacity in calling itself "Holy Russia," was the wide diffusion of monasticism and monasteries over the face of the Russian land. The secularizing pressure of the Imperial governments had merely proved in practice the extraordinary viability of Russian monasticism, and even led to its renewed flowering. The confiscation of monastery lands and the closing of some of the monasteries awakened in the monks new energies and the will to adapt by their labor. It also stimulated the spiritual revival of monasticism in the form of the glorious institution of *elders*. Paraphrasing again the earlier quotation, we might say: "Peter threw out a challenge to Russian monasticism, and fifty years later it replied by the appearance of Bishop St. Tikhon Zadonskii and the elder Paisy Velichkovskii; in another fifty years, with Saint Seraphim Sarovskii; and, again, fifty years later, with Bishop Feofan the Hermit [*Zatvornik*], the elder Ambrosius of Optina, and the host of his followers."

In brief, on the basis of all external and internal evidence, we should abandon the outworn, one-sidedly pessimistic appraisal of the Synodal period and learn to see in it a higher and historically ascending manifestation of the spiritual forces and attainments of the Russian Church.

Nicholas Zernov

THE ESTABLISHMENT OF THE RUSSIAN CHURCH

The traditional and unfavorable judgment of Peter's church reform is given by Professor Nicholas Zernov, a specialist in the history of the Russian Church and a well-known exponent of Russian Orthodoxy in England where he is professor at Oxford University. The attentive reader will note that the condemnation of Peter's church reforms is based entirely on a conception of the Russian Church that plays down its institutional aspects and public role.

The momentous changes which took place in the political life of Russia during the reign of Peter the Great (1682–1725) radically altered the relations between church and state. It is even possible to speak of the Russian Church as being "established" by Peter, for he replaced the free collaboration between two independent bodies, the church and the state, by a system of state control over all spiritual matters. This was a period which had far-reaching consequences in the history of Russian Christianity, for the present conflict between the communist state and the Orthodox Church is rooted in those remote years when the new Empire sprang up on the shores of the Baltic Sea. . . . The ecclesiastical changes made by Peter the Great were only a part of his general scheme for the reorganization of the country, and like all his reforms they were to a large extent the expression of his personality. Though undoubtedly the most outstanding ruler in the history of Russia, he was psychologically almost unbalanced, and all his actions were colored by his peculiar gifts and no less peculiar limitations. His grandfather and father, the tsars Michael (1613–1645) and Alexis Romanov (1645–1676) were renowned for their piety, and during their reigns the Moscow court was so strictly regulated by religious observances that it bore closer resemblance to a monastery than to the palace of a secular ruler. Peter destroyed this carefully built up fabric at one blow, and appeared before his astounded country as a typical Western monarch,

Reprinted with permission of the author, from Nicholas Zernov, "Peter the Great and the Establishment of the Russian Church," *Church Quarterly Review* [London] 125 (January–March 1938): 265–293.

wearing a military uniform and behaving after the manner of a foreign prince.[1] He ceased to be the Moscow Tsar, appointed by God Himself as the father of his people, and became the Emperor of Russia whose primary duty was to maintain the honor and glory of the new Empire. He transformed the country, which for almost six centuries had lived in complete isolation, into a European state and a strong military power.

. . . Every institution and every tradition which might be used by his adversaries as an instrument against his reforms had to be swept away and cast out of the new Europeanized Russian Empire. This attitude of the Emperor's was particularly noticeable in all his dealings with the church. To Peter it was the stronghold of the old Tsardom of Moscow and the refuge of all those who longed for its restoration. Peter the Great was not an atheist; he enjoyed even singing in the choir and reading the Epistles in the midst of the congregation. But his attitude towards religion was typical of the absolutist ruler of the eighteenth century. He had a strong sense of duty, he possessed a notion of justice, but he recognized no authority higher than his own will. Peter could respect Christians of genuine religious life, but he had no sense of the corporate life of the church, and he refused to admit that the church was an independent body obeying its own rules and pursuing its own aims as distinct from those of the state.[2] His whole ecclesiastical policy was inspired therefore by three concerns: 1. First of all by the fear of the church. He wished to eliminate any possibility of opposition from it, and therefore aimed at the destruction of such institutions as the Patriarchate or the church councils which could express the independent opinion of the church. 2. Secondly, he sought to familiarize the Russians with contemporary European civilization and to use the church as far as possible as an instrument for this purpose. He therefore favored those clergy who were willing to help him in this

---

[1] By their behavior and dress the Moscow tsars had borne a closer resemblance to ecclesiastical dignitaries than to secular rulers, and they divided their time between state duties and regular attendance at church services.

[2] One of the most striking manifestations of this spirit was the Imperial Order issued in 1722 which demanded under the threat of severe punishment that the priest should reveal to the government the secrets of confessions in all matters dealing either with the supreme interests of the state or with the safety of the Imperial family. This order has never been recognized by the church and as a rule it has not been obeyed by the clergy.

task, and gradually placed them in all key positions. 3. Thirdly, by his decision to appropriate ecclesiastical revenue for the needs of the army. He confiscated a large proportion of the church income and carried on a systematic war against the monks,[3] considering them to be an unproductive element in his country, a class which deprived the army of soldiers, and the state of taxpayers, and supported the spirit of opposition among the people. Peter's ideal was a well-ordered state where all the citizens served the same common cause, and faithfully obeyed the orders received from the monarch who was the living incorporation of the state's justice and wisdom, the final judge in all matters, both secular and spiritual.

Only towards the end of his reign did Peter the Great have time to embody his ideas in new institutions; most of them were, however, very hurriedly built up, and did not survive their founder. One of them proved however to be of exceptional durability and lasted until the fall of the Empire in 1917. This was the Most Holy Governing Synod with its lay procurator, the institution which according to Peter's plan was to secure the supremacy of the crown over the Russian Church.

The first step towards the establishment of the new ecclesiastical order was the Emperor's refusal to allow the election of a new patriarch after the death of Patriarch Adrian in 1700. Peter appointed the Metropolitan of Riazan, Stephen Iavorskii, as the *locum tenens,* and kept the church in this suspended state till 1721, when he presented the Russian episcopate with the new constitution. The latter was incorporated in a document called the "Ecclesiastical Reglament," which was composed by Theophanis Prokopovich, the Bishop of Pskov, chief ecclesiastical adviser to the Emperor.

This epoch-making document abolished the office of the patriarch and introduced in its place a collegiate body, known as the Most Holy Governing Synod.

This new organ had no precedent in the canon law of the Ortho-

---

[3] Being unable to abolish the monasteries altogether, Peter tried to limit their activities as far as possible. All the monasteries were obliged to take the old and infirm soldiers as their inmates; people were not allowed to take monastic vows without special authorization from the Emperor; and every educational and literary activity was strictly forbidden. Even the possession of paper and ink by a monk in his cell was declared to be a legal offense. This shows how much Peter feared the influence which the monasteries exercised over the Russian people.

dox Church and was copied by the Emperor from the West. It was composed of the president (Metropolitan Stephen), two vice-presidents (Archbishop Theodosius of Novgorod and Theophanis, Bishop of Pskov), and several members who were bishops, monks, and priests. They were all elected by the Emperor, all had equal votes, and every decision had to be approved by the majority. Peter called it a permanent council, but the Synod had nothing in common with the councils of the church. It was a collegiate organ, created by the state, controlled by the state, and responsible to the state only; its members were clerics, but they did not represent the church, for the church had no voice in their election.

Peter took great care to ensure the complete control of the crown over the Synod; it was not sufficient for him to impose on its members an additional oath of allegiance to him in which they declared, "I acknowledge the Monarch of all Russias, our Gracious Lord, to be the Final Judge of this College"; he also appointed as its supervisor a lay official, the Procurator of the Holy Synod, whose role was to represent the watchful eye of the Emperor himself, and without whose approval no decision of the Synod could be put into operation.

The lay procurator, who according to the language of the "Reglament" had to be "an officer, a good man, courageous and able enough to manage the Synodical affairs," became the central figure of the new institution.[4] Many of the procurators were actually officers of the army, and the fact that at the head of the Russian ecclesiastical government for two hundred years stood men possessing the mentality and wearing the uniform of a soldier was the symbol of the new relations between church and state.

Such was the body which the Russian Church had to accept as its supreme governing organ. Peter with his usual energy secured

---

[4] The history of the Synod displays a gradual but persistent growth of the procurator's power, which reached its climax during K. Pobedonostsev's rule over the Russian Church (1880–1905). The procurators especially increased their importance from the beginning of the nineteenth century when they reserved for themselves the right of direct communication with the Emperor. Although they had no voting power at the sessions of the Synod, nothing could be discussed by the bishops which was not proposed by the procurators. Every decision reached by the Synod had likewise to be approved by the procurators. If one adds to it that they acquired the right of presenting to the emperors the list of new candidates for the membership, and could dismiss in the same way those who contradicted their policy, their hold on the church becomes clear.

.its recognition by the bishops and abbots of the leading monasteries; they were visited by the Emperor's envoys and their signatures were separately collected. Under the Reglament the choice between banishment and unconditional approval was made clear, and the Russian Episcopate, without a single exception, preferred the latter. Even the Eastern Patriarchs under the diplomatic pressure of the Russian Ambassador were obliged to recognize the Holy Synod, this strange creation of the Emperor, as "their beloved brother in Christ."

The official motives for the reform were the greater impartiality and efficiency of an assembly of clergy over the rule of an individual prelate, and the necessity of combatting the misleading belief spread among the "simple" people that the Patriarch was the head of an institution independent of the state, and therefore equal to the Emperor. The hope of impartiality and efficiency was frustrated: the Synod has never shown any ability to deal effectively with the ecclesiastical government; but the danger of confusing the role of Emperor and Patriarch was utterly eliminated, for no one could regard the Synod, elected and controlled by the Emperor, as a competitor for his power.

Thus, the Russian Church found itself solidly incorporated into a new order on the Western pattern, which made the Emperor an absolute ruler of the country and the final judge in all secular and spiritual matters. The church itself received the humble place of a department of the state, one among other departments, controlled by a lay official representing the authority of the Godly Prince. This radical change in the relations between the church and the state was an inevitable consequence of the introduction into Russia of the Western political system, and as long as the bureaucratic Empire of St. Petersburg could last, the Russian Church had to occupy in the life of the nation the place appointed to it by Peter the Great.

One of the main problems raised by these momentous changes is the attitude of the Russian Church to the reform. From an outsider's point of view its passive acquiescence must appear as a great puzzle. The all-powerful church which dominated the hearts and minds of the Russian people for centuries, the church which only one hundred years earlier helped to rescue the country from the anarchy of the Time of Troubles (1598–1613), and on the eve of Peter's accession to the throne had produced an army of martyrs and confessors,[5] the same Church accepted in silence the drastic reforms which were so boldly inflicted upon it by the arbitrary will of the Emperor. It might seem that the Church of Russia was either already dead at the time, or agreeable to the type of alterations introduced by Peter. Such a description of the situation is frequently given, but it is definitely misleading.

The Church of Russia was neither dead, nor did it favor the new ecclesiastical order. It was decidedly opposed to it, but for several very important reasons it could not in any way resist the innovations and even had no means of expressing its disapproval. The causes of this paralysis of the Russian Church were deeply rooted in its past history. They were connected with some specific features of its organization and especially with the unique position held in it by the Tsars of Moscow.

Russia received its faith from Constantinople (988). At first the church enjoyed a great deal of independence from secular control, for till the fifteenth century the presiding bishop of the Russian Church, the Metropolitan of Kiev, was ordained and often even elected by the Patriarch of Constantinople and was responsible to him. The fifteenth and sixteenth centuries brought an important change into the relations of church and state in Russia. When the Byzantine Empire collapsed in 1453, the Russian Metropolitans began to be ordained in Russia; the decisive voice in their election was now the Princes of Moscow, who after becoming the sole rulers of Russia proclaimed themselves the autocrats [*Tsars*], the legitimate successors of the Byzantine *basileus*.

. . . [The Tsars of Moscow, as successors of the Princes of Moscow also inherited the latters' informal relationship between ruler and people. It was felt that the Tsar of Moscow, in spite of the size of the land over which he ruled, was like the father of the household.] This intimacy of relations between the Tsar and his people was especially pronounced in the affairs of the church. The Tsar of Russia had no legally established position in it, but he took the most active part in its life. It so happened that all the tsars of Russia until Peter the Great were not only devout members of the church, but

---

[5] Reference is here made to the Schism of the middle of the seventeenth century and the willingness of the "Old Believers" to suffer death and persecution rather than accept the reforms of the ritual introduced by Patriarch Nikon.

men whose predominant interests were in ecclesiastical affairs. No Russian could imagine a Tsar who would ever be other than a staunch supporter of church traditions. The tsars themselves also felt that their duty was to preserve peace and order both in state and church, and that they were responsible before God for the proper use of their power in these two spheres of Russian life. All the councils of the church were therefore convoked by the tsars, they personally selected members of the clergy who were to sit at its sessions, and they presented to them the questions for deliberation; if the tsars were dissatisfied with the decision of the council, they simply refused to confirm its acts, and these remained without operation (e.g., the Council of 1649 which was disapproved by Tsar Alexis). The Russian councils of the fifteenth, sixteenth, and seventeenth centuries were primarily consultative bodies gathered together by the tsars when the latter wanted to know the church answer to this or that problem of Christian life.

And yet in spite of all this power the Russian tsars would have been horrified if anyone had suggested to them that they were the judges or rulers over the church. They were in their own view nothing else than its faithful and obedient servants. The church for all the Russians of that period was a divine institution, a body which lived its own life and obeyed its own rules. The Tsar, like any other individual, could never change anything in its life or teaching without the consent of the other members, but he was responsible for the maintenance of order in the church and for the application of its eternal precepts to the daily life of the people entrusted to his charge. The tsars occupied exactly the same place in the life of the nation as a father in an ordinary Russian family, and in that capacity felt that they had to answer before God for the spiritual welfare of the members of their household and had to see that the services were attended, the fasts kept, and Christian instruction duly received.

This attitude was radically different from that of the Middle Ages in the West, where the hierarchy was identified with the church, and loyalty and obedience to the Pope was the usual expression of devotion to the church. In Russia the church itself as a corporate body was the object of devotion, the hierarchy and the laity had to serve it, each in their own way, but the layman had no hesitation in rebuking or even rejecting a representative of the hierarchy if the latter failed to maintain the tradition of the church.

The Russian Tsar was not above the hierarchy, and he never failed to show the most striking signs of his profound respect for the grace bestowed upon those in Holy Orders; on various solemn occasions he publicly expressed his humble submission to the power given to them,[6] but the distinction was always made between the Orders themselves and their holders. Russia and her tsars obeyed the Orthodox Church, but they expected the same obedience to it from the bishops and the rest of the clergy.

Thus the place of the Tsar in the Russian Church was different both from that of the Byzantine *basileus* and from the Western rulers; it had no precedents, it was not defined either by civil or canon law. It worked out quite satisfactorily as long as Russia was cut off from the rest of Europe, but as soon as it was brought into fellowship with the other Christian nations, and when it met with the rivalries and competitions which were raging there between the ecclesiastical and civil authorities, the insufficiency of the old system became immediately apparent, and it was Peter who took full advantage of the situation.

The main weakness of the Russian situation was that it ultimately relied upon the orthodoxy and piety of the tsars, and had no defense against any possible attack from that quarter. When the clergy or lay people preached a doctrine contrary to the traditional beliefs, then the church had weapons to combat this danger, but the possibility that the Tsar, the divinely-appointed father of the nation, could ever desert the truth and become the enemy of the church, seemed too remote to necessitate safeguards. Peter's attack came from the quarter which had always been considered as the very stronghold of undefiled Orthodoxy, and that is why both the clergy and people were unable to resist openly the policy of the Emperor.

This peculiarly Russian trust in the piety of the tsars was one of the main reasons for the failure of the church to defend its independence; the other factor which contributed to their weakness was the character of the Russian Episcopate. Episcopacy had always been an institution of the church which has found the utmost diffi-

---

[6] On Palm Sunday it was the Tsar who led the ass ridden by the Patriarch in a special procession that traversed the main streets of Moscow.

culty in conforming with the Christian spirit of love and service. Russia does not show any exception to this general rule. The Russian parishes with their elected clergy and many charitable organizations attached to them were very lively centers of Christian life; but the dioceses, in the proper sense of this term, had never been formed in Russia, for the huge regions ruled by the bishops had no organic life and were an artificial creation. The married priests were closely associated with their people, but this could not be said about the bishops who were elected from among the abbots of the big monasteries. They were very few in number, and led the life of the nobility. The bishops appeared to the rest of the clergy not as their Fathers in God, but as wealthy and unmerciful lords, who had only one kind of relation with the parishes, that of extracting exhausting taxation. Russia had up to the end of the seventeenth century only 17 dioceses, and this number was so inadequate that when the pious Tsar Theodor (1676–1682) suggested raising it at the Council in 1682, he gave the figure of 70 as corresponding to the real spiritual needs of the country. The proposal was turned down, however, by the bishops, for it endangered their huge incomes. The Russian bishops were not only few in number and isolated from the rest of the clergy, but they had even little contact among themselves, for the tremendous distances made this intercourse very difficult.

. . . The failure of the Russian bishops to defend the interests of the church would not in itself have been enough to paralyze the opposition to the Emperor. The Russian Christians were used to standing up for their traditions without the leadership of their episcopate, as was the case at the time of the ritualistic reforms (1653–1667). This time the situation was so confused, however, that even the most ardent churchmen were uncertain of what action to take. This was due not only to the Emperor's part in the antichurch campaign, but also to the character of the innovations he introduced.

The members of the Russian Church were taught by their Greek teachers that the essence of Christianity lies in doctrine and that for its defense every Christian ought to lay down his life and if necessary be martyred. To this the Russians added the belief that worship is of the same importance as doctrine—and for the sake of the purity of divine service they were ready to suffer and even to die, as they proved during the controversies of the seventeenth century. But

Peter's reforms affected neither doctrine nor worship; they were undermining those parts of church life, the value of which was not altogether ignored by the Russian Christians, but had been considerably neglected by them for the last hundred years. The final cause of Peter's success was therefore rooted in the deficiency of the popular conception of the church, which laid a greater stress upon ritualism and worship than upon a proper relationship between Christians. The real crux of the situation was that Peter was quite prepared to leave untouched the ritualistic piety so popular among the Russians. He was not interested in reforms of doctrine or worship, his goal was to deprive the church of its spiritual independence, and to make it one of the departments of the absolutist state. This was a challenge that had not been foreseen, and neither the clergy nor the people could face it properly.

. . . Two hundred years of submission to the state had left their traces on the Russian Church; most of them were of a negative nature, but some were positive. The spiritual isolation from which the Russian Church suffered during its Moscow period had been brought to an end, and that was a real achievement. Peter the Great forced the church to accept as its leaders men trained in the West, who brought with them fresh ideas and the appreciation of learning which was lacking among the Moscow Christians. . . . Increased contacts with the West raised the standard of education among the clergy which in the course of the nineteenth century reached the level of other European countries. . . . Signs of a wider and deeper spiritual life in Russia, especially in the monasteries, appeared towards the end of the eighteenth century, and they produced several monks of outstanding personality, among them St. Seraphim of Sarov (died 1832), one of the greatest saints of the Russian Church.

These were some of the positive contributions of the new order, but they were outweighed by the grave disadvantages which the Establishment brought upon the Russian Church. The worst evil was the spiritual submission of the church to the authority of the state. The Tsars of Moscow were autocrats, but their actions were judged by the church in the light of its teaching, as the actions of every other Christian. The Emperors of St. Petersburg were above such control, their will was considered to be right and beneficent independently of Christian standards. Compulsory silence was imposed upon the church on all political and social matters; the only province where it was left free was the domain of the personal life of its members. The result of this policy was the gradual decrease of church authority in all sections of Russian society.

This process was started among the upper classes, who began to despise the clergy for their lack of European education, and gradually arrived at the conclusion that the church of their country was an institution suitable only for uncouth and simple people who had not yet been admitted to the storehouse of modern civilization. When in the middle of the nineteenth century a new class of *intelligentsia* with its acute sense of social justice was born, its representatives took an openly hostile attitude towards the church, accusing it of subservience to the Imperial power. The same process proceeded among the lower classes of Russia. It started first with the criticism of the church for not being able to resist the reforms of Peter the Great. This dissatisfaction found its expression in the persistence of various sects of the type of the "Old Believers." Towards the end of the nineteenth century a sectarianism of a rationalist kind began to spread among the peasants, voicing their growing irritation at the silence of the church on social matters.

Thus the magnificent edifice of the Russian Church was continuously undermined from both sides, from one by the indifference of the Westernized nobility and the hostility of the radically-minded intelligentsia, and from the other by the growth of sectarianism among the peasants. In order to complete the picture of the disintegration of the Russian Church under the Establishment, the gradual bureaucratization of its life must be added. The church was treated officially more and more as "the department of the Orthodox confession," as one among numerous other state departments. The lay Procurators of the Synod were, for all practical purposes, the rulers of the Russian Church, controlling the dioceses through the special functionaries appointed for this purpose; the work of the diocesan bishops was limited practically to ordination to the priesthood, and their contact with their vast dioceses was systematically undermined by the frequent transfer from one see to another. The parish system was also ruined; the lay people were deprived of their right to participate in the affairs of the church, and the clergy were reduced to the state of functionaries whose very sermons were censored by government officials.

And yet in spite of all its degradation the church remained a living body, commanding the loyalty and love of the majority of the Russian people. It was paralyzed, its social activities were forbidden, its voice was heard no longer on matters of politics and economics, but it did not stop preaching the Gospel, it did not cease to administer the sacraments, nor did it fail to produce martyrs, missionaries, and saints.

S. V. Rozhdestvenskii
EDUCATIONAL REFORMS

By general consensus, modern Russian culture dates from the eighteenth century and is intimately related to Peter's reforms. Modern culture presupposes a relatively high level of intellectual sophistication and some sort of educational system to transmit and develop the cultural heritage. The reign of Peter the Great was, therefore, bound to be of crucial importance for the history of Russian education and the selection below, from the pen of S. V. Rozhdestvenskii (1868–1934), a most distinguished specialist of the history of Russian education, gives the background to Peter's innovations in this domain and a general assessment of their effect.

The period of the reforms of Peter the Great marked a profound divide in the history of Russian school education. The old Russian school had served exclusively as an instrument of church learning and as a rule it did not rise above the level of elementary education. Actually it did not even give an education but provided only the essential first tools with which an interested individual could, on his own, penetrate to the essence of the wisdom contained in the traditional code of the century's religious-ethical *Weltanschauung*. The

From S. V. Rozhdestvenskii, *Ocherki po Istorii Sistem Narodnogo Prosveshcheniia v Rossii v XVIII–XIX Vekakh* [*Essays in the History of the Systems of National Education in Russia in the 18th and 19th Centuries*], vol. I (St. Petersburg, 1912), pp. 1–5, 8–10. Editor's translation.

aims of secular professional education were utterly alien to the old Russian school. Applied science penetrated into Muscovy in the guise of purely practical "cleverness from overseas"; and the guardians of traditional virtue watched with eagle eyes that this "cleverness" did not extend beyond the confines of narrow practical application.

What service could this old elementary school render in the difficult period when the state had to master not only Western European technology in the narrow sense, but also applied science in the broadest sense; when for the first time Russian society was affected by the secular rationalistic *Weltanschauung* prevailing in the West at the end of the seventeenth century? The old school was helpless in meeting all the new requirements of state and society. Russia needed new schools, and these schools, which made their appearance during the period of reform, were not so much a green fruit grown on the poor soil of the old Russian education, but rather the seeds from which a comprehensive system of popular education could sprout in the distant future.

At the end of the seventeenth century, when the big reform movement was ripening in Muscovy, there was sketched for the first time the problem on which all important efforts and experiments in school reform during the eighteenth century were to focus. In the famous "privilege" of 1682 founding the Academy in the Zaikonospassk Monastery in Moscow, we see the first attempt at defining the new task of popular education not only from the point of view of the interests of the church, but of those of the state as well. In this project, for the first time, secular knowledge and clerical education were juxtaposed as two equally important branches of a single "wisdom-science," at the service not only of society's ethical progress but also of the state's power and welfare: "we learn to know the good and bad civil and religious affairs through a knowledge of things." The "wisdom-science" was "parent to the Tsar's offices and source of the discovery and improvement of all kinds of blessings; through it all monarchies obtain well-regulated institutions, justice, strong defense, and great territorial expansion." The Academy's program was to include "*civil* and religious sciences, beginning with grammar, rational, natural, and moral philosophy, and also theology, which teaches divine things and [the ways to] the cleansing of conscience" and also "knowledge of ecclesiastic and *secular* law and all other liberal arts." Access to the Academy was to be given to persons of all classes. "This educational institution established by Us, the Great Lord [i.e., Tsar] should be free and common to people of all rank, estate, and age, provided that they are of the Eastern Christian Orthodox faith and come for the sake of learning all the virtuous sciences blessed by the Church." For success in sciences "diligent youths" were to receive adequate compensation from the sovereign, "and upon completion of the liberal arts" they would be granted "ranks corresponding to their intelligence." Except for those of noble birth no one who did not complete the liberal arts [course] was to be admitted to [higher] state ranks of *stol'nik, striapchii,* etc. Only learning and manifestly meritorious performances in military or other government business was to give access to these ranks. Thus, for the first time, scholarly education was made a necessary condition for the right to be in government service. From a material point of view the Academy was to be given security by lavish grants from the Tsar and the private donations of individuals from all classes. Finally the Academy received the right of trying its own members and students on the basis of a special "academic law," "except for murder and other big crimes."

As is well known, this broadly conceived plan of a state school for all classes with a full program of clerical and secular education did not succeed. The search for higher spiritual and secular knowledge could not avoid being subjected to the church spirit prevailing at the time; on the soil of old Muscovite culture the depository of the "liberal arts" had to become, in S. Soloviev's well-known characterization, "the citadel erected by the Orthodox Church for withstanding the unavoidable clash with the non-Orthodox West." Thus, for the first time, on the eve of the reform period, the school question had been put broadly from the point of view of the interests of the state; but the latter did not yet dare to separate itself from the interests of the church.

If on the basis of the old Muscovite order the effort at mastering the liberal arts had led to the creation of a professional theological school clearly aiming at the defense of church traditions, then under the new conditions of the reform period, the same effort could not but adapt to the state's needs which so profoundly permeated all of Peter's reforms. After returning from his trip abroad during 1698–1699, the Tsar apparently still had the old intention of making the Moscow Academy not only into an ecclesiastical, but also into a secular school. In a conversation the Tsar had with Patriarch Adrian, the Moscow school was given a double goal: general education and professional training. "The teachings and light of the Scriptures are divine knowledge which man needs above all things. And those who have studied well in this school should be put to various use: church and civil service, military occupations, architecture, and healing medicine." "The excellent and skillful instruction in all things that is given in this school should keep people from studying the liberal arts with foreigners who do not correctly speak our slavonic tongue, who are also of a different faith, and who might, in the course of their instruction, teach the children their heresies, and as a result, great harm may be done to the children and to our holy church; and from [the foreigners'] ignorance, injury to our language as well." The difficult war that began soon thereafter put an end to the naive belief that it was possible to combine in one school the aims of a general education in the spirit of the old religious view of the world with those of professional training—clerical and secular. The immediate needs of government service, the hasty preparation of specialists in various branches of this service took precedence.

The first professional schools had originated in response to the pressure of practical needs at various moments of Peter's reform, they depended on the complex circumstances of this or that specific moment. They could not, therefore, form into a single, orderly, planned system, and they represented various branches of professional education with unequal success. Nor were the government's energy and initiative the same in all of the various branches of professional education. The greatest energy was naturally displayed in the organization of military education, for military requirements were the major stimulus to reform. The efforts to establish "feeders" of juridical education were much weaker, for it seemed possible to satisfy the immediate needs of the new administrative institutions by means of the practice of service itself, turning the latter into a kind of apprenticeship. Lastly, there appeared purely professional ecclesiastic schools, since the clerical service was less subject to reform than the military or civil services; and since its needs could be met on the basis of old Muscovite practices.

If it is true that the only stimulus to the establishment of various branches of professional education were the needs of state service, if in the words of Vladimirskii-Budanov the concepts of service and education were merged, and "the government saw in education the interest of service, while private individuals saw in it only [the source of] material benefits," then the question arises: what role is to be assigned to this kind of education in the history of Russian school education in general? Should we not conclude that Peter's creation of professional schools for the preparation of specialists in various branches of state service—sailors, artillerists, engineers, officials— was an episode of great importance in the history of state service and technical knowledge, but that it was of no significance in the history of education? Such a conclusion would be erroneous. The professional training hastily and crudely set up by Peter—in addition to responding to the direct intentions of the legislators—also answered to real needs in Russian life; it served not only practical requirements but also the broader cultural interests of society.

As A. Pypin has observed, at times the necessity of circumstances transformed the means of professional training into tools for general education. Thus, in 1697 Peter sent abroad a first group of young courtiers, and he ordered them to study those special sciences which would turn these young men into specialists-navigators. But in fact, the result was different: "Of the first group of 1697, not one became a real navy man. But the trip had general educational value: the group of young Russian boiars became more or less well-acquainted with the general tenor of European life, they saw new customs, and for the first time they could appreciate these customs or, at any rate, they could be impressed by the great artistic and scientific productions [they saw]. Having been aroused for the first time, their curiosity was to develop into a passion for assimilating those intellectual and artistic productions that had apparently become a necessity [to them]. The first travelers became neither shipbuilders nor admirals, but most of them subsequently filled important posts in the internal administration and in diplomacy; and most became more or less experienced and conscious executors of

Peter's designs." Indeed, in his co-workers Peter valued not only technical mastery, "clever fingers," but also a clear head, an independent outlook, and initiative. The varied activity that accompanied at that time any [state] service and its preparation demanded considerable intellectual development and strength of character. The typical [public] figure of the Petrine period was not a narrow specialist who had achieved perfection in his specialty and who had been completely absorbed into it; no, he was a master of all trades, capable of tackling unaccustomed new business on his own, "capable of surveying at a glance a whole field of knowledge—be it artillery, fortification, or mineralogy, geology, geography, history—and come away from it enriched." The very conditions and requirements of life that moulded the character of Peter's contemporaries reduced the danger that lurks behind every narrow, professional, craft training: the danger of deadening routine that depresses the mind and destroys energy. The professional education of the first half of the eighteenth century suffered rather from the opposite extreme: a lack of permanence and of a continuous tradition in its aims and contents.

Paul N. Miliukov

SECULAR SCHOOLS UNDER PETER THE GREAT

After making a most important contribution to our knowledge and understanding of Russia's social and economic conditions under Peter the Great (see the selection above), P. N. Miliukov left the world of scholarship to become the leader of the liberal Constitutional Democratic Party (so-called "Cadet Party") in the last decade of the Tsarist regime. But during moments of inactivity forced on him by the repressive measures of the imperial government, Miliukov undertook a major work of historic synthesis, Outlines of the History of Russian Culture, *which he completed only on the eve of his death*

From P. N. Miliukov, *Ocherki po Istorii Russkoi Kul'tury* [*Essays in the History of Russian Culture*], Jubilee edition, vol. II, part 2, Paris, 1931 (izd. "Sovremennyia Zapiski"), pp. 732–743. Editor's translation.

in exile. In connection with this work of synthesis Miliukov made an exhaus-
tive study of all available sources pertaining to the formation of Russian
political thought and culture in the eighteenth century. This naturally led him
to a close examination of the schools established by Peter.

The selection below conveys some of the difficulties encountered in laying
the groundwork for modern education and culture in Russia. As seen by
Miliukov, the difficulty stemmed mainly from the fact that education and
culture were first viewed exclusively as instruments of state policy and goals,
made compulsory and forced on an unwilling and ill-prepared society.

While scholastic textbooks were being introduced into the academic
curriculum by the brothers Likhuda,[1] the 16-year-old Peter was hard
at work on his notebooks of mathematics. In a style that did little
honor to his rhetorical and dialectical abilities and also grossly vio-
lated the rules of grammar and spelling, Peter worked out the rules
of addition and subtraction and solved problems in artillery and
astronomy. Everyone knows the results of these mathematical exercises: five years later, sporting a sailor's outfit, Peter was repeating
in broken Dutch greetings and curses in Arkhangel'sk, Russia's only
harbor at the time. Still five years later, in the same sailor's outfit,
but with a somewhat larger Dutch vocabulary, Peter was sawing and
filing in Amsterdam. Upon his return home he demanded that all
Russians who wanted to serve be capable of sawing, filing, building,
and navigating ships as he was himself.

The most direct way of acquiring this knowledge was to go
abroad, as Peter himself had done, and as he compelled many of
his contemporaries to do. But abroad the Russians proved too little-
prepared and could not properly benefit from the trip. . . . For this
reason, during his first trip abroad (1698) Peter hired the Englishman Farquharson as teacher of mathematics and navigation. In 1701
the "school of mathematical sciences and navigation" was established in the Sukharev Tower in Moscow and Farquharson began to
teach navigation to Russian youth—"some voluntarily, some under
compulsion."

In this fashion, alongside the professional school of theological
studies there arose in Moscow another professional school, that of
navigation. The government's attitude with respect to the aims of

---

[1] Two Greek brothers who taught at the Slavonic, Greek, Latin Academy in Moscow
in the second half of the seventeenth century.—Ed.

education had not changed. As had been the case previously, science and schooling had to serve the practical needs of the state. It was only the nature of these needs that had changed: instead of correcting church books and protecting the faith, it was now a matter of transforming the army and navy. In establishing the first Russian secular school the young Reformer was least interested in satisfying the needs of general education. But life itself corrected the omission. The sailors who returned from their study trips abroad and who graduated from the school of navigation had to be used not as specialists in their field, but as generally educated people. They became administrators, diplomats, teachers, builders, geodetists, engineers, etc. Peter soon had to realize "that not only for navigation was this school needed." In any case, the school of navigation had a military-naval character, and it preserved this character after moving to Petersburg in 1715 where it received the name of "Naval Academy."

The two academies, the "naval" and the "slavonic-greek-latin," soon served as foundation for a whole network of elementary schools that Peter set up in the provinces. It is this creation of a network of secular and ecclesiastical schools in Russia that marks Peter's reign as a completely new epoch in the history of Russian education. Without the two academies in the capitals the provincial schools could never have been established, for there would have been nowhere to obtain teachers from. With respect to the provincial schools, the "naval" and "slavonic-greek-latin" academies played the role of teachers' colleges. In turn, the provincial schools were to serve as preparatory grades for the schools in the capitals: the lower secular school gave elementary mathematical knowledge and the lower ecclesiastical school imparted philological knowledge.

The year the school of navigation moved to Petersburg, Peter ordered that there be sent to every province two of its students who had completed their work in geometry and geography, "for teaching in science young children of all classes." As a consequence of this decree, there were opened in the following year (1716) twelve schools in various Russian towns; between 1720 and 1722 thirty more schools were added. These new schools taught arithmetic and geometry and were called "cypher" schools. Fortunately we are in a position to determine the results obtained by the cypher schools during the first period of their existence. According to information gathered in 1727 slightly over 2000 pupils had been enrolled in these schools, voluntarily or under compulsion. With respect to their class origin the pupils were distributed as follows:

1.	from the clergy	931	45.4%
2.	soldiers' children	402	19.6%
3.	children of clerks	374	18.2%
4.	children of artisans	93	4.5%
5.	children of noblemen and squires	53	2.5%

But this composition was not maintained for long. No sooner had these schools been established than various classes of the population began to protest against this novel school obligation. The artisans were the first to petition that they be exempted from sending their children to school, for the children should stay in the stores and learn their father's craft. In 1720 the government satisfied their request and the cypher schools lost part of their enrollment. But more significant still proved to be the competition between the ecclesiastical and the cypher schools.

Ecclesiastical schools made their appearance in the provinces in obedience to the rules of the Spiritual Regulation[2] that compelled bishops to set up diocesan schools attached to their sees (1721). In compliance with the rules, forty-six diocesan schools were opened in the course of the next five years, 1721–1725. Thus, in the last years of Peter's reign, almost every provincial capital had two schools, a secular and an ecclesiastical. Students had to be driven into either school by force, and naturally competition developed between the two. The Synod demanded that all children of the clergy attending the cypher schools be returned to the diocesan schools. In this way a large number of pupils was withdrawn from the cypher schools. The magnitude of the loss can be gauged from the fact that after the withdrawal of the children of the clergy and of the artisans, fourteen cypher schools were left without any pupils. These schools had to be closed and their teachers returned to the Naval Academy. In the other twenty-eight cypher schools there remained almost exclusively the children of clerks. In 1727 there remained

---

2 Spiritual Regulation [*Dukhovnyi Reglament*], the legislative act (issued 25 January 1721), embodying the new organization and principles of Peter's church reform.—Ed.

only 500 pupils out of the 2000 enrolled at first. The causes for this drop are graphically illustrated by the following table:

1. children of artisans and clergy withdrawn 572 37%
2. fled, returned home, or did not appear 322 20.8%
3. graduated after completion of course 302 19.9%
4. illiterates, idiots, incapables 233 15%
5. taken into various branches of state service
   before completion of course 93 6%

More than one-third of those who left school before completion had been withdrawn compulsorily; more than one-fifth left school voluntarily; one-seventh were dismissed by the schools themselves; one-seventh entered service without completing the course; and only for one-fifth of the cases did the school accomplish its purpose.

The question of the very existence of the secular school was raised immediately after Peter's death. Peter had put the administration of the cypher schools in the hands of the Ministry of the Navy (College of the Admiralty) because their teachers were drawn from the Naval Academy. Now (1726) the Admiralty was trying to get rid of this responsibility and renewed Peter's earlier proposal (1723) of combining the cypher schools with the diocesan schools. But the Holy Synod objected to the merger, for in general it was not well-disposed to "secular maritime sciences." "To impart the knowledge of arithmetic and geometry without giving theological instruction is not the clergy's business. For this reason we request that the cypher and geometry schools remain under secular administration," declared the Synod in 1727. It was only because of this refusal that Peter's cypher schools lasted until 1744. At that time there were only eight schools left out of twenty-eight; and of these eight the three largest were combined with garrison schools. Garrison schools attached to regiments had been established in 1732; they were maintained at regimental cost and the teachers were officers and non-commissioned officers. Besides reading and writing, these schools also taught military drill, arithmetic, artillery, and engineering.

Peter's secular school did not prove very long-lasting. Its remnants were preserved as part of the military schools that took over portions of its curriculum. In this form it rendered an important service to Russian culture: even in the first years of the reign of

Catherine II it was only in garrison schools that one could find individuals with an elementary knowledge of arithmetic.

Let us now look at the fate of the diocesan schools established, as we have noted, according to a provision of the Spiritual Regulation. These schools were directly supervised by the local bishop, not by the lay authorities. State authorities did not interfere in their operation, as they did in the cypher schools. The government had no concern in providing a teaching staff for the diocesan schools. The teachers were recruited rather haphazardly; in the best of cases they were students of the academy of Moscow and even of the academy of Kiev; in other cases ordinary local clergy became teachers. In any event, the recruitment of teachers as well as the very existence of the diocesan schools depended on the good will of the diocesan authorities that had to maintain them at their own expense. Whenever a diocese changed hands schools might be set up or discontinued. Active prelates like Job of Novgorod, or Pitirim of Nizhnii Novgorod, Dmitrii of Rostov, Gabriel Buzhinskii of Riazan' raised the level of the schools and filled them with hundreds of pupils. Other bishops allowed the pupils to return home, closed down the schools completely or did not even open them at all under the pretext of lack of funds or teachers. The programs of instruction also depended on the means available and the zeal of local authorities. The best schools taught a program that approximated that of the academy in Moscow and included all the liberal arts. In most cases, however, the curriculum was limited to grammar and rhetoric. In some cases, as for example in the school at Viatka, the pupils learned only how to read and write, as teachers of more advanced subjects were unavailable. Incidentally, it was necessary sometimes to rest content with imparting only reading and writing because of the great need for parish priests. In the school of Nizhnii Novgorod, for example, of 832 pupils, 427, more than one-half, contented themselves with going through the primers only, and immediately afterwards they were ordained priests, deacons, etc.

As pupils were recruited in less harsh a way than the students of secular schools, the percentage of deserters was much lower in the diocesan schools. In 1727 there were forty-six diocesan schools in Russia, they had 3056 pupils, and of these only 239 deserted. We should add, however, that of the remaining 2827 almost one-half

(1331) belonged to ten schools in three Ukrainian dioceses (Kiev, Chernigov, Belgorod). Thus in Great Russia proper the number of pupils was slightly higher in the secular than in the diocesan schools. In some cases the secular schools were ahead of the diocesan in terms of the level of their instruction. But as we have noted Peter's secular schools had but a very brief flowering. The diocesan schools, on the other hand, proved more stable. Without any decrease, almost fifty diocesan schools survived until the time they were transformed into seminaries.

Their very transformation into seminaries was a consequence of their prosperity, while the transformation of cypher schools into garrison schools was the result of decline. The diocesan school was transformed into a seminary and its curriculum extended to the level of an academy by the introduction of intermediate and advanced grades, in addition to the elementary. Besides reading and writing, the full curriculum included grammar, rhetoric, philosophy, and theology. . . . Such a program tended to transform the diocesan school from an elementary into a secondary educational institution, and in turn it became the focus for the lower type of schools that were arising within the confines of the diocese. . . . [With the exception of Novgorod where the change took place in the first years of the eighteenth century], the diocesan schools began to be transformed into seminaries about 1737 when a general decree was issued to this effect. But the high cost of the transformation delayed the establishment of seminaries until the accession of Catherine II. After the first impulse given by Peter to the ecclesiastic schools, their further development proceeded slowly, as had been also the case of the secular schools. . . . In the reign of Catherine II the full program was introduced in only eight seminaries. (In 1738 there were seventeen seminaries with 2589 students and in 1764 twenty-six with 6000 students.) . . .

With an acquaintance of the fate of the cypher and diocesan schools we have almost exhausted the question of Russian school organization in the first half of the eighteenth century. The ground for a continuous development of Russian secondary education had been laid in this period, but not even this much can be said of the primary-school system. Peter's efforts in this latter respect remained completely fruitless. . . . But from the organization of the schools in the first half of the eighteenth century, let us turn to the goals they pursued.

As its first characteristic feature we should note that the Russian school of that time did not aim either at bringing up its pupils or at imparting general education to them; it aimed mainly at giving technical training for professional purposes. This was a point of view inherited in its entirety from the seventeenth century; only the eighteenth century deduced from it the necessity of a very comprehensive organization of the schools. This is the reason why some scholars have felt that the eighteenth century had introduced something radically new into Russian pedagogy. In fact, however, a truly pedagogical point of view was as alien to the schools of the period we are considering as it had been to the schools of the seventeenth century. Both institutions saw the pupil merely as an object of pedagogical action. If he came on his own, the school treated him the way old-fashioned master craftsmen treated apprentices: on the basis of a voluntary contract.

If the pupil was sent by the government, learning became a form of [state] service. For the service he received a salary, for nonfulfillment of his obligations he was subjected to the punishment specified by the service [regulations]. The responsibility of a pupil did not, therefore, differ from that of an adult person. A fault was equated with a regular violation of the law and punished like a crime. The task of "education" was limited to the setting up of external discipline. For absences, pupils were fined; for "impertinence" they were beaten with rods; for more serious misconduct they were given lashes in the schoolyard. Retired soldiers were in attendance in the classrooms, armed with a whip "and if some student misbehaves, he [the soldier] ought to strike, regardless of his [pupil's] family origin."

Neither upbringing nor "education" entered into the duties of the Petrine school. The new school of mathematics did not aim at the development of the mind but only at the acquisition of essential technical know-how. Only accidentally, to the extent that some preliminary general knowledge was a prerequisite for technical training, did the school acquire some functions of general education. Following upon the acquisition of preliminary knowledge came the professional training: a general common preparation was given [the pupils] for the sake of this latter training. The Reformer's guiding idea was that the school had to prepare for various branches of the state service, and to this end it had to be professional. In doing so, as we have said, Peter took over the old seventeenth-century viewpoint. But to the single professional goal of the seventeenth-century Muscovite school—preparation of the clergy—he added a whole line of other state tasks.

Peter's first idea had been to entrust the execution of these tasks to the Muscovite school. At any rate, upon his return from abroad Peter had the following interesting exchange with the Patriarch Adrian. "Thanks to the Lord's mercy we have a school; and let persons who have studied in this school with intelligence be put to all kind of uses: ecclesiastical service, civil service, military service and engineering, and medical service." Soon, though, the Tsar was bound to notice how far removed the clever rhetoric of medieval learning was from the real modern sciences he was in need of. As there were no special schools, at first his collaborators had to acquire the necessary learning directly in service, through practice: the naval officer learned his craft on a ship, the civil official in the office, the doctor in the hospital, the apothecary in the pharmacy; exactly in the same way as before Peter's time the priest had been trained in a church and the merchant behind the counter. Of course this was not adequate. At the first opportunity professional training had to be given a school framework.

Once these schools had been established, they became obligatory for those for whom service had been a compulsory obligation earlier. It is for this reason that attendance at Peter's military school in itself became an obligation of the service class. At the same time the school became class-bound; and if the class-bound character did not become implanted immediately, it is only because at first the government valued the presence of anyone who was desirous to study, regardless of his origin. As the historian of the Naval Academy has noted, "not many noblemen entered this institution voluntarily; it was men from lower ranks [*raznochintsy*], not noblemen, who came willingly." This did not prevent a differentiation from taking place in the subsequent careers of members of these two groups. "Young men from the lower classes, *raznochintsy,* having completed the first two grades and learned how to write and count, terminated their studies and were assigned as clerks to various offices in the Admiralty or as assistant architects, pharmacists, etc. The children of the nobility went on to higher grades for further study and for service in the army and navy. With the transfer of the academy to Petersburg it became an exclusively military school and gave preference in admission to noblemen, and wealthier noblemen at that. The school's lower grades were left open in Moscow for pupils from the lower classes. It is from among the latter that were recruited the teachers of the cypher schools." The same observation could be made in the case of another military school of Peter's, that of engineering (founded 1712). It too had been destined exclusively for the nobility. In the absence of students from the nobility the school was filled up with *raznochintsy,* and it became a strictly noble institution only at the time of its transfer to Petersburg (1719). The third school, for artillery (1712), continued to teach sons of gunners in its lower grades for a very long time; higher professional training was given only to the nobility and only the latter were admitted to higher military careers. . . . The class character of these schools became firmly established after Peter's death. . . .

Alongside the development of these schools' class character, there took place a definition of the particular range of knowledge that was to be characteristic of the nobleman's education. Included among the "noble" or "knightly" subjects were, above all, modern languages, fencing, and dancing. It was this curriculum that determined the program of the first school of general studies in Russia. Naturally, not all noblemen could attend the educational institutions in the capital. Those who did not attend them had to undergo schooling through "practice" in the guard regiments, and rise to the higher ranks through service.

Another branch, besides the military, that since Peter's time has required special training, was the civil service. For the performance of civil administrative duties it was increasingly necessary to be familiar with political, juridical, and economic sciences. The government endeavored to set up a professional school for this branch too. But it met with the nobility's old prejudice against "office" service. The school did not materialize, as there was no adequate social material for it. Peter insisted in vain on the necessity of preparing for the civil service, and in vain he entreated "not to hold this training against members of prominent and noble families, for without it no one can be promoted to higher and ministerial ranks. . . ." Not even the introduction of jurisprudence into the curriculum of schools for the nobility could force the noblemen to study this subject. Of 245 noblemen enrolled in the Noble Corps of Cadets[3] in 1733 only 11 took jurisprudence. Noblemen who had been sent to work in offices for a practical acquaintance with administration did not want to work together with clerks and had to be returned to military schools. . . .

All of this leads to the conclusion that under Peter and his immediate successors Russian society needed first of all *elementary* education and was looking for it wherever it could find it within the limited resources available. The government, on the other hand, needed men with *professional* training and made all possible efforts to drive the youth of all classes into the kind of professional schools that would prepare them for discharging their fathers' and grandfathers' duties. Lastly, *general education* was little valued for itself by either the government or society. This is the reason why the government first limited itself to the opening of a set of special schools to satisfy its own immediate requirements, leaving the remainder to time and society's own efforts.

[3] Corps of Cadets (*Shliakhetnyi kadetskii korpus*)—a privileged school for children of the nobility established in 1731.—Ed.

IV THE SOVEREIGN EMPEROR AND THE OPPOSITION

Michael Cherniavsky

THE SOVEREIGN EMPEROR

The changes wrought by Peter had still another dimension for the Tsar's contemporaries: religious and symbolic. The process of secularization of both nature and symbolism of political power—which produced some of the most anguished as well as enthusiastic reactions—is described and discussed by Michael Cherniavsky, Professor of History at the State University of New York at Albany. His perceptive analysis reminds us of the significance that images, myths, and symbols have in political thought. His observations provide the background and set the framework for the dynamics of Russian historical consciousness since Peter the Great.

> *The Russian tsar must be terrible and fierce!*—M. Gorky

In the kaleidoscope of Peter's reforms one can pick out those which imply a new stage of secularization of the state: abolition of the patriarchate, the establishment of the Governing Synod of the Church under a lay bureaucrat, the law permitting members of the reigning dynasty to marry foreign princesses who are not converted to the Orthodox faith. All this was symbolized by the new title—*Imperator*—which the Senate, established by Peter himself, offered to the Tsar upon the conclusion of the victorious war with Sweden. It was perhaps equally well symbolized by the consequent elimination of the epithet *"tishaishii,"* the "most-gentle," from the liturgy.

The change, of course, was not instantaneous. Peter himself, and those around him, necessarily employed traditional formulas and expressions for traditional actions and habits, even when trying to express their new conceptions and ideas. In his memoirs I. I. Nepluiev describes a scene between himself and Peter. Nepluiev had come to thank the emperor for his appointment as resident to Constantinople; the new ambassador fell at Peter's feet, whereupon the emperor raised him up and said:

> *Don't bow, brother; I am placed here [to supervise] by God, and my duty*

> *is to see to it that anyone unworthy is not rewarded, and anyone worthy*
> *is not deprived; if you will be good [effective]—you will be doing good*
> *not to me but more to yourself and your fatherland; and if you will be bad*
> *—I shall be the claimant, for God demands from me that I should not*
> *allow the stupid and the evil any opportunity. . . . Serve with faith and*
> *truth! at first God, and following Him, I will have to support you.*

This could have been said by Peter's father, Tsar Alexis, as an expression of theocratic humility; and Nepluiev's action, his *proskynesis,* embracing the feet of his Tsar, was as traditional as Peter's words.

Nor is this the unique example. Nepluiev's colleague, Nartov, recorded that on one occasion Peter had said, "What is the difference between God and the tsar if both are offered the same respect?" and on another occasion, again to encourage a servitor, the emperor said,"Even . . . though God is high [up], and the tsar is far [away], nevertheless a prayer to the former and service for the latter will not be in vain." Peter's use of the Russian proverb of the seventeenth century indicates his purpose: to maintain the association of God and the tsar, but also to point out the distinction between the two, conveyed in the difference between prayer and duty. If anything, these statements reveal a greater humility on the part of Peter than on the part of his predecessors, expressed in a desire to diminish the gulf between the ruler and his subjects, which would be very much in character for the traditional image of Peter, with his dislike for ritual, pomp, and ceremony. That a change in Russian conceptions did take place, nevertheless, a change which necessitates interpreting Peter's words by other than seventeenth-century standards, is shown rather symbolically in the records of the same two men, Peter's loyal followers. While at his post in Constantinople, Nepluiev heard of the death of his emperor; he concluded his praise of his master with the following words: "And may the Lord put his soul, which worked so much for the common good, among the righteous." For Nepluiev there was no question, any longer, of the saint-prince, saintly in function and in essence; the best he can hope for is a place among the righteous for Peter, the first emperor from whom everything in Russia derived. Nartov, too, reacted to Peter's death; his conclusion was a different one: "While Peter the Great is no longer with us, yet his spirit lives in our souls and we, who have had the happiness of being with the monarch, will die faithful to him and will carry to the grave our passionate love for the god on earth [*zemnomu bogu*]."

For Nartov also, there was no question of the saint-prince, of the pious orthodox tsar; what he sees is the *deus terrenus,* not the image of God, but a god himself. Neither of the two men seem to have thought within the framework of the myths we have studied, for both of which the keystone was the equation *God-Prince.*

The denial of the theocratic foundation of the ruler-myth under Peter, the disappearance of the "Pious and Most-Gentle Tsar" could have two alternative consequences within the old Russian tradition of the saint-prince: the rejection of a tsar who no longer corresponded, in his personal attributes, to the ideal image, or a new and possibly greater exaltation of the tsar on a different ideological foundation. The first alternative was reflected in popular reaction to the Tsar, which, although heterogeneous, can be ordered in a psychological if not chronological pattern. A conversation about the Tsar's observance of fasting-days took place in 1701 between the priest Paul and the architect Tarasy: in answer to the priest's claim that "the Great Sovereign could not do such a thing as to eat meat during the Great Fast [at Easter] for only the Germans do that [*sc.* eat meat]," the architect said that "He, the Great Sovereign, is himself the son of a German." The meaning of this remark becomes clear when we consider the events of that time. In 1699, while Peter was abroad in Europe, the infantry regiments founded by Ivan the Terrible and stationed in Moscow, the *streltsy,* revolted. While the rebellion was put down with incredible brutality, by 1705 the regiments were restless again. This time they tried to gain the support of the Cossacks. Their emissaries informed the Cossacks that the Tsar was a changeling, substituted at birth for a daughter born to Tsaritsa Nataliia, or (a more convincing rumor) that the young Tsar had died or had been killed on his European journeys, and that a German changeling ruled over Russia with the purpose of damning all of her souls to perdition.

The conclusion to be drawn from this is evident: an evil tsar could not be a true tsar, and evil was measured (particularly since the seventeenth century) in the myth of the ruler by the degree of his impiety, as an implicit antithesis to the piety which was the supreme expression of the tsar's personal goodness. The emphasis remained on the person of the tsar. The popular opposition to Peter did not envisage removing the Tsar for his sins and malfeasance; it simply did not admit the possibility of the Tsar ever having such vices, and introduced the changeling legend in order to account for the existing conditions. The historical logic of this reaction is quite clear: the Russian prince, saintly in his person, became, with the rise of the state, the guardian of orthodoxy and thereby the guarantor of salvation for each Russian; hence the saintliness of the ruler, expressed in his piety, was of direct concern to each Russian, for it determined not only the existence of the tsar, but of Russia as well. The impious tsar could not be a true tsar, but what did this mean for the fate of Russia? Time and again the answer is given to us by the many men who claimed, in private and in public, that Peter was the Antichrist. In terms of the theory of Moscow the Third Rome, and of the role assigned in it to the tsar, the logic of this claim is unassailable. The Antichrist heralded the end of the world, which was to follow the fall of the Third Rome, and hence of orthodoxy. The final logical step was taken by the thousands of the schismatic Old Believers who immolated themselves in their forest communities at the approach of the tsar's officials or soldiers.

In a recent and stimulating article on the Three Romes, Robert L. Wolff, discussing the power of the ideology of autocracy, wrote: "If a state rests on generally accepted assumptions, it is almost impossible to challenge those assumptions without damaging the structure of the state."[1] This seems a rather idealistic interpretation of history. It is doubtful whether the *streltsy,* the Cossacks, or even the Old Believers rebelled because of Peter's impiety; the power of the myth is revealed rather by the fact that the opposition, rebellion, and self-immolation were considered justified by this impiety. In other words, those in opposition to Peter translated their grievances into the language of the myth. Insofar as they justified their actions by denying the further validity of the myth of the ruler, the popular uprisings denied the validity or even the reality of the state.

But if some in Russia were led, by the abolition of the eschatological, religious tradition, to an apocalyptic conclusion, others found a different solution to the problem of the different image of the tsar.

[1] Robert L. Wolff, "The Three Romes: The Migration of an Ideology and the Making of an Autocrat," *Daedalus* (Spring 1959), p. 306.

Rejecting, or perhaps indifferent to the theocratic justification, Nartov concluded that Peter the Emperor was god on earth. Here, too, the argument was consistent. The saintly prince, Christlike in his being, became the godlike tsar in order to lead Russia and the world to salvation; the end of the eschatological focus meant the existence of the state for its own sake and meant that the tsar, godlike for the sake of Christ, was now god for his own and the state's sake. Or, to parody the famous claim of the medieval French kings—*Rex Franciae imperator est in regno suo* [The King of France is emperor in his realm]—one could say of Peter, *Imperator Rossiae deus est in imperio suo* [The emperor of Russia is god in his empire]. Nartov, of course, is rather extreme; but the Russian myth of the Christlike prince, saintly in his person, was, in a sense, strengthened when Christ became irrelevant to the secularized prince, and when therefore the divinity of the prince lost any outside referent or control. In this sense Peter, in secularizing the image of the Russian tsar, created true absolutism, for the myth of the person of the prince remained, but without any standard of judgment to be applied to it. That some of those close to Peter were aware of the possibilities of the Tsar's new image is indicated in the testimony offered under torture by Tsarevich Alexis, Peter's son, at his trial for treason in 1719. Tsarevich Alexis said that his teacher Viazemsky had told him that: "Stepan Beliaev and the church choir sing in front of your father—'Whenever God wills it is the state of nature conquered,' and other such verses; they sing all this, tempting your father; and he is so pleased that they equate him with God."

Both the reactions to Peter presented here were extreme ones. The majority of the Russians, one can argue, were not aware of such a revolutionary change in the image of the Tsar. In folksongs and tales, Peter, frequently confused with Ivan the Terrible, represents, like his predecessor, the forceful, violently active, ruthless but just Russian tsar. Yet it is difficult to avoid the conclusion that, if there was not a revolutionary change in the ruler-myth, there was at the beginning of the eighteenth century a process of crystallization, of increasing explicitness consequent on the establishment of the secular state. In other words, the change in the tsar's image was not caused by Peter; rather, he spelled out the necessary implications of the process in the Russian state and society.

FIGURE 2. Tsar Alexis (Aleksie Mikhailovich). (From *Portrety, gerby i pechati Bol'shoi Gosudarstvennoi Knigi 1672 g.* [St. Petersburg, 1903], plate 32. Courtesy of Slavonic Division, New York Public Library; Astor, Lenox and Tilden Foundations.)

FIGURE 3. Peter I—engraving by J. Houbraken based on a portrait by K. Moor, 1717. (From D. A. Rovinskii, *Podrobnyi slovar' russkikh gravirovannykh portretov*, III [St. Petersburg, 1880], col. 1576. Courtesy of Slavonic Division, New York Public Library; Astor, Lenox and Tilden Foundations.)

To illustrate this change, we may be permitted a short digression at this point, for nowhere is it more strikingly manifested than in the realm of iconography. The portrait of Peter (Figure 3), contrasted with that of his father (Figure 2), speaks for itself: instead of the pectoral cross, the crown, and the *barmy,* we see Western armor; instead of the orb and scepter, two decorations showing a naval battle (on the left) and the plan of St. Petersburg (on the right); instead of the traditional, awesome, ringing titles, the inscription—not even in Russian—PETRUS PRIMUS RUSSORUM IMPERATOR.

If the Emperor's portrait, however, can be explained away as a personal preference on Peter's part—his Westernized idea of himself

FIGURE 4. Peter I and Ivan V in the "Thesis of Obedovskii"—engraving late
seventeenth century. (From: D. A. Rovinskii, *Podrobnyi slovar' russkikh
gravirovannykh portretov*, III [St. Petersburg, 1880], col. 1531. Courtesy of
Slavonic Division, New York Public Library; Astor, Lenox, and Tilden Foundations.)

as emperor—more convincing evidence is presented by two engravings, both executed during Peter's lifetime. The first one (Figure 4).
done in 1691, summarized in the most fantastic way all the aspects
and nuances of the ruler-myth: it shows in the foreground the two
co-tsars, Peter and his older half-brother Ivan V; behind them, reced-
ing into the background, are two other pairs of co-rulers, the Byzan-

tine emperors Basil and Constantine, Arcadius, and Honorius. Above them, under the medallion with the image of St. George, is the inscription: "God, Lord of heaven and of earth, one and triune, is well disposed towards the triunely reigning pairs, Arcadius and Honorius who ruled as one, Basil and Constantine; and now Ivan and Peter." Poised above them is the double-headed eagle, symbol both of Byzantium and of Russia. In the center of his body is a medallion with the image of St. Vladimir, and along his wings are the names of nine Russian rulers.[2] Under the right head of the eagle is St. Alexis, "creature of God,"[3] and under the left head is the image of Tsarevich St. Dimitry of Uglich. The eagle is being handed a sword by the princely passion-sufferer, St. Gleb, while his brother, St. Boris, hands the eagle a lance entwined with olive. To either side of them are medallions of Tsar Feodor Alexeevich and Tsar Alexis, respectively. The heads of the eagle are crowned by John the Baptist and St. Peter the apostle, backed up by two saints each. Above the central, large crown is the Virgin, holding a book with the words "Through Me Tsars reign" inscribed on it. The Virgin herself is being crowned by the three persons of the Trinity, with God the Father and Christ holding up the crown.

The [engraving] demonstrates what could be accomplished when Russian myths were treated in a symbolic fashion by the sophisticated and Westernized theologians and philosophers of the Kiev Academy of the seventeenth century. In a rather large space there was represented the image of Russian tsardom: Byzantium, St. Vladimir, Tsars, Grand Princes, saints and martyrs, and above them all the Trinity, symbolized, below, by the two young Tsars.

The second of our engravings was done only twenty-six years later (Figure 5). At the top we see Peter, wearing armor with an ermine cloak over it, a sword at his side and a field marshal's baton in his right hand. Above his head, in the rays of a radiant sun, two cupids bear the new imperial crown. Behind him is a chain made up of medallions with the ground-plans of fortresses captured by the Tsar. To his right is a painting of the combined Russian fleet, and to his

---

2 The Grand Princes Vsevolod Iaroslavich, Vladimir Monomakh, Iziaslav, Sviatoslav, Iaroslav, the tsars Ivan IV, Feodor, Vasily Shuisky and Michael.
3 *Sviatoi Aleksei, bozhii chelovek:* the term was used to denote a kind of holy fool, child-like and half-witted, belonging to God.

left is a representation of the naval victory at Greinham. He stands at the base of an inverted pyramid; the nine steps that compose it are nine victories won by Peter. Serving as background to the central image of Peter and his victories are portraits of thirty-three Russian rulers beginning with Riurik, who is shown at the very peak of the pyramid. A comparison with the *Great State Book* would show that at least in one respect the portraits differ, for none of the princes or tsars is wearing a halo. But such a comparison would be meaningless, for we learn that all the thirty-three portraits were based by the artist on a similar dynastic group portrait of the Dukes of Brandenburg.

Iconographic evidence is certainly not conclusive. But it is suggestive of at least a certain mood. The road from the theocratic tsar to the sovereign emperor was traveled rather quickly by the court circles, the writers, the official ideologues. The ancestors, whether Brandenburgian or Russian, serve as a background in a literal sense; the saints and martyrs are replaced by the victories, and at the head of it all, replacing the Trinity, stands the tsar, the new god on earth.

Peter's own conception of the state and his role within it would fit clearly within the ideology of enlightened absolutism, where the ruler was the first servant of the abstract and depersonalized state which all men served. Again and again he expressed his ultimate purpose as the service of Russia, who was the enduring and the absolute, and who, manifested by the Ruling Senate (*Pravitel'stvuischii Senat*), crowned him for his labors with the triumphant title of emperor. What this meant was the evolution of an abstract, impersonal image of the ruler. The new title, unfamiliar and strange-sounding, symbolized pure political power. In this sense it was an antithesis to the "body natural" tsar, an antithesis indicated in the contrasting appellations of the ruler, *"Batiushka Tsar'"* (Little Father Tsar) and *"Gosudar' Imperator"* (Sovereign Emperor), epithets which remained in use until 1917. The contrast is even sharper if one remembers that, along with the imperial title, Peter also received from his Senate the title of *"Otets Otechestva"* [Father of the Country]. *"Batiushka Tsar,"* widely used in the seventeenth century, remains the popular epithet, emphasizing the person of the tsar and his relation as a person to his subjects, as against the official and depersonalized sovereign. The symbolism inherent in the antithesis can be carried further, however. Timofeev,

FIGURE 5. Peter I—engraving by Picart, 1717. (From D. A. Rovinskii, *Podrobnyi slovar' russkikh gravirovannykh portretov, III* [St. Petersburg, 1880], col. 1616. Courtesy of Slavonic Division, New York Public Library; Astor, Lenox, and Tilden Foundations.)

describing the Time of Troubles, portrayed Russia as a widow, for her husband the true tsar had died. The tsar was Russia's bridegroom as Christ was the bridegroom of the Church, and *"Batiushka Tsar"* was paralleled, until 1917, by the commonest epithet for Russia, *Matushka Rus,'* "Mother Russia." Hence the image of the saint-prince and later pious tsar, the emphasis on the person of the prince, implied a distinction between the tsar and Russia at the same time that it emphasized the indissoluble bond between them. The husband-tsar carried the burdens of Russia on his shoulders, acting because of his personal qualities as mediator between his children and God as his model, Christ, had done. The emperor, however, was the father of *his* country and, to remove even the possibility of incestuous relations, *otechestvo* (fatherland) is neuter, while *Matushka Rus'* is feminine.

A distinction between the *Imperator* and the *Rossiiskaia Imperia* was lacking, however, despite Peter's efforts to endow the image of *"Rossiia"* with life. An interesting illustration of these efforts is Peter's treatment of the feast day of St. Alexander Nevsky. The relics of the saint were transported from Vladimir to St. Petersburg in 1723, and the feast day was changed from November 14th, the day of Nevsky's death, to November 23, the day of the saint's burial in Vladimir. Peter, however, ordered yet another change, to August 30, the anniversary of the victorious peace treaty with Sweden, on which occasion Russia became an empire. The saint-prince was put to work not for the salvation of Russian souls but for the glory of the imperial state and its new capital, St. Petersburg, whose patron he became. The separation between the emperor and the state which Peter sought did not, however, come about; in Russia (as elsewhere) the line between the ruler's "I am the first servant of the state" and "L'état c'est moi" could not be perceived.

The explanation for this is not very hard to find, at least in terms of political theology. The Petrine reforms were the culminating point for the evolution of the secular state; for that very reason many of them were designed to eliminate the outworn symbols and rituals of the former eschatologically oriented Christian society and therefore tended to emphasize sharply the ideological difference between past and present. Hence, for many Russians, the Russian empire appeared as something quite different and new, created *ex nihilo*. But, at the same time, the emperor carried with him the whole tradition of the ruler, Christlike in person and in power, a tradition which, when Christ became irrelevant, made of the emperor a god on earth. When the contemporary and admirer of Peter I, P. N. Krekshin, wrote: "Our father, Peter the Great! You have led us from nonexistence to existence . . . you have enlightened us and glorified us . . . The drops of sweat of your labors was our aromatic myrrh which perfumed the glory of Russia to the ends of the world," he was pointing out the fact that the new Russia was formed and defined by the Emperor, that it was contained in him. That Krekshin himself was aware of the implications of his statement he showed when he continued in his "Notes," "If those who possess blessed papers [dela] of Peter the Great or had been eye-witnesses of great deeds will not desire to submit [all this information] for the collection and glorification of true and most-glorious deeds of Peter the Great, they shall be ungrateful servants [raby], they shall be called those who have concealed the talent of their Lord [Gospoda], and not the sons of the fatherland. Then our enemies will mock us and will proclaim: 'While the Sovereign is worthy of such a State, the people are unworthy of such a Sovereign.' "

Into this brief statement Krekshin managed to pack the tangle of strands which made up the myth of the Sovereign Emperor. Peter the Creator is reinforced here by the ambiguity in the application of the parable of the talents. For Russians, not as Christians but as "sons of the fatherland," the emperor is the true "Lord." His thoughts and his deeds motivate and determine the newly-created paradise, Russia, and the people must be worthy of entrance into it. A distinction is drawn between the Russian people and the state, a political abstraction, created by and contained in the emperor.

And in fact, whatever his personal motivations and qualities or vices, Peter himself demonstrated the identity of the tsar and the state, the submergence of the feeble idea of the secular Russia in the old and powerful myth of the Russian tsar. Nowhere in the whole complicated bureaucratic structure established by the Emperor do we find anything that can be called an institution: a "Governing Senate" or a "Most Holy Synod" ordered about and disciplined by noncommissioned officers of the Guards could hardly be called institutions, but rather were executive extensions of Peter's personal will.

Despite all his formal attempts, the Emperor ruled by means of persons, not institutions, and the original appellation, "The Lords Senate" (*Gospoda Senat*), changed to "The Lords Senators" (*Gospoda Senaty*). The identification of the Emperor's will and the state in this case was so complete that it could not tolerate the intrusion of an abstraction represented by an institution.

The nature of this problem is most clearly revealed in Russian law, a subject deserving of a whole study unto itself, but which will be used here only for the purpose of illustration. Despite the ever-growing complexity of the Russian law codes, culminating with the *Ulozhenie* of Tsar Alexis in 1649, there does not seem to be any theory or conception of positive law. There was only the absolute, over-arching Natural Law, the Divine Order, absolute justice, of which the tsar was a manifestation: the "Animate Law." The reasons for this must be sought in the concrete complexities of Russian history, and the problem is made the more difficult by the fact that one finds no speculations and discussions about the nature of law. Yet a partial explanation, which bears on our problem, was provided by the same metropolitan Pitirim who wished to canonize Stolypin. To justify the chaotic administrative decrees of the various ministers, the metropolitan proclaimed in 1915 that they too, as well as the tsar, have the Holy Ghost upon them. Reporting this, the Russian poetess, Zinaida Gippius, ironically drew the right conclusion: "Grace is above laws." That this principle prevailed in seventeenth-century Russia can be seen in the judiciary role of the tsar. In effect the tsar did not really legislate; each case that reached his presence was decided separately, on its own merits, even if the decision was based on precedent. The significance of this principle was that it placed the tsar outside the framework of legal thought. In the medieval West the problem of the *princeps legibus solutus est* was solved by positing the prince as both above and below the Law; above it in his power to make law, below it in his princely moral will which led him to accept the Law voluntarily. In Russia, however, the saint-prince stood completely above the Law, and the assurance of justice was provided by his personal sanctity rather than by his relation to justice. So, too, it was the piety of the "Most-Gentle and Pious Tsars" which guaranteed justice; i.e., the personal qualities of the tsar as man rather than his princely functions.

Inner piety is a quality difficult to measure, however, and only its outward manifestation, adherence to ritual, customs, and traditions, limited the former tsars in their exercise of judicial power. The evolution of the secular state at the time of Peter I, by its abolition of old customs and traditions in the tsarist ritual, abolished the standard by which the person of the ruler could be judged and thereby abolished the distinction between the emperor's personal will and Law or law. To put it another way, Law in Russia did not serve as a middle term between the tsar and the people, but, identified with the *person* of the tsar, served to emphasize the identity of the ruler and the state. In this case the rejection of the tsar as a person, the denial of his piety or sanctity, should have led to the rejection of all his laws, and of the Russian state as such, and this was the position taken by the more extreme opponents of Peter I. The Old Believers, rejecting Peter I as a changeling or as Antichrist, fled the state physically, and refused to acknowledge or obey the most innocuous decrees or regulations.

The secular, absolutist state in Russia, as elsewhere, was symbolized by the final step in the evolution of the ruler-myth: for, if the rationale in the case of the saint-princes was the sanctification of power by the person, and in the case of the pious tsars the sanctification of the person by power, now power sanctified power. In a strange and ironic way the state of Peter I marked, in the Russian context, a reversion to an older form or conception. One could argue that Peter's Russia signified the victory of the khan over the basileus; the tsar-emperor ruled Russia as his private property, for which he was responsible to no one; the source of his power lay in itself, in its ability to conquer, rather than in any unique quality or myth of Russia itself. One instance of such a view is found in the law of succession promulgated by Peter in 1722. During two centuries the Grand Princes of Moscow tried to establish the principle of primogeniture for the Grand Principality as against the right of the Khan to invest whomever he pleased with the throne of All Russia. The sixteenth and seventeenth centuries saw the full acceptance of this principle, and the end of the Riurikid dynasty in 1598 appeared to Russian society as a catastrophe. Yet Peter's law of 1722 gave the reigning emperor the right and power to nominate his successor as he chose, without any specified limitations. The issue, of course, does not lie in the political circumstances, in Peter's desire to exclude from the throne the progeny of his son Alexis; as it turned out, the Emperor had not nominated anyone before his death. But the form in which Peter clothed his political considerations indicates both the degree of abstraction and absolutism that the image of the ruler had reached and the persistence of an old tradition, reaching back to the time before the concept of the state really existed, and Russia was regarded as the private property of her princes. The vitality of this tradition was revealed in a rather paradoxical way as late as 1905: opposing the intention of Nicholas II to grant the Constitution of 1905, one of the Grand Dukes argued that Nicholas had no right to do this, i.e. to give up part of his power, for "la Russie appartient à toute notre famille."

The final symbolic step in the evolution of the autocratic ruler, truly secular and truly absolute in the sense of owing nothing to anything outside of himself and limited by nothing outside of himself, took place in 1742. Beginning with the coronation of Elizabeth, the Russian rulers crowned themselves in the ceremony performed in the Cathedral of the Dormition in the Kremlin; the senior archbishop only handed the crown to the emperor (or empress), who then placed it on his own head. We find no hints as to the possible reason for this change in the coronation ritual; the three preceding imperial coronations of 1724, 1727, and 1730 show no changes or indications of change. Yet the self-crowning, which began in 1742, reflected more accurately the new myth of the ruler than did the traditional ceremonies during the first part of the century. The Sovereign Emperor was emperor *sui generis,* containing within himself all power and the source of all power, completely secular, or, what is the same thing, deified. And, ironically enough, the history of the eighteenth century in Russia substantiated the new image of the sovereign first revealed by Peter I. The male line of the Romanovs ended five years after Peter's death, in 1730, with his grandson Peter II; the rest of the century saw three empresses, one of them (Catherine II) a German princess quite unrelated to the Russian dynasty, and an emperor (Peter III), a Duke of Holstein, related by blood and not at all by culture or ideology. All of these were playthings of the Russian gentry which made up the Guards regiments stationed in the capital. Certainly, if our chronicler of the Time of Troubles, Ivan Timofeev, could see this pageant of rulers, he would have had to give up his standard of suitability. How to determine the proper and natural tsar, not a "slave-tsar," when none of the old categories would apply? There was not really a dynasty one could identify, no sanctity one could feel, no piety one could admire. The Sovereign Emperor was such an abstraction that a German woman could fill the position.

This is not to say that the traditional forms of the ruler-myth were abandoned. Archbishop Feofan Prokopovich, the ideologist of the Petrine state, in his formal exhortation at the coronation of Peter II in 1727, spoke of the emperor as God's vicar, the elect of God; for his Christian virtues the emperor will be associated in heaven with the saintly tsars, his ancestors. And, praising Peter I, Feofan still called him Christ. Yet it is significant that in the chief work of the new ideology, *Pravda Voli Monarshei* (The Justice of the Monarch's Will), written in 1722, the archbishop only referred to the "Christian Sovereign" or "Christian Monarch," never to the Orthodox one. The reason for this new formula is not difficult to suggest; Feofan was the leader of the Westernizing, bureaucratic, secularized upper clergy supported by Peter I. As Peter I borrowed the forms if not the content of Western eighteenth-century absolutism, so his archbishop borrowed the forms of political theory provided by the West. For our problem, however, the change from "Orthodox" to "Christian" is meaningful. Certainly, the "Christian Sovereign" is theologically as correct as the Orthodox one; but it did mean a break from the image of the tsar who was tsar because he was Orthodox, because on him depended the fate of all men's souls; it did mean a greater depersonalization, a greater abstraction of the ruler. All the European rulers were Christian, hence all had equal and identical power. This last conclusion is not explicit, but implicit it certainly was, both in the logic of the argument and in relations with European princes. One can imagine what effect Peter's acceptance of the small German princes as equals would have made on his saintly predecessor, Ivan the Terrible.

It is useful at this point to pause and delimit more precisely the aspects of the ruler-myth with which we have been concerned, and also to remind ourselves of the obvious qualifications and *caveats*. For the purpose of exposition, the chronological method served very well to show the changes in the myth of the ruler, through well-defined stages, during the centuries. Yet this linear exposition is, in a sense, a distortion of historical reality. In the evolution of the Russian secular state the expected shift took place from medieval political theory to that of early modern absolutism; in theological terms one can describe it as a shift of emphasis from Christ, the manifest deity, to God the Father, abstract and impersonal. The secular state did not arise with Peter I, however, but developed through the centuries; as one Russian jurist wrote, Peter I put into practice what was theory under Ivan the Terrible. The ideological problems created by the secular state also existed for centuries, and hence the solutions for these problems overlapped. In other words, the Sovereign Emperor did not displace the Most-Gentle Tsar; with the shift of emphasis toward the "emperor," the image of the Orthodox Father Tsar continued to exist, partially contained in that of the emperor, partially living alongside of the latter, or even in opposition to it. Contained in both these images, as well as continuing an independent existence, was the image of the saint-prince with its emphasis on the person of the ruler. The changes which could be rung upon these themes are shown by the various images of Peter I described here: Sovereign Emperor and Antichrist, pious Christian monarch and Earthly God; and, in the course of the eighteenth century, attempts were made to synthesize the images of the ruler. . . . The difficulty of synthesizing the myth, however, was [great]. . . . While the image of the emperor, such as Peter, could and did contain the various aspects of the ruler-myth, presenting one or another facet to particular groups or individuals, these aspects were intrinsically antithetical. But while the tension between the "saint-prince" and the "orthodox tsar" was mainly theological and hence subdued, while the medieval saintly prince could and did merge into the early Orthodox and Pious Tsar, the antithesis between the latter and the image of the new imperial sovereign was quite explicit. One could be the sovereign emperor without being the pious Russian tsar. In fact, a very large minority of Russians, the schismatic Old Believers, drew the extreme conclusion: beginning with Peter I, to be the emperor meant *not* being the tsar. For masses of Old Believers Peter and his successors remained Antichrists exactly because they were emperors. The more extreme groups refused to pray for the ruler; that is, in effect they refused to recognize the existence of the state as such. When, following a temporary liberalization of government policy, the Old Believers, in 1799, agreed to pray for the Emperor Paul I, they insisted on praying for

". . . the Great Sovereign, Tsar Pavel Petrovich of All Russia" but would not include the title of emperor nor the official form of the prayer.

What all this meant was that a split along class lines was taking place with regard to the Russian image of the ruler. While for the Old Believers "emperor" meant Antichrist, for the mass of the Russian peasantry the ruler simply remained the *"Batiushka-Tsar,"* the traditional, pious, Most-Gentle Russian Tsar. A number of reasons can be suggested for this. The split along social lines had existed, of course, for a long time. It was manifested by the Cossacks in the sixteenth and seventeenth centuries, in their rejection of even the pious and most-gentle tsars and the growing state, and in their appropriation during the Razin revolt of a personal and private ruler in the person of the Tsar's son. Yet the natural social oppression and resulting antagonism does not explain the problem. That the masses reacted against the Petrine monarchy is not surprising, considering the monstrous new burdens it imposed on them. In the sixteenth century, however, burdens as monstrous imposed by Ivan the Terrible did not produce a comparable ideological reaction, even if one considers the Time of Troubles as part of the same period. The difference seems to be in the fact that by the eighteenth century the myth of the ruler had acquired sufficient complexity, a sufficient number of different aspects, facets, and possible interpretations to perform the function of myth: to allow individuals and groups to express, with ever-growing variety, their personal and collective problems and aspirations within its framework. In the event, the difference between the image of the ruler held by the upper class, created and educated by Peter's new Empire, and that held by the mass of serf peasantry would be central.

Alain Besançon

EMPEROR AND HEIR—FATHER AND SON

The new image of the ruler was not accepted by everybody, beginning even within the imperial family itself. The dramatic clash between Peter the Great and his oldest son and heir, Alexis (1690–1718) was truly symbolic of the conflict between two cultures, two worlds, as well as of the perennial genera- tion gap (only this time in reverse). The actual events of Alexis' trial and death have not been completely unravelled, but their political and cultural significance is clear. In addition, and this is the great contribution of Alain Besançon's analysis, the episode revealed the subconscious—personal and historical—motivations at play and thus became another element in the chain of national and historical myths that shaped modern Russian consciousness.

The article reproduced here is from a book that deals with the most basic myths of Russian history as they were produced by the collective unconscious of the Russian people and its cultural élite. Professor Alain Besançon is a young French historian who has done original and pioneering work in the frontier region between psychoanalysis and history. He is at present Directeur d'études at the VIᵉ section of the École des Hautes Etudes pratiques of the Sorbonne.

The Tsarevich Alexis grew up in his mother's—Tsarina Eudoxia— environment, a remnant of old Muscovy. After Peter had sent his wife to a convent, Alexis was raised in traditional fashion in the old palace in Moscow. He resembled his grandfather, Tsar Alexis. His sloth, slowness, contemplativeness, apathy, and flaccid sensuality can be accounted for by his constitution and education, as well as by that old Russia which Peter was endeavoring by all means to put into motion. That is why Peter treated Alexis as he did Russia. He gave him German tutors, insulted him, beat him, enrolled him into his regiments where he had him raise supplies, build fortifica- tions, seek out and execute deserters, and forward reports. All this at the age of seventeen or eighteen. Moreover Alexis had to learn German, French, geometry, nautical science. . . . Peter locked his son, as he did Russia, into the vicious circle of despotism. He wanted the slave to act consciously and freely while remaining a

Reprinted with permission of the author and publisher, from Alain Besançon, *Le Tsarévitch immolé—La symbolique de la loi dans la culture russe* (Paris: Librairie Plon, 1967), pp. 111–122. Editor's translation.

slave. He wanted the puny, beaten, terrorized child to display his Herculean father's unfettered joyful activity and tireless energy.

The crisis broke in October 1715. Peter sent a long admonition. Recalling the Swedish war and Russia's glory, he wrote: "All this, with the help of the Almighty, has been accomplished through my own poor efforts and the faithful labors of other true sons of the fatherland. When, however, after contemplating the happiness God has granted to our fatherland, I turn my eyes on my posterity, it is a sorrow hardly less great than my joy that overcomes me in seeing you, the heir, completely incapable of guiding the affairs of the state. Yet, it is not God Who is the cause, since He has not deprived you of reason nor of all your bodily strength; for while you are not very strong you are not completely debile either. . . ." Peter went on to reproach Alexis for his want of taste for military exercises and then continued:

> And as I am a man and subject to death, to whom shall I leave what, with God's help, has been sown and the little that has already been raised? To him who in imitation of the lazy slave of whom the Gospels tell us that he buried his talent in the earth, that is who threw away everything that God gave him! I also remind you of what an obstinate and evil spirit you are possessed. How often have I scolded you, and not only scolded but also beaten you, and how many years don't I talk to you? But all this to no avail, useless and vain; you don't want to do anything but stay at home and enjoy it while elsewhere everything goes wrong. . . . Sadly reflecting on this and seeing that I cannot turn you to good through any means, I have decided to write you this last will and wait a little longer; perhaps you will reform sincerely. If this does not happen, be advised that I shall completely deprive you of the inheritance, like a gangrenous member. . . . Indeed, God willing, I shall do it, for since I neither have nor will spare my own life for my fatherland and people, why should I spare you, a good-for-nothing?

What the father demanded of his son he demanded of Russia too: identification with him, his energy, his labors. But at once the son discovered the tactics of avoidance. He translated the threat, which in Peter's mind had only a corrective purpose, onto the sacrificial plane enhanced by tradition. In accepting, nay asking, for the punishment Alexis preserved his own autonomy and his values conformant with those of the culture into which he had been steeped. After three days therefore, he answered:

Gracious Sovereign-Father! This 27th day of October 1715, on the day of my wife's burial,[1] I have read the letter received from you; and I cannot say anything except that if because of my worthlessness you deign deprive me of the inheritance of the Russian crown, let it be according to your will. And of this I beg you, Lord, most humbly: whereas I see myself most inadequate and useless for this task, as well as devoid of memory (without which one can't accomplish anything) and weakened in all my intellectual and physical forces (as a result of various illnesses) and incapable of ruling such a people, a task which requires a man not as rotten as I. Therefore, with respect to the heritage—may God give you long years of health!—I do not pretend to it and shall not pretend to it even if I had no brother (but now, thank God, I have a brother to whom God grant many years of health); and to this I take God for witness upon my soul. . . . I entrust my children to your will; as for myself, I only request sustinance to my death. Submitting all this to your decision and gracious will, I am your lowly slave and son Alexis.

Alexis' answers enraged Peter. This escape into abasement forced him to reveal the truth in his demands. Ostensibly he wanted to reform his son, that is, make him like himself. Peter bared his soul and asked Alexis to participate in his own harshness. But with respect to identification Alexis had managed but a pale imitation: his solitary drunkenness aped the epic drinking bouts of the Tsar; and Euphrosynia, the Finnish serf girl whom Alexis had taken for his mistress—as his father had done with a Livonian servant[2]—would betray him and become the instrument of the father's wrath. Now Alexis was withdrawing and behaving as submissively as, deep down in his heart, his father wished him to. Thus Alexis refused complicity in Peter's murderous wish. In so doing he behaved in the same way as did those Russians who escaped into the forest and, waiting for the Last Day, sang:[3] "No salvation down here, none. Evil alone rules us, evil. Death alone can save us, death! . . . Fire awaits us, fire."

[1] Sophie-Charlotte of Brunswick-Wolffenbüttel died while giving birth to a son, the future Emperor Peter II (1727–1730).
[2] Peter the Great eventually married his mistress, Maria, a servant girl whom his generals had picked up in Riga during the war. In 1721 Peter crowned her empress under the name of Catherine. She ruled after his death from 1725–1727.
[3] Reference to the more radical members of the Old Belief who refused to recognize the Tsar and his agents. Rather than pay taxes or serve in the army, they escaped into the woods and mountains. Upon approach of the imperial agents they would often commit suicide by burning themselves to death. See Robert O. Crummey, *The Old Believers and the World of Antichrist—The Vyg Community and the Russian State, 1694–1855* (Madison: University of Wisconsin Press, 1970).

What Alexis asked for was a private life; this Peter granted to no Russian. That was the time when thousands of schismatics were withdrawing into the "deserts": "Find, my beloved ones, mountains and caves. Sink, my beloved ones, into the abyss of the earth . . . where I would not see the scandal of this world."

It is not enough to say that Alexis was under the influence of the "long beards."[4] He was the living incarnation of the world that Peter seared in vitriol. Hence his paternal rage, for he held in his imperial hands, in the person of his son, all of Russia as if assembled by magic and which he was about to kill, asking for its own consent to do so.

Six weeks later the Tsar reiterated: "Though you have reached maturity, do you help me in my unbearable sorrows and labors? Alas, not at all! And as everyone knows you even hate my deeds which, without sparing my health, I have performed for my people. And of course, after me you will destroy them. For this reason you cannot remain, as you wish, neither fish nor fowl. And either you mend your ways and sincerely become worthy of being an heir, or be a monk. . . ."

Alexis answered the next day in two lines: "I desire the estate of monk and for this I implore your gracious consent. Your slave and worthless son." As Soloviev[5] has noted, "the son was triumphing over the father." There remained nothing for Peter but to grant tonsure to his son—and this he was not ready to do—or to postpone decision. The Tsar hesitated for several months, then, from Copenhagen, he came back to the charge, 26 August 1716: ". . . therefore, now, since you had enough time for reflection, take a decision immediately upon receipt of this letter: either the first or the second [way]. . . . We confirm this and everything must be decided finally, for I see that you are only wasting time in your usual sterility."

For the first time, then, Alexis had a movement of revolt. His entourage . . . was perhaps encouraging him: "A monk's cowl is not nailed on the head; it can be taken off." But he committed the mistake, unforgivable to a Russian, to seek security by emigrating.

[4] Those who did not accept Peter's reforms and continued to wear beards in spite of the prohibition against them.
[5] Sergei M. Soloviev, 1820–1879, most prominent Russian historian of the nineteenth century, the founder of modern scientific historiography in Russia. Author of a monumental history of Russia in twenty-nine vols.

To emigrate was to violate one of the oldest and most deeply engrained taboos of Russian society. Ambassadors crossed the border only at the price of a thousand ceremonies which made palpable the sacred nature of the boundary of a power and of a faith. . . . But Alexis' gesture reveals one of the meanings of this interdiction. To leave is to break the sacrificial relationship, to refuse the suffering necessary. ". . . Shall a man leave his father and his mother": this is forbidden forever if it is true that the oedipal suffering must be borne to the end. The law inherent in this situation demands cleaving to the source of pain. Rarely does a Russian emigrate without remorse and without a sense of committing desertion for which he will not atone during his entire life. . . .

"You have left and sought foreign protection like a deserter," Peter wrote to Alexis. "This is unheard of not only among our children but even among our most distinguished subjects! What an insult and disappointment to your father, what a shame for your fatherland!"

Alexis returned. He had obtained a written and public promise of pardon and a partial guaranty for permission to live in a village with Euphrosynia. Thus began the Tsarevich's passion.

We need not unravel the nature of the family conflict, not because it cannot be surmised but because it is not in itself a genuine historical problem. What we are interested in is not the neurotic element per se but its relationship to collective representations. However, one must not be the dupe of Peter's own justifications which have been so readily accepted by historians. According to them, Peter's motive was to secure an acceptable succession. But after he had killed his son Alexis there remained a boy by his second wife, a child of three, retarded and sickly. After this boy's death the following year, Peter was to have only another stillborn son. He then promulgated the incredible law of 1722 which permitted the sovereign to deed the empire to whomever he pleased, the way God disposes of the world. But Peter could not make up his mind, even on his deathbed, to designate anyone. We have reports that during his last illness, in his delirium "he was heard to say that he had sacrificed his own blood" and that he ordered paper to be brought. "I leave everything . . ." he wrote, but did not finish and died. The empire fell to the Livonian servant girl. One should, therefore, not rely too much on the argument from reason of state which only serves as imperfect rationalization for unreasoning behavior and passionate excess.

We are not attempting a clinical reading of this sinister episode, but there is a political reading—even though the reality of individual experience remains central. The murder of the Tsarevich takes place in a world that is in the process of secularization; even more it is an element and a factor of this secularization. It was not Peter's intention to sacrifice his son for the sins—in the Christian sense—of the Russian people or his own. He wanted Alexis tried for an actual, legally defined crime, for a crime against the state. But on this issue the Tsar is faulted by the son who takes on and sticks to the traditional Christian role. Hence the horror of the endless interrogations in which Alexis acknowledges a sin of which he is not accused, but cannot confess crimes of which he is innocent.

As soon as Alexis returned from abroad Peter reneged on his promise of unconditional pardon: he made it dependent on the denunciation of accomplices. Alexis also had to make a solemn renunciation of the throne. It took place in the Cathedral of the Dormition in the Kremlin on 3 February 1718. "I, undersigned, affirm on the Holy Gospels that because of my crime against His Majesty, my father and sovereign . . . I am deprived of the inheritance of the Russian throne. This I recognize to be just on account of my guilt and indignity. . . ." The same day an imperial manifesto was published: ". . . Although he, Our son, is deserving of death on account of such repulsive deeds, especially his bringing dishonor on Us by his flight, his slanders, and his opposition to his Lord, We however, taking pity on him in Our paternal heart, forgive him and free him of all punishment. But on account of his worthlessness We cannot in all conscience let him be heir to the Russian throne after Our death."

There remained the denunciations. Alexis underwent seven interrogations in all, at first in writing. Peter conducted the affair personally. Alexis first gave the names of those who had counselled and helped him in his flight, Kikin, Viazemskii, Tsarevna Maria Alekseevna, V. Dolgorukii, who were immediately arrested and tortured. Then he named Glebov, Demid, and the Archbishop of Rostov, Dositheus, who were also tortured. At the same time the separate case of Ilarion Dokukin, a small official of the artillery department, was being investigated. Dokukin had handed the Tsar, publicly in church, a copy of the new oath of allegiance[6] to which he had affixed an addendum which voiced the sentiments of the oppressed: "Because the God-protected Tsarevich Alexis has been unjustly chased and deprived of the throne of the All Russian Tsar, I—on my Christian conscience and before God's tribunal and the Holy Gospel—do not take the oath and do not kiss the life-giving cross and do not sign in my own hand. . . . Even though the wrath of the Tsar be on me for this, let the will of my Lord God Jesus Christ be done, and I, Christ's slave Ilarion Dokukin, by His Holy will am willing to suffer for the truth. Amen, amen, amen."

In March Alexis was invited to witness on the Red Square the execution of those he had denounced: the wheel for the Archbishop of Rostov, Demid, and Dokukin, empalement for Glebov. . . . The others, with tongues cut out and nostrils slit were sent to forced labor. Yet Peter was still confronted only by an elusive state of mind, a *non possumus,* a will for martyrdom. All the testimonies had yielded but gossip, allusions, complaints; it was impossible to prove the existence of a plot.

At this point Euphrosynia turned into the helpmate of her sovereign. She revealed statements made in her presence by her princely lover while he was a refugee in Italy. Hearing of riots he was said to have remarked: "With the help of God perhaps we shall return in joy." He was alleged to have said: "When I shall rule, I shall live in Moscow and Petersburg will sink to the status of an average town; I shall not maintain any fleet and keep an army only for defense. I shall not make war on anyone and shall be content with the old possessions [of the empire]. In winter I shall reside in Moscow and in the summer in Iaroslavl'." He also was to have said: ". . . I don't know why my father does not love me and wants to make my brother heir, though he is only a baby; and having done this my father hopes his wife, my stepmother, to be clever, and after his death there will be woman's rule." He also was alleged to have thought of taking refuge with the Pope. And then, having learned of a vague plot in the army, he replied to the person who asked him

---

[6] Upon Alexis' renunciation of the throne, the baby Peter (son of Peter the Great by his second wife, Catherine) was proclaimed heir, and all Russians had to swear an oath of allegiance to him. This was done in a church, every subject kissing the cross and signing his name (or putting a cross) beneath the official proclamation.

whether he might join the insurgents that perhaps he would do it if invited.

The crime was that of intention. But in his heart Peter had at last taken the decision to "sacrifice this unworthy son to the good of the people." However, while giving free rein to his light-hearted sadism, Peter wanted—as Voltaire says—that the nation itself condemn the prince. By associating to this death the new Russia he had reared, Peter was securing a complicity based on blood. Alexis did not, therefore, die "for the common weal of the people." He is the sign of the schism that the Petrine reforms introduced into Russian society and the watershed in Russia's history between *a before* and *an after*. Alexis was as much the gangrened member that is cut away as he was the expiatory victim.

The legal basis of the accusation remained the *Slovo i delo Gosudarevo* (Word and deed pertaining to the sovereign), a category of crimes for which, since the mid-seventeenth century, the ordinary course of justice was suspended and the case directly remanded to the tsar's jurisdiction. No distinction was made between commission and omission of an act. The category of crimes was expressive of royal theophany: the crime against the sovereign is as a crime against God. It illustrated the paradox of the process of secularization which goes through theocratic confirmation: by appropriating omniscience and omnipotence the sovereign is temporarily haloed by the light of Mt. Tabor.

From this derives the drama's strange end which mixes judicial comedy, sacrificial meal, and family tragedy. "I suffer," declared Peter, thus finding his way back to the ancestral tradition of the burden of punishment and the loneliness of Gethsemane; "it is difficult for those who do not know this affair to decide on my innocence; God [alone] sees the truth." For this reason, as Boris had submitted to Patriarch Job the question of Dmitrii's death,[7] so did Peter lay the matter before the clergy which he had enslaved. ". . . We wish that as teacher's of God's word you, hierarchs and clergy, issue not any kind of decree, but uncover and render for Us a true precept and argument, based on God's commandments and the examples

---

[7] Dmitrii, last son of Ivan the Terrible, died under somewhat mysterious circumstances, at age 10, in 1591. His death ended the old dynasty and permitted the chief minister, Boris Godunov, to ascend the throne.

and rules of Holy Writ, what punishment is deserved by Our son's accursed and Absalom-like design." But the bishops answered that the sovereign power does not come under the judgment of its own subjects but acts as it sees fit without having to take counsel with lower ranks. If Peter wants to make an act of pardon he will do as Christ did when he forgave the prodigal son. If he wants to punish he will find examples in the Old Testament. "In short, the heart of the Tsar is in the hands of God. Let him chose the side to which God's hand bends him," the clergy wrote on June 18.

At the same time the Tsar was setting up a high court composed of more than one hundred dignitaries of all ranks, the image of the new Russia. Peter declared to the group: ". . . do not consider that you are to judge my son, the son of your sovereign; without taking into consideration the person, do what is right and do not imperil your souls or mine, so that our consciences be pure on the Day of Reckoning and our fatherland unharmed." These few lines expressed the major contradiction: Peter wanted an impersonal sentence rendered in the name of the state and demanded it for the sake of his own soul, for the fate of the kingdom and of the world was to be decided in it. Without stretching the meaning very greatly, we could interpret this as follows: I am asking you to play the comedy of the modern state because the salvation of the most pious Tsar and of the Orthodox realm is at stake.

On June 19th the Tsarevich was put on the rack and given twenty-five blows [of the knout]. It is only then that he compensated his father for the suffering he, Alexis, had inflicted on the Tsar by turning the other cheek, allowing to be spat upon, and escaping into abjection. That day, for the first time, Alexis consented to confess what was hidden at the bottom of his Christian passivity. He acknowledged having once said to his confessor: "I wish the death of my father." And the priest had answered him: "God forgive you, we too wish for his death." At last Peter had found in his son the necessary complicity; it was a complicity complementary to his wish and symmetrical to the murderous intent. The way was free to death and forgiveness.

Everything was accomplished in one week. Peter asked three new questions whose nature was barely political but familial and personal, proving that some intimacy had been recaptured.

1. Why had he not listened to me or done anything that pleased me or anything good, but done only what leads to sin and shame?
2. Why was he not afraid and did not fear punishment for not listening to me?
3. Why did he desire the succession by other means than obedience?

Alexis answered as required: Because I have lived with my mother, servant girls, and bigots. I took advantage of my father's absences to frequent priests and to drink with them and, following their example, I began to detest not only my father's deeds but his very person. I wanted to succeed by bad means because I have strayed from the true path and I then had to look for foreign help. I would have accepted the emperor's [of Germany] assistance.[8] To the second question he answered, "only my bad disposition was the reason that I was not afraid and did not fear punishment for not listening to my father, I confess it sincerely. And though my father frightened me, it was not the fear that becomes a son, it was such as to draw away from him and not do his will."

Again the prince was tortured, fifteen blows [of the knout] this time. He confirmed everything. The same day the court rendered its verdict. It reminded that the condition for the imperial pardon—say everything and conceal nothing—had not been fulfilled; that the prince acknowledged to have sought the succession during the lifetime of the sovereign, even at the price of rebellion and foreign intervention; that he had hidden his wish for the death of his father; that he was unworthy of pity. Unanimously, by virtue of the commandments of both Old and New Testaments, the canons of the Holy Fathers of the Church, the laws of Roman and Greek emperors, as well as on the basis of Russian law, the court, in all conscience, felt that he had merited death. "Although as slaves and subjects we render this verdict with contrite heart and tears and we declare that as the subjects of autocratic power we are not worthy of rendering such a high judgment, particularly with respect to the son of our most gracious autocratic Tsar and Lord." . . .

Under the date of 26 June 1718, the following entry was made

---

8 Charles VI (1711–1740) was Tsarevich Alexis' brother-in-law. He gave him asylum first in the Tirol and then in Naples when Alexis escaped from Russia.

into the register of the garrison of St. Petersburg: "At 6 p.m., Tsarevich Alexis, kept under guard in the Trubetskoi Bastion, gave up his
soul to God." It is of little importance to us whether or not Alexis
succumbed to the torture of a new session, perhaps even at the
hands of his father. The next day the Tsar informed his people of the
exemplary significance of the event, a significance which their history and religion had taught the Russian people to give to all such
events.

After receiving notification of the sentence, Peter averred, he was
torn between paternal forgiveness and the good of the state. It is
then that God in His goodness resolved his doubt by recalling his
son Alexis from this world. But in accordance with his Christian
duty, before he died, Alexis confessed, received communion, and
called his father to his side; and Peter came, forgetful of the sorrows
his son had caused him. And with many tears and much contrition
Alexis confessed and acknowledged all the crimes against his father
and asked for forgiveness which the Tsar dutifully accorded him as
a Christian and as a father. . . .

Eugene F. Shmurlo

THE OPPOSITION OF THE TRADITIONALISTS

*It is common knowledge that there was great resistance to Peter's innova-
tions. Usually this resistance is ascribed to the backward traditionalists, to
those concerned only with the preservation of hoary external forms. The
enemies of Peter's reforms, it is often thought, were either incapable or unwilling to understand the necessity for Russia to join up with Western civilization and the advantages of being a modern and dynamic nation. Eugene F.
Shmurlo (1853–1934), whose main work was on Russia's religious and cultural relations with the West, tries to describe and explain the deeper reasons
for the popular opposition to Peter's reforms.*

From Eugene F. Shmurlo, *Petr Velikii v Otsenke Sovremennikov i Potomstva, Vyp.
I, XVIII vek [Peter the Great in the Judgment of Contemporaries and Posterity—
fasc. I, the 18th century]* (St. Petersburg, 1912), pp. 1–6. Translated by Mirra Ginsburg.

The era of Peter the Great has long since become a part of history. Two centuries separate us from the reforming work of the first Russian Emperor. Much water has flowed since then, and yet we still seem to be under the spell of that period, as if we had not yet emerged from its troubled, feverish days and are still unable to deal with it altogether objectively. The spirit of Peter is still alive among us, and at moments we are ready to think that the royal reformer has left us only yesterday, that he has not as yet had time to become a historical personage. Nor can we think of him as we do Ivan III, or the Terrible Tsar, or even Tsar Aleksei Mikhailovich, who was only a single generation away from the Reformer. These rulers have receded into such a distant past that we are able, to quote the poet, to speak about them, "hearing indifferently of good and bad." Not so with Peter. His "good" is still palpable and visible; his "bad," at moments, still makes it difficult for us to breathe. The great Emperor posed in all their sharpness questions that we have not yet entirely resolved to this day. Willy-nilly, we still live in an environment of concepts and practical activities which he had been the first to invest with immediacy and sharp definition.

This proximity to Peter's epoch inevitably affects our appraisal of it. The lack of historical distance has interfered with proper perspective, and the literature devoted to Peter's reforming activity is more reminiscent of the speeches in a courtroom, defending or indicting a defendant, than of the calm analysis of scientific historical criticism.

The movement which created the era of transformation began in the seventeenth century. The terrible depredations suffered by our country at the beginning of that century compelled us to awaken from long hibernation and to give serious thought to our shortcomings. Although the basic mass of Russian society continued to vegetate in its old inertia, a small handful of progressive people had already separated itself from it. This handful consisted of all who were no longer satisfied only with past traditions, with the way of life inherited from ancient times. The fact of which they were most keenly aware was the lack of *education,* and the need to borrow it from where it was available, from the West. Thus, two directions gradually began to emerge—the old Russian and the European. Equally dissatisfied with contemporary life, they offered different cures; the minority sought the remedy abroad, while the majority wanted to fence the country in against the heterodox with an even higher wall than that erected by the Mongolian yoke and the centuries-old alienation of the Russian people from its brothers in blood and spirit.

But not all the opponents of the West opposed education as such. They merely sought it in the direction hallowed by ages, from Orthodox Byzantium, firmly clinging to old traditions and shunning innovations. At the same time, the Schism had divided the very mass of the people into two hostile parts. Thus, the process of movement had begun, and it was so strong and elemental that nothing could stop it any longer. But society itself still lived its old life, far from the knowledge that it had already broken from its moorings, that it was on the move. There was no awareness as yet that the present moment was essentially already the eve of great events. If those people had been shown one day how far they had progressed from the preceding day, they would have rejected the idea with distrust and indignation. Yet on the morrow they would themselves enthusiastically unfurl the new flag and defend it with stubborn fanaticism.

Such was the society into which Peter was born. He posed directly and openly the question which, I believe, should be regarded as the starting point of all his state activity: should the country deliberately vegetate in its past, or should it eagerly seek knowledge from those who possess it? Should it lock itself up within its corner and shut out the light of truth, or should it throw its doors open to this light, dispelling the accumulated darkness of many years? . . . Peter seemed to be asking: shall we look backward at the road by which we have come, and seek our models there, or shall we admit that, in order to possess happiness, we must win it by work and struggle, we must go forward without fear of borrowing from others and association with other men? Should we preserve the old, the Tsar seemed to be asking, merely because it was old and handed down from our forebears? Or should we obey the voice of reason, if it proves that the new is genuinely better?

In old Muscovy the wheel of life turned much too slowly. The Muscovites looked mostly backward, alarmed at the idea of increasing ever so slightly the speed of the locomotive that was dragging the unwieldy train, Russia, along the road. The motto of Muscovite Russia was: "Be careful; see that you do not lose the good things handed down from *yesterday*." Peter's banner carried another slogan: "Forward, do not fear change, seek to bring about a *tomorrow* that will be better than today."

This was the answer Peter chose, and the country began to move, at a rapid, dizzying pace. Let us not forget that the *goals* set by the Tsar-reformer were being realized by *means* which in themselves were capable of arousing resistance and opposition: the old Russia knew nothing of respect for persons, and consistently used physical force in place of moral persuasion. The energy with which the Russian Tsar sought to implant the new knowledge; the autocratic faith in the rightness of the program and the methods for its achievement; the extraordinary nervous tension in which the Tsar kept the country for more than a quarter of a century—all this evoked the admiration of some, and filled others with dread. Men of the old school, swept up by the rushing hurricane, could not but move, run with it, for they were an organic part of the state organism which had been brought into motion. But they moved against their will, offended in their most cherished feelings. In Peter's reform it is necessary to draw a sharp line between the sound kernel of truth and the unnecessary, often downright revolting incrustations—the unwholesome casing into which this truth was wrapped at the time. A true son of his age, Peter had no respect for the person and was far from the thought that the individual has his own world of legitimate desires, habits, ideas, and convictions. No wonder his attitude provoked a burst of fiery indignation, and bred the bitterness of indelible grievance.

Indeed, let us try to put ourselves into the place of Peter's opponents. "Holy Russia," they felt, must shun alike the infidels in the East and the foreigners in the West. And yet science, this newfangled foreign importation, had to be received precisely from foreign, infidel hands. Is it any wonder that Peter's call to culture acquired, in the eyes of the adherents of old Muscovy, the significance of a religious, national question? It might be suggested that, addicted as they were to letter and form, they feared not so much science itself as the wrappings in which it was delivered to us. But what if it were so? Was their reaction so much worse than the fanaticism with which the other side argued that, by merely exposing one's chin and dressing in bob-tailed clothes, one could become an educated man? Can they be blamed for coming to see their religion, their commandments embodied in their very beards and long caftans, in fasting and in shunning infidels and men of alien beliefs? After all, they had absorbed these ideas with their mothers' milk! The most authoritative people had instilled these concepts in them. They had been taught repeatedly that the only proper dress for attending God's church was the traditional Russian dress; might those who donned foreign clothing be accurst, for they likened themselves to the infidel. Shaving the beard was "an abomination before God," for it brought man down to the condition of apes, dogs, and cats. In the Old Testament, beards were shaved "as an insult and a punishment." And if this was so, could it be that all of Russia had now become a land of criminals?

And so, the Russian people were inevitably led to ask themselves: where were truth and justice when an entire people was so thoughtlessly insulted? . . . The beard, as Buslaev justly observed, became "the symbol of Russian nationality, the Russian past and tradition." To shave one's beard was to distort the image of God. The Stoglav,[1] the *Kormchaya* Book,[2] the patriarchs and church laws had all forbidden shaving as a heretic notion, an assault on the purity of the Orthodox faith. What right do we have to say that the beard, to the sincerely pious man, was a mere form, an empty signboard, when, in his conviction, the ban went all the way back to the Oecumenical Councils and was established by the rules of the Holy Apostles, which forbade performance of the funeral mass [*otpevanie*] for deceased beard-shavers and prohibited the reading of the *Sorokoust*[3] and the offering of communion bread for the commemoration of their souls? The critics may prove the error of the references to the Fathers of the Church; yet, since this idea, whether correct or incorrect, had come to be accepted, could it have been ignored and spurned? And this is why we read without the shadow of a smile a foreigner's report that some men carried their shaven beards under their coats, in the hope that, when their final hour came, the beard would be buried with them, giving them an opportunity to vindicate themselves before the Highest Judge. These convictions were a part of their

---

[1] Stoglav—decisions (one hundred chapters, hence the name) of the church council held in Moscow in 1551.—Ed.
[2] Kormchaia Book (*kormchaia kniga*)—collection of Russian canon law based on the Byzantine *Nomokanon*.—Ed.
[3] *Sorokoust*—prayer for the dead (to be read for forty consecutive days following the person's death).—Ed.

religion, and this religion was being outraged and insulted. Everything they had become accustomed to, everything that had become to them a sacred, spiritual need, was now vanishing forever. A man of convictions and self-respect can far more easily endure physical pain than allow mockery of his moral world, of all that expresses his innermost "I." There can be no doubt as to the action to be taken in the latter case: challenged to battle, the man will snatch at any available weapon with all the desperation of hopelessness.

It is said that the traditionalists failed to distinguish between form and content, frantically clinging to the beard and the caftan in the naive faith of their soul-saving properties. But the real tragedy of the situation stemmed from the belief of the opponents of innovations that the European forms concealed the most abominable content. Subsequent generations would unravel this complex question (but at the cost of how much effort? and even then, to what extent?). They would sift out the sound grain from the unnecessary chaff. In the meantime, in the eyes of the vast majority, Peter's measures were shaking the very foundations of church and state. The antinational, non-Orthodox character of these measures—this was the root cause of the conflict. The minds of the outraged believers turned to comparisons with Grishka Otrepiev—and who was worse in the eyes of the Russian people than the False Dimitrii?[4]

The figure of the Tsar grew ever more terrifying, extraordinary, and gigantic in the imagination of the adherents of ancient tradition. He was turned into a super-human creature, possessed by the devil, born of an impure virgin—the Antichrist himself. . . . "Ah," said his contemporaries, "this is why he hobnobs with the Germans, this is why he has introduced the recruit system and brands the recruits with a red-hot iron—the brand of the Antichrist. This is why he tortures the *streltsy,* and why he killed his own son! Now it is clear why he does not observe fast days, why he stole eight years from God,[5] robbed Jesus Christ of His primacy, and took the title of Patriarch.

[4] Grishka Otrepiev, the False Dimitrii, gave himself out to be the youngest son of Ivan the Terrible. He reigned for a few months after the death of Boris Godunov in 1605.—Ed.
[5] "Robbed eight years"—The Old Believers and many traditionalists believed that there was a discrepancy of eight years between the Western-style calendar adopted by Peter the Great (in 1700) and the old Muscovite calendar which reckoned from the Creation of the World.—Ed.

This is why he shaves his beard, why he has donned a short coat, assumed the visage of a beast and wears the curls of a dog; this is why he has levied new taxes and assessments upon the Christian world. . . . There have been seven Antichrists. According to the Holy Writ, an eighth is to be born. And now he has come in the person of Peter. It is the Antichrist, the Antichrist who sits on the throne!"

This dreadful talk was heard in all corners of the Russian land, among all strata of society. It was the talk of peasant women and soldiers' wives, serfs and monks. These incendiary ideas were secretly nurtured or openly spoken by the squire, the peasant, the beggar, the old men living on monastery charity, the dissenter, the townsman, the captain of dragoons and the retired ensign. The epileptic soothsayer, the nun, the deacon and the priest, each in his own way, harped on the same tune: "What kind of a Tsar is this? He has devoured the whole people, the Germans have got the best of him! It's high time we got rid of him!"

The government vainly tried by cruel executions to quell the abusive talk; it vainly sought to counter the clandestine literature with its own, citing the authority of Bishop Dimitrii of Rostov and distributing popular prints to argue its points. The denunciations of the Tsar went on openly and without fear; the defamers were certain that the mass of the people was on their side. Dimitrii of Rostov's writings in defense of shaving had no success. As for torture and execution— of what avail were executions? . . . There were many who went of their own will to the Preobrazhenskii Department,[6] who, knowing in advance of the tortures awaiting them, yet, obedient solely to the voice of their conscience, declared: "This is my business with the Tsar: I have come to tell the Tsar that he is destroying the Christian Faith." Such men were not to be intimidated by executions. People perished, died by the hundreds in terrible torment. But, alas! Peter remained, in the eyes of hundreds of thousands, the accurst Antichrist, the Jew of the tribe of Dan [*zhidovin ot kolena Danova*], but not the father-Tsar, not God's anointed. Popular discontent continued to grow, and all the terrors of the torture chamber merely increased it ten-fold.

---

[6] Preobrazhenskii Department [*Preobrazhenskii Prikaz*]—office in charge of internal security and the secret police.—Ed

V HISTORICAL ASSESSMENTS

Sergei F. Platonov

PETER THE GREAT NOT A REVOLUTIONARY INNOVATOR

In the first selection from the pen of this distinguished historian, we have read a high estimate of the accomplishments of Muscovy in solving Russia's traditional diplomatic and political tasks and problems. It will not come as a surprise, therefore, to find Platonov arguing that, however impressive and exciting Peter's personality, the Emperor did little that was radically new; that he only followed in the footsteps of his Muscovite predecessors; and that like them, he was not always successful in solving Russia's basic problems.

Our approach to the description of the era of transformations stemmed from a conviction that this period has been predetermined by the entire course of Russia's previous history. We have therefore examined the essential features of pre-Petrine life as it had evolved up to the moment when Peter began his work. We then acquainted ourselves with Peter's upbringing and the circumstances of his childhood and youth, in order to understand the development of the reformer's personality. And, finally, we have studied the character of Peter's reforming activity in all its aspects.

What are we to conclude from our study of Peter? Was his activity traditional, or did it represent a sharp and sudden revolution in the life of the Muscovite state, for which the country was entirely unprepared?

The answer is quite clear. Peter's reforms were not a revolution either in their substance or their results. Peter was not a "royal revolutionary," as he is sometimes called.

To begin with, Peter's reform was not a political revolution. In foreign policy, Peter closely followed the old directions and fought the old enemies; he achieved unprecedented success in the West, but he did not resolve by his successes the old political problems in relation to Poland and Turkey. He did a great deal toward the attainment of the cherished aspirations of Muscovy, but he did not complete all that had to be done. The conquest of the Crimea and the partitions

From Sergei F. Platonov, *Lektsii po Russkoi Istorii* [*Lectures on Russian History*], edited by I. Blinov (St. Petersburg, 1904), pp. 457–460. Translated by Mirra Ginsburg.

of Poland under Catherine II were our nation's next steps forward, directly continuing the work of Peter and of old Russia.

In domestic policy, Peter did not leave the seventeenth century far behind. The organization of the state remained the same. The fullness of sovereign power as it had been formulated by Tsar Aleksei in the words of the Acts of the Apostles, was given more extensive definition under Peter in the Military Regulation, in decrees, and in the philosophic tracts of Feofan Prokopovich. Local self-government, which had been a class institution, unpolitical in character before Peter's day, remained the same under Peter. Bureaucratic institutions continued to be superior to the organs of self-government of the social classes, and although the outward forms of the administration were altered, its general nature remained unchanged. Under Peter as before him, the administration was based on a mixture of principles: personal and collegial, bureaucratic and estate-based.

Nor did Peter's work bring about a social revolution. The position of the various classes within the state, as well as their mutual relationships, remained essentially unchanged. The attachment of social classes to state obligations remained in full force; only the manner in which these duties were rendered was changed. Under Peter, the gentry had not yet attained the right to own people as a matter of class privilege; it owned the peasants' labor merely because it needed material security to perform service to the state. The peasants had not yet lost their personal civil rights and were not regarded as full serfs. The course of history led to progressive intensification of their bondage, but, as we have seen, this process had begun before Peter and was completed after him.

It is equally impossible to see any revolutionary significance in Peter's economic policy, its objectves or its results. Peter gave clear definition to the goal toward which his predecessors had already moved in halting steps—the goal of raising the country's productive capacity. His program for the development of the nation's industry and trade had already been familiar in the seventeenth century—to Krizhanich[1] theoretically, and to Ordyn-Nashchokin practically. The results achieved by Peter did not place the national economy on a new foundation. Agricultural labor remained the principal source of

[1] Iurii Krizhanich (died 1683), Croat writer and priest, is frequently considered the ancestor of Pan-Slavism.—Ed.

the nation's wealth. Possessing after Peter's death 200 factories and plants, Russia continued to be an agricultural country, with but a weakly developed industry and trade.

Culturally, Peter cannot be said to have brought anything radically new into Russian life either. The old cultural ideals had begun to be questioned before him. The problem of new foundations in cultural life had come into sharp focus in the seventeenth century. Tsar Aleksei had already in part been a representative of the new tendencies, and Tsar Feodor had embodied them fully. In this respect, Tsar Peter was their direct heir. But while his predecessors had been the pupils of Kievan theologians and scholastics, Peter was the pupil of Western European bearers of Protestant culture. Peter's forebears troubled themselves little about disseminating their knowledge among the people, while Peter regarded this as one of his chief tasks. In this he differed substantially from the seventeenth-century sovereigns. Thus, Peter was not the originator of the cultural trend, but the first ruler who ventured to carry out the reform. The results of his activity were very great: he gave his people the widest opportunity for material and cultural association with the entire civilized world. But one must not overestimate these results. Under Peter, education affected only the upper strata of society, and even there only to a small extent; the mass of the people retained its old outlook.

But if, as we see, Peter's activity introduced nothing that was radically new as compared with the past, why did his reforms acquire among later generations, and even among Peter's contemporaries, the reputation of a radical state revolution? Why did Peter, who acted along traditional lines, become a royal revolutionary in the eyes of Russian society?

There are two main reasons for this. One may be found in the attitude of society toward Peter; the other, in Peter himself.

Russian society was tremendously impressed by Peter's broad and decisive reforms, in striking contrast to the cautious and slow policies of the government of Muscovy. This society lacked the sense of historical tradition which was so strong in Peter's genius. Near-sighted Muscovites explained both the foreign undertakings and the domestic innovations of the Tsar by his personal whims, views, and habits. They contrasted specific innovations with equally specific customs of long standing, and concluded that Peter was mercilessly destroying their past and traditions. Behind the abolished and newly established particulars of social life they failed to see the general nature of the old and the new. Public opinion had not yet reached the capacity to generalize on such a level as to be aware of the fundamental principles of Russian national and social life, and it dealt only with individual facts. This was why Peter's contemporaries who witnessed the innumerable innovations, both large and small, felt that Peter had turned the entire life of the country upside down, leaving no stone of the old edifice in place. They regarded transformations in the old order as its total destruction.

This impression among contemporaries was furthered by Peter himself. His conduct, his entire manner of action, suggested that Peter was not merely changing the old forms, but that he hated them passionately and fought to abolish them. Instead of improving the old, he seemed to be driving it out and forcibly replacing it by new ways of life. This frenetic attitude toward his work, the militant character of his activity, the needless cruelties, the coercion and severity of his measures—all these were the results of impressions left by the experiences of Peter's childhood and youth. Having grown up in the midst of enmity and strife, having seen both open rebellion and secret opposition, Peter did not enter upon the path of reform in a calm and even spirit. He hated the milieu which had poisoned his childhood, and the dark aspects of the old life which had given rise to that milieu. Therefore, in destroying and changing the old ways, he brought into his activity as a monarch also the feelings of a man who had suffered because of them. Compelled to fight for power and independence at the beginning of his reign, Peter preserved his fighting methods to the end. Initially faced by open enmity, and even later feeling the hidden resistance of society, Peter constantly fought for what he believed and considered right and useful. This explains those aspects of Peter's reforming activity which lent his reform the features of a sharp and forcible revolution.

In its essence, however, this reform was not a revolution.

Georgii V. Plekhanov
PETER THE GREAT—
AN ORIENTAL DESPOT

Georgii V. Plekhanov (1856–1918) was the father of Russian Marxism and its most distinguished theoretician. Unlike present-day Soviet (so-called Marxist) historians, Plekhanov fully accepted Marx's own opinion of Russia's social and economic backwardness. Following up suggestions made in the eighteenth century and by some writers of the Romantic period, Marx singled out "Oriental despotism" as a special type of social organization in which the absolute ruler (and his bureaucracy) had control of the major tools of production. Applying this notion to his analysis of Russian history, Plekhanov underscored his country's backwardness and argued for the absolute necessity of rapid Westernization, which for him meant the introduction of economic dynamism and a form of capitalist-bourgeois society (before proceeding to a socialist revolution and order). In the incompleted History of Russian Social Thought, *his only work of genuine historical scholarship, Plekhanov developed this point of view with respect to Russia's cultural and ideological Westernization in the seventeenth and eighteenth centuries. In carrying out his innovations Peter relied on the traditional methods of "Oriental despotism" (i.e., state compulsion and direction), argued Plekhanov. And this conclusion led Plekhanov to question the effectiveness of the reforms in providing the framework for a genuine Westernization of the country.*

Western European theoreticians of enlightened despotism frequently gave expression to their conviction that "compulsion" was necessary. Our Peter has also been called an enlightened despot; this is of course justified. But speaking of Peter's enlightened despotism, we should never forget the particular traits which distinguish the despotism of Oriental monarchies from the absolutism of West European states. The Oriental despot has the right to dispose of the property of his subjects at will; in the absolute monarchies of Western Europe the state could dispose of its subjects' property only within the limits set by law or custom. We should stress that the difference was not due to some kind of moral superiority of Western monarchs over Oriental rulers; it was exclusively the result of the different relationships prevailing among social forces. But the fact remains that in carrying out

From Georgii V. Plekhanov, *Istoriia Russkoi Obshchestvennoi Mysli* [*History of Russian Social Thought*], vol. II (Moscow, 1918), pp. 91–97. Editor's translation.

his reform Peter possessed the unlimited power of an Oriental despot. And he made full use of this unlimited power.

Aiming at the development of Russia's productive forces he began by indissolubly binding to the state all the forces already available. During his first trip abroad he hired many foreign mining specialists. Upon his return he actively promoted the development of mining in European Russia and in Siberia. To insure the success of this endeavor, in 1700 he granted everybody the right to prospect for ores throughout the whole Empire, *regardless of the landowner's will.* Landowners on whose estates ore deposits were found received preference when petitioning for permission to build factories on these estates. If they did not want to, or could not, take advantage of this privilege, the right was made available to anyone desirous of establishing this kind of new enterprise who had the means to do it, "so that God's gift should not lie idle underground." Those who hid the existence of ore deposits or who prevented others from establishing mines were subject to corporal punishment and death. However accustomed the inhabitants of Muscovy might have been to the state's cavalier treatment of their property, yet the new violations of their property rights resulting from Peter's concern for the development of mining provoked them at the least to passive resistance. Unable to oppose the imperial edicts openly, the landowners took their revenge on the prospectors. "It has become known to Us [Peter] that prospectors of ores and minerals are subjected to much injury and persecution," and as a result the College of Mines was ordered to make a full investigation of the situation.

No less typical were Peter's measures for promoting pearl fishing. A decree of 1716 demanded that no obstacles be put in the way of Captain Velishev and his men in their search for pearls. Velishev received the right to hire men experienced in this field. But should these men not wish to be hired by Velishev, the latter could compel them by force, though paying them 3 rubles a month and seeing to it "strictly" that they work well.

In need of good timber for his fleet, Peter *de facto* made state property of forests. It was at this time that many forest reserves were created, reserves that could not be touched even by their owners. The cutting of ship timber was punishable by death, though Peter found it convenient to alleviate the penalty subsequently: the cutting down of oak trees was punished by the tearing of nostrils and hard labor. Even this penalty was found to be too harsh, as you will agree, and it was replaced by a money fine: 15 rubles for an oak, 10 rubles for any other tree. But recidivists were still subject to have their nostrils torn out and be exiled to hard labor.

In the interest of the state, fishing preserves were taken out of private ownership. In May, 1722, order was given to distribute among large landowners—proportionately to their holdings—fine fleeced sheep that previously had been kept on state farms. Even those "who did not want to receive these sheep" were compelled to accept them. In other words, the raising of fine fleeced sheep became a duty in kind imposed on the population for the sake of developing textile production. To this end—which was closely related to the needs of the newly created army—landowners received not only sheep but also shepherds. Nobody asked the shepherds whether they wanted to become the possession of this or that owner, as nobody had asked the pearl fishers whether they wanted to be hired by Captain Velishev. The working population of the country was treated like the property of the state. The learning of trades also became an obligation for the sake of "the interest of the state." In 1712 it was ordered to select from all provinces 315 young men among the best smiths and carpenters and to train them in the making of rifle barrels, locks, and stocks. In addition, in every province two persons had to be trained as saddlers for the regiments [garrisoned in the province]. Men skilled in these crafts had to work for the state at the first demand of the government. In 1709, forty thousand men, not counting masons and bricklayers, were sent to Petersburg for the city's construction. In 1711 craftsmen were requisitioned in the provinces for work in the Admiralty, etc.

Peter's attitude to the working population is best illustrated by the following incident: In 1712 he ordered Sheremetev "to purchase peasants among the Livonian population and to send them to Russia for settlement in less fertile areas so that, with their help, the Russians might be taught better farming methods." Unexpectedly, the enterprise turned out well. In view of the large number of prisoners of war it was not necessary to purchase native peasants. Sheremetev replied to the Tsar: "You have ordered, Sire, to purchase and send Livonians and "Finns" [*chukhnia*], but thanks to your Lordship's luck I will send the people without having to buy them. I can send more than one thousand people, but it will be difficult to transport them." In spite of the last mentioned difficulty, six hundred people of both sexes were sent to Moscow.

In Europeanizing Russia Peter carried to its extreme logical consequence the population's lack of rights *vis-à-vis* the state that is characteristic of Oriental despotism. The Tsar-reformer did not stand upon ceremony with the working population ("the Monarch's orphans"), but neither did he find it necessary to stand on ceremony with the service people ("the Monarch's servants"). The acquisition of technical know-how (for example, navigation and instruments) also became one of the many forms of duties in kind: it became the "tax in kind" of the nobility. We know that the nobility performed this duty poorly; nevertheless they fulfilled it to some extent. For his part, the head of the state valued the nobility only to the extent that they fulfilled their obligation to serve and to prepare themselves for [state] service. Peter did not tire of impressing on the nobility the fact that it was only through service that its members became noble and differed from the mean, i.e., common, people. But if only service made the nobleman "noble," it was natural to give right of nobility to any meritorious individual. This is what Peter did. By virtue of the decree of January 16, 1721, anyone who had reached the rank of commissioned officer [*ober ofitser*] was given hereditary nobility. The following year, establishing the famous Table of Ranks, Peter explained that members of the nobility by birth would not receive a rank until they had rendered services to the state and the country. A few years earlier, in February, 1714, it had been forbidden to promote to officer rank those servicemen of noble family who had not gone through service as soldiers in the guards and "who were not acquainted with the fundamentals of soldiering." According to the Military Regulation of 1716, the "Russian nobleman had no other way of reaching officer status except through service in the guards." As a result, the regiments of the guards became primarily noble units. In one guard regiment that consisted entirely of children of the nobility there were up to three hundred enlisted men bearing the title of prince.[1] "In the guards," writes Kliuchevsky, "the nobleman lived like an ordinary

---

[1] The so-called personal regiment, leib-regiment, organized 1719.—Ed.

soldier; quartered in the regimental barracks he received soldier's rations and performed all the duties of an enlisted man." The noble enlisted man frequently found himself under the orders of someone of common origin who had reached his rank through merit. In this way rank took precedence over birthright. This situation was in accordance with social and political developments that can be traced from the times of Ivan the Terrible on: the *oprichnina*[2] had been introduced to compel birthright to bow before service. In this respect, by Europeanizing Russia, Peter brought to their culmination the very traits that likened his Empire to Oriental despotism. It is to misunderstand the pattern of service to see in it a sign of democracy. . . . In fact it has nothing in common with democracy; it is diametrically opposed to democracy. Under the [service] system everybody, save one person, is enslaved, while in democracy all are free, at least in law. . . .

The patrimonial monarchy of Muscovy respected the individual less and scorned legality more than the fiscal and police states of the West. The patrimonial monarchy was very unfavorable ground for the development of culture. In spite of this, even before Peter, we have encountered a few individuals in Moscow who were sincerely carried away by Western customs and science. The more so we might expect that such persons, while not ceasing to be exceptions, would become less rare under Peter and his successors. And indeed, ever since Peter's reforms, there is no end of sincere admirers of Western culture. It is among them that Russian public opinion and social thought developed. One of Peter's closest assistants, Prokopovich, who himself belonged to their ranks, has called them the "learned host."

---

[2] *Oprichnina*—special corps of military servicemen organized by Ivan the Terrible to curb and destroy the old noble families.—Ed.

B. H. Sumner

PETER'S ACCOMPLISHMENTS AND THEIR HISTORICAL SIGNIFICANCE

The late Warden of All Souls (Oxford University), B. H. Sumner (1893–1951), brings an Englishman's common sense and detachment to his discussion of the relationship between Peter's reforms on the one hand, and parallel trends in Western Europe and the radical transformation wrought by the Soviet regime, on the other.

Peter was an iconoclast: he broke with many externals, and with the ritualistic, traditional orthodox manner of life that hitherto had been part and parcel of the nationalism and religion of the court and the magnates and landed families, and in some degree of the bulk of the Russian people. He was lay and secular in his interests, aims, and habit of mind and of life; rationalism and utility were uppermost. He had dynamic energy, violent unbreakable determination, and unfailing courage: therewith he triumphed in the long run over all his adversities, defeats, and setbacks—except one, and that one curiously enough his defeat at the hands of the Turks, in 1711, on the Pruth. He was a patriot, devoted to Russia, not sparing his subjects, but least of all himself, in unremitting service to her. He worked upon her "like nitric acid on iron." He was untiring in his plans for the development of Russia's economic resources, particularly her industries, and among those especially metallurgy. In this he had much success, and the great iron and copper industries in the Urals owe their origin to Peter. He was the initiator of what may be called modern education in Russia, not confined to one class, though mainly confined to the immediately useful and the technical. He devoted great attention to Asiatic lands and to Siberia, marched in person into Transcaucasia in war against Persia, sought out Central Asian routes to India and initiated the first successful search for a Northeast passage, discovered shortly after his death by Behring. He made the Russian navy out of nothing. He remade the Russian army on the model of the up-to-date European armies of that day, armed for the greater part with

From B. H. Sumner, "Peter the Great," *History* 32 (March 1947): 42–49. Reprinted by permission of the publishers and B. H. Sumner's executors.

flintlocks and bayonets, well-equipped with a varied artillery, in the end munitioned for the most part from Russian resources. With this army and navy he defeated Sweden, ultimately, after twenty-one consecutive years of war; and Sweden ranked among the foremost military powers of the day, and had in her King Charles XII, a military leader who was the compeer of Marlborough and Prince Eugene, however lacking he was as a statesman. (Thanks to Creasy, Macaulay's schoolboy used to know of Poltava, for it is numbered among his fifteen decisive battles of the world—the only Russian one to be so: Poltava, "the Russian resurrection," as Peter and his wife Catherine refer to it in their intimate letters.) With this army and navy Peter gained for Russia the Baltic provinces and the mouth of the Neva, where he founded his new capital, St. Petersburg, achievements which obviously enough during the last seven years have been brought home again and again to the Russian people.

Such are some of the salient aspects of Peter's character and deeds which link up easily enough with much that is of absorbing interest to the Soviet Union. But I would like at this point to utter a caveat against facile comparisons which are often made between Peter and Stalin or Lenin, or between what was accomplished under Peter and what has happened in the last thirty years in Russia. There is, in my opinion, nothing truly corresponding to the October Revolution in Peter's transformation of Muscovy into Russia—or indeed in any period of Russian history. Peter stood for a new outlook on life, but not for a radically new type of society or of state. He has often been compared to a thunderstorm, with blinding, searing lightning, with drenching but fruitful and irrigating rain, a thunderstorm in spring from a clear sky. That is an untrue comparison. The thunderstorm had been slowly working up, growing and flickering on the horizon, long before it burst with Peter. His methods were extreme and violent and shocking to many, perhaps most, of his subjects—so had been Ivan the Terrible's methods a century and more before him—and in that sense he may be called revolutionary; as Herzen styled him: "un jacobin anticipé et un terroriste révolutionnaire," who wrought "grimly and terribly against the will of the people, relying on autocratic authority and personal strength." But he did not seek either to build upon entirely new foundations or to sweep away the essentials of the Muscovite social structure. Especially, he not only did not change the basic fact of serfdom: in various ways he extended serfdom and clamped it down more heavily. His achievements were not very great, even though many of them were undone or warped after his death, but they constituted a great era of reforms, rushed through at breakneck speed, rather than a revolution in comparison with so all-embracing and far-spreading and profound a revolution as that begun in 1917.

There is, however, one respect in which Peter and his effects may perhaps be said to constitute a revolution in a sense. For two hundred years he has divided Russia, very broadly speaking, into two groups. Already his contemporaries were ranged against each other, some opposing him in the name of "the old and ancient faith of holy ortho- dox Rus," others supporting him in the name of "the new European science and culture, of 'enlightened' Petrine Russia." On the con- clusion of the Great Northern War in 1721 Peter was officially ac- claimed as "Father of the Fatherland, All-Russian Emperor, Peter the Great." On his death in 1725 his favored ecclesiastic, Feofan Proko- povich, Archbishop of Novgorod and ruler of Peter's newly created Synod, preached a funeral oration lauding him as "having raised Russia as from the dead," and comparing him to Samson, mighty man of arms, Japhet the creator of a fleet, Moses the lawgiver, and Solo- mon the wise. That on the one side. But also on his death there ap- peared an unsparing cartoon, one of the most popular of the cheap woodcuts that for so long circulated underground in Russia, entitled "The mice bury the cat." Many rejoiced that Antichrist was no more, that "the bloodsucker," "the cruel beast of prey" had gone to join Beëlzebub from whom he had sprung. For many their dearest wish was that St. Petersburg should be abandoned, and Moscow should once again be the capital; and so it was for a very brief span. The two cities symbolized the opposed attitudes to Peter and all that he stood for.

Thus from the very time of Peter himself there appears what has been called "the ideological schism"—*ideologichesky raskol,* the word *raskol,* schism, harking back to the great religious schism in the sixties of the seventeenth century—"the ideological schism" between the conception of Russia as part of Europe and of Muscovy as a world of her own, neither Europe nor Asia. In eighteenth-century literature, for obvious reasons public expression could not be given to direct criticism of the personality or role of Peter and hence to direct discussion of the fundamental problem "what is the nature of Russia, what is her future?" (This actual formula was coined much later by the historian Kavelin in writing of Peter in 1866.) But the subsequent publication of the manuscripts of Shcherbatov[1] and Radishchev[2] show that in Catherine the Great's reign there were definitely formulated highly critical views of the direction given to Russian life and culture by Peter, "the mighty [*vlastny*] autocrat, who destroyed the last signs of rude freedom in his fatherland" (Radishchev). At the beginning of the nineteenth century with Karamzin,[3] in his later period of old-style, nationalist-patriot, there is openly posed, and in the grand manner, the question how Peter and his work should be evaluated in terms of Russia's national life and future. Thenceforward, above all in the great controversies between the Westerners and the Slavophiles, this question is regarded as fundamental in the historico-philosophical disquisitions on the relation of Russia to Europe, on the place of Russia in the world, on the meaning of "national culture" or "national spirit," of orthodoxy, the *mir* (the village commune) or of governmental power. It is perhaps true to say that the reign of Peter has been for Russians, and not at all only for Russian historians, what the French Revolution has been for five generations of Frenchmen. The interpretation of Peter and his reforms has been a political declaration of faith; it has tended to be part and parcel of a view of life, whether primarily religious or mystical, rationalist or materialist, conservative or liberal.

This prolonged public debate has as its central theme, as I have said, the problem "what is the nature of Russia and what is her future?" Because it turned so frequently upon Peter the Great another problem of equal importance was raised: can a centralized, dictatorial government impose successfully from above, radical changes, or a revolution, especially at extreme speed and by violent means? These, as I see it, are the biggest reasons why Peter the

---

[1] M. M. Shcherbatov (1733–1790), historian and conservative critic of Russian manners and public life.—Ed.

[2] Alexander N. Radishchev (1749–1802), considered the first member of the Russian *intelligentsia*. His major work, *A Journey from St. Petersburg to Moscow*, is an impassioned indictment of serfdom and autocracy.—Ed.

[3] Nicholas M. Karamzin (1766–1826), writer and historian; usually considered the spokesman for a nationalistic and "conservative" view of Russian history and politics.—Ed.

Great has filled so large and so disputed a place in subsequent Russian history, and they raise issues of universal import which make the study of Peter and his times almost as absorbingly interesting to us as to his fellow countrymen. In the last eighty years, however, there has come about so great a change in our historical knowledge of seventeenth- and eighteenth-century Russia, that these issues are now raised in less simple form in relation to Peter.

In the great cultural struggle between what may be loosely described as the adherents of the old, *stariny,* and the adherents of the new, *novizny,* there are two points most of them had in common with the others. They were weak, sometimes adsurdly weak, in their historical knowledge, especially of the earlier centuries and the pre-Petrine Russia. Secondly, they were agreed in placing the greatest emphasis on Peter himself and on regarding his reign as a catastrophic, dividing watershed. For Lomonosov[4] or Shcherbatov, Karamzin or Chaadayev,[5] Byelinsky[6] or Kireyevsky,[7] Herzen[8] or Aksakov,[9] Dobroliubov[10] or Khomiakov,[11] Peter was a giant and a genius, a thunder tempest, whether deforming with lightning or enriching with rain, a cataclysm, whether the regimenting despot importing narrow foreign bureaucrats and noxious foreign ways, or a bogatyr, the enlightened autocrat, who, in the words of Byelinsky, "opened the door for his people to the light of God and little by little dispersed the darkness of ignorance."

---

[4] Mikhail V. Lomonosov (1711–1765), poet, historian, grammarian—the leading figure of Russian cultural life in the eighteenth century.—Ed.

[5] Petr Ia. Chaadaev (1794?–1856), author of the "Philosophical Letters" (published in 1836) that started the Slavophile-Westerner controversy.—Ed.

[6] Vissarion G. Byelinsky (1811–1848), writer and literary critic, ardent Westernizer. —Ed.

[7] Ivan P. Kireyevsky (1805–1856), one of the spiritual founders and leaders of Slavophilism.—Ed.

[8] Alexander I. Herzen (1812–1870), writer and publicist, a prominent member of the circle of Westerners in the 1840s and later founder of the populist orientation of Russian socialism.—Ed.

[9] Aksakov—there were two brothers, Konstantin (1817–1861) and Ivan (1823–1866)—prominent Slavophiles. Ivan eventually moved very close to Panslavism in the 1870s.—Ed.

[10] Nicholas A. Dobroliubov (1836–1861), writer and critic, a leading representative of "Nihilism" in the 1860s.—Ed.

[11] Alexis S. Khomiakov (1804–1860), a leading figure of the Slavophile movement, his main contribution and interests lay in theology and the philosophy of history. —Ed.

Thus Peter was emphatically the Great for both sides, whether for good or for evil, and what he did was something wholly novel, a paroxysm of revolution. Since the 1860s a series of Russian historians, beginning with the monumental Soloviev, have exploded this idea that Peter worked as it were on a *tabula rasa,* that he came as it were out of a clear sky. Some, though not many, of these historians have also belittled his capacities, "written him down" on the whole, and minimized his personal share in the reforms with which his name is linked. It is now generally recognized that Peter, in almost all spheres of his activities, had his precursors; that seventeenth-century Muscovy was in travail with something new, that Peter's reforms did not, with certain exceptions, mean a complete break with the past but rather an immense jolt to the past, and the infusion in a strong, sometimes scalding jet of the new that had hitherto been only slowly and tentatively trickling into Muscovy. That is not to decry Peter or his work, but to make them more comprehensible.

If you take eight essential fields in which Peter wrought profound changes, you will find that in all of these there were beginnings in the generation before him, and sometimes much further back than that. That applies to the greater part of his foreign policy, to his army reorganization, to his reorganization of the central government, to his reorganization of taxation and serfdom, to his employment of foreigners in Russia and education reforms, to his insistence on compulsory service, to his economic and industrial developments, and lastly to his break with the prevailing traditional and ritualistic ordering of life typified in so much of seventeenth-century orthodoxy. I can think of only four changes wrought by Peter (though they were great and lasting) which had either nothing leading towards them in the immediate past or so very little that it scarcely counts. These were the education of Russians abroad, the abolition of the Patriarchate, the creation of the navy, and the making of a new capital, St. Petersburg. Further, however much in many ways Peter was enamoured of the West and borrowed from it, he did not do so indiscriminately or wholesale, and he remained thoroughly Russian. It is a striking fact that Miliukov, who was perhaps the strongest of Peter's critics among recent historians, should sum up on Peter's reforms thus:—"Their fortuitousness, arbitrariness, individual stamp, and violence are necessary elements in them. Despite their sharply antinational externals, they are entirely rooted in the conditions of national life. The country received nothing but the reforms for which she was fitted."

I have mentioned in passing Peter's foreign policy. His imposing success in this field had, as we all know, one novel and lasting result of the greatest consequence: Russia at a bound, in thirty years, became one of the European powers. Contemporaries in Europe were well aware of this sudden portent, and many, British included, were much disturbed by it. When Peter came to England in 1698, his capture of Azov and league against Turkey had inspired no alarms. On the contrary, a congratulatory poem of welcome coupled William III with Peter as "Christ's firmest Pillars and the Christians' Prop" on the West and East, "whose powerful Work Subdues both Mahomet and the Christian Turk"; and it closed, "May Roman Conquests be outdone by Thee And Czar to more than Caesar then extended be." By the close of the Great Northern War this polite hyperbole had turned into an ominously true prophecy in the eyes of many British, and Hanoverian, statesmen. For them the balance of power in northern Germany and the Baltic had been all too rudely upset, and Peter's new creation was in secret denounced as "that fleet which will disturb the world whilst it is steered by ambition and revenge." They were apt in effect to re-echo Burnet's words: "How long he is to be the scourge of that nation or of his neighbors, God only knows." Others who were not concerned with affairs of state judged differently, and one main current of eighteenth-century British opinion on Peter tended to be most impressed with the idea that here was a great example of Reason, forcing men to be obedient and civilized, as well as progressive. Thanks to Peter, in the words of Voltaire, the Russians "ont fait plus de progrès en cinquante ans qu'aucune nation n'en avait fait par elle-même en cinq cent années."

Suggestions for Additional Reading
and a Bibliographical Note

The figure of Peter the Great has dominated the development of Russian social and political thought, as well as Russian historical writing. As a matter of fact, the historiography of Peter the Great provides an almost perfect mirror for the Russian intelligentsia's views on the past and future of Russia, their relationship to the West, and the nature of the social and political problems confronting their country. Here we can give only the barest of outlines of this interesting and important aspect of Russian historical consciousness and writing. (For a survey of Russian historiography see Anatole G. Mazour, *Modern Russian Historiography,* Princeton, 1958.)

Throughout the eighteenth century Peter the Great was the object of the most uncritical and enthusiastic admiration. He was credited with the modernization and civilization of Russia by opening it up to Western influences. His reign, it was believed, marked a completely new epoch in Russian history, and everything that had preceded it was both barbarous and of no interest any longer. Quite naturally, such an attitude could not be maintained when a strong feeling of national pride, developed after Russia's successful struggle against Napoleon, and when the influence of German Romanticism, with its love for the medieval and popular past of a nation, had made itself felt in the second quarter of the nineteenth century. Peter the Great began to be seen not merely as the titan who single-handed had created modern Russia all of one piece, but rather as one of several —albeit the most important perhaps—figures who had helped to shape the destiny of the Russian nation.

Two interpretations of Peter's role were advanced, each acknowledging his powerful impact, but giving a different evaluation of its nature and result. According to one school, Peter was the originator of Russia's Westernization, and he was admired for having broken with the traditions of Muscovy. Those who accepted this view of Peter's reign, the Westerners, went on to argue that the direction given by Peter should be maintained and his work completed by Russia's becoming a truly Western nation politically (through constitutional reforms) and socially (through the abolition of serfdom). Opposed to this interpretation were those who saw in Peter's reign a great national tragedy. Indeed, they argued, by breaking radically with the Muscovite past, Peter had interrupted the normal, traditional evolution of Russia and, worse still, he had created that almost unbridgeable gap between the common people (the peasants) and the educated upper classes. The task, therefore, was to renew contact with the pre-Petrine past, undo the harm done by Peter's Westernization, go back to the values and traditions of the Slavic (i.e., Russian) people; hence the name of Slavophiles given to the advocates of this interpretation. Clearly, neither Westerners nor Slavophiles were interested in an objective study of Peter's reign, for they viewed it exclusively in terms of their philosophic, national, and political predilections.

After the great controversy between Slavophiles and Westerners (which filled the 1840s and 1850s) had died down, it became possible to engage in a dispassionate and scholarly study of Peter's life and work. Begun by the patriarch of modern Russian historiography, Soloviev, it was continued by such prominent historians of the late nineteenth and early twentieth centuries as Kliuchevsky, Platonov, Miliukov, of whose work representative excerpts have been given in the present volume. A great number of valuable monographs on limited aspects of Peter's reign were also produced and primary sources published in scholarly fashion. In spite of these efforts, however, many aspects of Peter's life and times still need studying; nor has all relevant documentation been made accessible and analysed. As a result, no historian has as yet dared to tackle the tremendous job of a scholarly and comprehensive biography of Peter or a rounded study of his reign.

The Revolution of 1917 and the seizure of power by the Bolsheviks brought about a new orientation in Russian historical writing and at the same time put historiography under the strict supervision and direct control of the Soviet state and the Communist Party. The result was to make almost impossible any objective and dispassionate study of Russia's past, and especially of the reign of Peter I. There is no need to describe here how the study of Peter's reign fared in the Soviet Union, for it has been excellently done by Cyril E. Black in the article "The Reforms of Peter the Great" in the volume which he edited, *Rewriting Russian History* (New York, 1956), pp. 242–270.

Further references are available in *Istoriia SSSR, Ukazatel' sovetskoi literatury, 1917–1952,* vol. I, Moscow, 1956.

Peter the Great and his reign have attracted the curiosity and interest of foreign, as well as Russian, writers. For an annotated list of writings by foreigners in the eighteenth and nineteenth centuries see R. Mintzloff, *Pierre le Grand dans la littérature étrangère* (St. Petersburg, 1872). The older Russian writings are listed by E. F. Shmurlo, *Petr Velikii v russkoi literature* [Peter the Great in Russian literature] (St. Petersburg, 1889).

Readily available in English, but quite outdated and to be used with great caution are the biographies by E. Schuyler (1884), K. Waliszewski (1897), and Stephen Graham (1929).

The best short survey available in any language is B. H. Sumner, *Peter the Great and the Emergence of Russia* (London, 1950). Equally valuable is the short study by R. Wittram, *Peter der Grosse—der Eintritt Russlands in die Neuzeit* (Berlin-Goettingen-Heidelberg, 1954). In recent years a few popular biographies and histories have been written by H. Lamb and I. Grey in English, H. Vallotton and R. Portal in French, and H. Kersten in German. A suggestive attempt at seeing Peter's reign in terms of contemporary Europe, unfortunately not well executed, is to be found in L. Jay Oliva, *Russia in the Era of Peter the Great* (Englewood Cliffs, N. J., 1969).

A comprehensive study of the life and reign of Peter the Great has appeared recently in Germany: Reinhard Wittram, *Peter I Czar und Kaiser—Zur Geschichte Peters des Grossen in seiner Zeit,* 2 vols. Göttingen (Vandenhoeck & Ruprecht) 1964. It is the best—judicious and full—treatment of Peter I's reign available to date, but it is a bit traditional in its emphasis on diplomatic and military affairs.

On Peter's diplomacy in specific instances—besides the general histories of Europe in the eighteenth century—one can usefully consult Sir J. A. R. Marriott, *Anglo-Russian Relations 1689–1943* (London, 1944); B. H. Sumner, *Peter the Great and the Ottoman Empire* (Oxford, 1950); D. Gerhard, *England und der Aufstieg Russlands* (Berlin, München, 1933); W. Mediger, *Moskaus Weg nach Europa* (Braunschweig, 1952). The Soviet point of view is to be found in B. Kafengauz, *Vneshniaia politika pri Petre I* [Foreign policy under

Peter I] (Moscow, 1942); and S. A. Feigina, *Alandskii kongress—Vneshniaia politika Rossii v. kontse Severnoi Voiny* [The Aland Congress—Foreign Policy of Russia at the end of the Northern War] (Moscow, 1959). There is a new splendid biography of Peter's great enemy, the king of Sweden: R. M. Hatton, *Charles XII of Sweden* (London, 1968).

On economic and social history see the relevant chapters in Jerome Blum, *Lord and Peasant in Russia from the Ninth to the Nineteenth Century* (Princeton, 1961). The article of S. Blanc, "A propos de la politique économique de Pierre le Grand," *Cahiers du Monde russe et soviétique* 3 (January 1962): 122–139 is an informative and critical discussion of the problem.

For an interpretation of Peter's reign on the status and evolution of the élite, see Marc Raeff, *Origins of the Russian Intelligentsia—The Eighteenth Century Nobility* (New York, 1966). On education see the relevant chapters in N. Hans, *History of Russian Educational Policy, 1701–1917* (London, 1931) and the more recent Alexander Vucinich, *Science in Russian Culture—A History to 1860* (Stanford, 1963).

On cultural affairs and literature see D. Čizecskij, *History of Russian Literature from the IXth Century to the End of the Baroque* (The Hague, 1960); D. S. Mirsky, *A History of Russian Literature,* ed. F. J. Whitfield (New York, 1955); Harold B. Segel, *The Literature of Eighteenth Century Russia—A History and Anthology,* I (New York, 1967); L. R. Lewitter, "Peter the Great, Poland, and the Westernization of Russia," *Journal of the History of Ideas* 19 (October 1958): 493–506; E. Winter, *Frühaufklärung (Der Kampf gegen den Konfessionalismus in Mittel- und Osteuropa und die deutsch-slawische Begegnung)* (Berlin, 1966). On the Petrine Church, consult the recently published account by James Cracraft, *The Church Reform of Peter the Great* (Stanford, 1971).

The most useful general histories of Russia are: V. O. Kliuchevsky, *Kurs russkoi istorii* (5 vols, several eds., most recently Moscow, 1956–1958)—the complete English translation (New York-London, 1911–1913) is very poor; K. Stählin, *Geschichte Russlands* (4 vols. in 5; Berlin, 1930–1939; reprinted 1962); P. Miliukov, Ch. Seignobos, L. Eisenman, *Histoire de Russie* (3 vols.; Paris, 1932—English transl. C. L. Markman, New York, 1968). For an analytical summary there is

Marc Raeff, *Imperial Russia 1682–1825: The Coming of Age of Modern Russia* (New York, 1970), with a comprehensive bibliographical essay.

Peter the Great has been the subject of several interesting works of Russian literature. The following are available in English translation: A. Pushkin, *The Bronze Horseman;* D. Merezhkovsky, *Peter and Alexis;* Alexis Tolstoi, *Peter the Great.*